T

Ser

G000320387

The Message of James
The tests of faith

Titles in this series

The Message of James

The tests of faith

J. A. Motyer
formerly Principal of Trinity College, Bristol

Inter-Varsity Press

Inter-Varsity Press
38 De Montfort Street, Leicester LE1 7GP, England

© J. A. Motyer 1985

First published 1985
Reprinted 1988, 1990, 1991

British Library Cataloguing in Publication Data
Motyer, J. A.
   The message of James: the tests of faith.————
   (The Bible speaks today)
   1. Bible. N.T. James————Commentaries
   I. Title   II. Series
   227'.9106   BS2785.3

   ISBN 0–85110–744–3

Set in 11 on 12pt Garamond by Nuprint Services Ltd, Harpenden, Herts

Printed and bound in Great Britain by
Richard Clay (The Chaucer Press) Ltd, Bungay, Suffolk

Inter-Varsity Press is the book-publishing division of the Universities and Colleges Christian Fellowship (formerly the Inter-Varsity Fellowship), a student movement linking Christian Unions in universities and colleges throughout the United Kingdom and the Republic of Ireland, and a member movement of the International Fellowship of Evangelical Students. For information about local and national activities write to UCCF, 38 De Montfort Street, Leicester LE1 7GP.

General preface

The Bible speaks today describes a series of both Old Testament and New Testament expositions, which are characterized by a threefold ideal: to expound the biblical text with accuracy, to relate it to contemporary life, and to be readable.

These books are, therefore, not 'commentaries', for the commentary seeks rather to elucidate the text than to apply it, and tends to be a work rather of reference than of literature. Nor, on the other hand, do they contain the kind of 'sermons' which attempt to be contemporary and readable, without taking Scripture seriously enough.

The contributors to this series are all united in their convictions that God still speaks through what he has spoken, and that nothing is more necessary for the life, health and growth of Christians than that they should hear what the Spirit is saying to them through his ancient – yet ever modern – Word.

J. A. MOTYER
J. R. W. STOTT
Series Editors

TO GEOFF AND PHYLLIS BROWN

Contents

Author's preface

In 1970, Inter-Varsity Press kindly published some studies of mine on James under the title *The Tests of Faith*. Little or nothing remains here of that earlier book. Everything has been re-written, much has been added, and at a number of points I have changed my mind. This is as it should be, for the Word of God is an endless treasure and an ever-fresh teacher.

I have been greatly helped throughout by the perceptive and detailed help given by Dr John Stott, the Series Editor. It is a pleasure to record his kindness and to express my gratitude for it.

ALEC MOTYER

Chief abbreviations

Adamson	James Adamson, *The Epistle of James (The New International Commentary on the New Testament*, Eerdmans, 1976).
Alford	H. Alford, *The Greek Testament, A Critical and Exegetical Commentary* (Rivingtons, 1880).
AG	William F. Arndt and F. Wilbut Gingrich, *A Greek-English Lexicon of the New Testament and Other Early Christian Literature* (University of Chicago Press and Cambridge University Press, 1957).
AV	The Authorized (King James') Version of the Bible (1611).
Barnes	A. Barnes, *Notes on the New Testament,* vol. X (Blackie, n.d.).
Blanchard	J. Blanchard, *Not Hearers Only: Bible Studies on the Letter of James,* 4 vols. (Word Books, 1971-74).
Calvin	J. Calvin, *Commentaries on the Catholic Epistles* (Edinburgh, 1855).
Davids	P. B. Davids, *The Epistle of James (The New International Greek Testament Commentary,* Paternoster, 1982).
Knowling	R. J. Knowling, *The Epistle of St James (Westminster Commentaries*, Methuen, 1904).
Laws	Sophie Laws, *A Commentary on the Epistle of James* (A. & C. Black, 1980).
LXX	The Old Testament in Greek according to the Septuagint, 3rd century BC.
Mitton	C. L. Mitton, *The Epistle of James* (Marshall, Morgan & Scott, 1966).
NEB	The New English Bible (NT 1961, [2]1970; OT 1970).

9

CHIEF ABBREVIATIONS

NIV	The New International Version of the Bible (NT 1974; OT 1979).
Plumptre	E. H. Plumptre, *The General Epistle of St James (The Cambridge Bible for Schools and Colleges,* Cambridge University Press, 1901).
Ropes	J. H. Ropes, *A Critical and Exegetical Commentary on the Epistle of St James (International Critical Commentaries,* T. & T. Clark, 1978 reprint).
RSV	The Revised Standard Version of the Bible (NT 1946, ^{2}1971; OT 1952).
RV	The Revised Version of the Bible (1885).
Stevenson	H. F. Stevenson, *James Speaks for Today* (Marshall, Morgan & Scott, 1966).
Tasker	R. V. G. Tasker, *The General Epistle of James (Tyndale New Testament Commentaries,* Tyndale Press, 1956).
Ward	R. A. Ward, 'James' in *New Bible Commentary,* Third Edition (Inter-Varsity Press, 1970).

Introduction

As soon as we read through the letter of James we say to ourselves, 'This man was a preacher before he was a writer.' He addresses his readers as a preacher addresses his hearers, directly, pointedly. *Do not be deceived,* he says (1:16), or *Do you want to be shown?* (2:20), or *Know this* (1:19). He is capable of rounding on those whose errors he wishes to expose (4:13; 5:1); he calls attention with many a 'behold' to things he does not want them to miss (3:4–5; 5:4; *etc.*). Imaginary (but very relevant) objectors make their appearance (2:18); rhetorical questions keep attention alive (2:4–5, 14–16; 5:13); homely illustrations abound – horses, rudders, fires (3:3–6), springs of water, gardening (3:11–12) and farming (5:7) – and startling statements jolt the congregation awake: *Count it all joy when you meet various trials* (1:2); *You do well. Even the demons believe* (2:19). And over and over again the warmth of the vital relationship between preacher and congregation is maintained as the word *Brethren, My brethren* and *My beloved brethren* come through the lips straight from the heart (*e.g.* 1:2, 16, 19; 2:1, 5, 14; 5:7, 9; *etc.*).[1]

We cannot help asking ourselves, therefore, if a spoken original lies behind the letter as we have it, and if this is not the explanation of the often curious abruptness with which James seems to swing from one topic to another.[2] A preacher with his striking abilities must often

[1] J. H. Ropes (pp. 10ff.) gives a detailed and fascinating account of the Greek literary form known as the 'Diatribe' – spoken, popular moral addresses going back as far as Diogenes and the Cynics (early 4th century BC). He sadly notes that 'whatever literary precipitate in written form their discourses may once have had' vanished long ago. Later examples do, however, survive and the similarities with James are plain.

[2] P. B. Davids (p. 22) proposes a 'two-tier' background for the letter of James: first a series of homilies and then an epistle in which a redactor edited the pieces together. His appeals to the work of a redactor are, however, unnecessary and unconvincing.

have faced the questions frequently enough addressed to lesser practitioners of the art: Had you thought of publishing your sermon? Don't you think this material ought to have a wider audience and influence? We must not, of course, walk too far along the road of imagination, but there is no doubt that the 'letter' reads like sermon notes in which the preacher wrote down the main outline he wished to follow and the main paragraphs of material which he wished to present, but waited for the inspiration of the moment to develop each point and to build bridges between the individual topics he was handling. We shall note many examples of this possibility in our studies of James, but for the moment we must concentrate on this, that like every good sermon, James' letter was constructed with a clear plan, with an introduction, a well-subdivided central section and a conclusion designed both to bring the sermon back to the point where it started and also to take account of the teaching which has emerged en route.

The introduction and conclusion balance each other in this way:

Introduction (1:2–11)	*Conclusion* (5:7–20)
The need for **patience** (1:2–4) and **prayer** (1:5–8)	The need for **patience** (5:7–12) and **prayer** (5:13–18) and **care** (5:19–20)
in all the contrasting circumstances of life (1:9–11)	in all the contrasting circumstances of life.

The theme of 'care' (5:19–20) arises from the major teaching on that subject in chapter 2 in the same way as the conclusion's re-emphasis on the danger of an unguarded tongue (5:9, 12) looks back to the topic of 3:1–12. But the coincidence of subject-matter between the introduction and the conclusion is striking: here are truths significant enough to come first in the letter and important enough to be repeated at the end – patience and prayer.

The central content of the letter (1:12 – 5:6) carries the *theme* of the *birth* (1:13–19a), *growth* (1:19b–25) and *development* (1:26 – 5:6) of the Christian. Not all growth is true growth; true Christian growth can be assessed by noting whether certain specific developments are taking place:

a. Recapitulation of the introduction (1:12): through *trials*, by *patience*, to the *crown*.

b. **Birth** (1:13–19a): though the old nature remains active (13–16) the Father has brought us to new birth by his word (17–19a);

c. **Growth** (1:19b–25): we grow by hearing (19b–20), receiving (21) and obeying (22–25) the Father's Word;

d. **Development** (1:26 – 5:6): there are three notable developments which are the characteristics of true Christian growth:

1:26	1:27a	1:27b
The controlled tongue	Care for the needy	Personal purity of life
Detailed study of: Care for the needy (2:1–26)	Control of the tongue (3:1–12)	Personal purity of life (3:13 – 5:6)

We shall see later why James states the three lines of Christian development in one order (1:26–27) and then studies them in detail in a different order (2:1 – 5:6). At present we are (so to speak) examining the wood, not the trees. As we do so, we see what a wonderfully thorough, painstaking teacher James is – and how very realistic!

The 'conflict' theme

The Christian is literally 'born for battle'. Before James tells us about the miracle of that birth which comes to us by the Father's will, through the Father's word (1:18), he reminds us that, Christians though we are, the old nature is still virulent and active within us (1:13–16). The new birth does not solve the conflict, nor give us an automatic victory. Nor does it put us beyond the reach of temptation or of the possibility of falling; the new birth in fact brings us into the arena where the old nature and the new nature battle it out. It is for this reason that James follows his teaching on the new birth (1:18) by explaining growth, making it clear that this is a prolonged struggle, a fight against odds.

Furthermore, the enemy within, the old nature, is not our only problem: there are also all the various ills, trials and temptations of life. The church is not only still in the world but is dispersed throughout the world (1:1). Christians are a special people, but not a protected species. Indeed, there is a sense in which they ought to expect even more than their share of the buffetings of life. This is because patient endurance of all sorts of tribulations is, in fact, God's appointed way forward for his people to the maturity (1:4) and crown (1:12) he wills for them. Ask James, 'Does the road wind up-hill all the way?' and hear him reply, 'Yes, to the very end.'

In all this James is no different from all the other teachers God has given us in the Bible. But he is different from teachers who have arisen and still arise, saying that there is an easy way to holiness – an experience, a technique or a blessing which will waft us effortlessly, even if not necessarily painlessly, to permanent loftier heights of living. All such teachings are not only without scriptural foundation – and so very plainly contrary to the teaching of James – but they are in fact recipes for disaster. They disappoint for this very reason, that there was never any hope that they could succeed. They are not God's way. 'Begin as a baby,' says James (1:18). Grow from infancy and babyhood through adolescence to adulthood (1:19–25). Make sure your growth is a true, Christian development, and remember that it is by leaping life's hurdles that you get to the tape.

A Christian life-style

The holiness to which James calls us is a holiness which is lived out in this world, but which marks us off from it (1:27b). When he develops this theme (3:13 – 5:6) he calls us (3:13) to the *good life*, but he speaks more characteristically when he warns that *friendship with the world is enmity with God* (4:4).

Those who can look back through thirty or forty years of Christian experience will recall that teaching about separation from the world used to be far more prominent then than it is today. Those who became Christians at any point up to the mid-1940s were carefully (and with loving intent) made aware by their seniors what was proper for a Christian not to do, where not to go, how not to dress. We must not doubt the serious and pure intention which lay behind this teaching, nor mock what was so plainly meant for our good; yet we were fundamentally misled. We were drilled in a reactive holiness: whatever happened to be the current fashion in the 'world' (*i.e.* society outside the Christian fellowship) must be contradicted by the Christian. We were called simply to react against surrounding social norms.

As we look around us today, however, the abandonment of the old reactive separation from the world has led to a forgetfulness of the concept of separation, and for very many Christians what goes in the world goes in the church. If everyone does it, why should not the Christian? We need to discover and live by positive Christian standards – not reacting against the world around us, but responding obediently to the Word of God within the world around us. James wrote his letter just for us.

The recovery of the local church

One of the outstanding ways in which the difference shows between Christians and the surrounding world is in the quality of fellowship which should mark the local church. The church is God's family, in which all members are *brethren*. If this word sounds to us sexist, then we must look beyond the maleness of the word to the reality of the family relationship which we have to each other as children born of the same Father (1:18). Rather than be offended because James uses the masculine word, let the loveliness of the repeated *brethren, my brethren, my beloved brethren* sink into our minds and hearts until there is born in us a determination that *our* church will be like that. Let it be a fellowship of rich and poor (1:9–11), who alike consider their faith their greatest wealth (2:5); a fellowship of care where brother or sister never goes away in need (2:15), where the tongue is guarded lest it disrupt (4:11–12; 5:9) and where heavenly wisdom in all its peace (3:17) produces that soil of true oneness in which righteousness can come to harvest (3:18). Though James writes as one who can, with authority, address the universal church (1:1), the only actual authorities he mentions in his letter are the Word of God and the elders of the local church (5:14). We need to recover this 'local' vision. If the world around us saw the problems of its own animosities, divisions and deprivations solved in the microcosm of the local church, we would need no more special evangelistic efforts, for the life of the church would be like the light of a city set on a hill which cannot be hidden.

'Not a needy person among them'

James was a member of a church which was so exercised about the needs of brothers and sisters that it could be said that there was 'not a needy person among them' (Acts 4:34). Nothing was held back in the face of the prior consideration of lifting another's burden. The right to hold private property was never disputed (*cf.* Acts 5:4) and there was no attempt to institute a 'Christian commune', let alone a Christian communism, but one great rule operated: they sold possessions and goods and (lit.) 'used to distribute to all, *as any had need'* (Acts 2:45 and 4:34). Their aim was not to dispose of goods, but to meet needs. Out of this setting came James' letter – and, as we shall see, it came out of his heart too.

The theme of the poor and the rich recurs in the letter (1:9–11; 2:1–7, 14–17; 4:13–17; 5:1–6). James re-echoes what Jesus said about the difficulty of the rich entering the kingdom. He does not hide the fact that affluence can breed arrogance, can assume the right to special treatment and even be deceived into thinking that wisdom comes with wealth; neither does he hide the fact that the poor are the special targets of the love of God and that the fruits of poverty in spiritual terms can be great. But his great call is that all believers should hold whatever of this world's good they possess in trust for the needy.

We should rejoice that in our day a concern for a world of want has to such an extent revived. James, however, might want to ask us two questions. First, has our concern to meet need yet reached the point noted in Acts, where nothing was held back if it could be used to dispel need from the fellowship? Very many Western Christians are far and away better off financially than their wildest dreams ever led them to expect – but if giving is measured not quantitatively (how much given?) but in terms of the poor widow who gave all, in Mark 12:44 (how much left?), we have no reason to be proud. Secondly, James might ask, Did you in fact realize that the meeting of needs is not peripheral, nor optional, but central and obligatory to your faith? If only we can hear James' testimony on this point, what a commitment to meeting the needs of others must follow! Right at the heart of our salvation stands the Father who *of his own will brought us forth* (1:18). This means that spontaneously, without any commanding or compelling, he was moved by forces within his own heart and nature to reach out to us in our need. Compassion is the outflow of his nature. If this is so, then concern for the needy is not, so to say, an external duty which we seek to impose on ourselves; it is part of the Father's likeness in us his children, and in this way it is proof of the work of grace in our hearts.

16

The unsuspected factor

There is another proof of the work of grace in our hearts. Like a doctor who comes to a patient and says, 'Let me see your tongue,' James examines our tongues, not only as an index of spiritual health but – and this is the surprise – as a key to spiritual well-being. Of course, in this too he is not innovating but bringing out in a particularly striking way an emphasis which runs right through the Bible. Peter, for example, says, 'He that would love life and see good days, let him keep his tongue from evil and his lips from speaking guile' (1 Pet. 3:10). But he is quoting Psalm 34:12–13 – in other words, this is something on which the whole Scripture is agreed.

James has his own way of saying this, by means of his illustrations of horse, ship and fire (3:2ff.): if only we can master the tongue, then we can control all the energies of our lives (the horse), we can steer our way through all the winds of circumstances (the ship), and we can set bounds around the fiery and destructive forces within our sinful natures (the fire). The tongue is the master-key to it all: this is the biblical psychology James teaches. Practical to the last, and knowing that mastery and constancy are problems which really vex us, he will not allow us to run pell-mell after some new experience or some freshly proffered remedy. The answer lies within ourselves.

It is at points like this that we need to give our most careful attention to the Bible, for it is opening up truths we would not otherwise suspect to be significant. The holy life is our direct responsibility and at its heart . . . the tongue!

But who is James?

These, then, are some of the current and practical issues on which we are addressed in this carefully organized sermon-on-paper. But who is the preacher, this gentle *James, a servant of God and of the Lord Jesus Christ* (1:1)?

There are three men called James in the New Testament: James the son of Zebedee,[3] one of the inner circle of the apostles; James the son of Alphaeus, probably to be identified with James the younger or 'little James';[4] and, thirdly, James, son of Joseph and Mary, the Lord's

[3]Mk. 1:19; Acts 12:2; *etc.*
[4]Mk. 3:18; 15:40. See the excellent discussion in J. W. Wenham, *Easter Enigma* (Paternoster Press, 1984), pp. 36ff.

brother.[5] It is usually thought that James son of Zebedee was martyred at too early a date (AD 44) for him to have been the author of the letter. Even this, however, cannot be maintained for certain. Nothing in the letter absolutely forbids a date as early as James the son of Zebedee, and certainly the arguments proposed for later dates lack impressiveness. The only reason for excluding 'little James' from authorship is the tenuous one that nothing is known about him! The same, as a matter of fact, applies to Jude, known only for his name and his letter. But long-standing tradition attributes the letter to James the Lord's brother. It was not until the sixteenth century that this attribution was disputed, but since then serious questioning has continued. The candidature of James the Lord's brother is still widely maintained by specialists, but there is at least equal support for the view that the letter is the work of an unknown author, probably working at some point between AD 70 and 130.

One question regarding authorship is raised both by those who hold that the Lord's brother was the author and by those who believe that the letter belongs to a later date: the quality of the Greek in which it is written. All agree that the author was a person of linguistic skill and sensitivity, and ask whether James the Lord's brother, with his humble background, could have risen to these literary heights. For some this is a pointer away from James the son of Joseph and Mary; for others it is a matter of sufficient importance to require some adjustment of their theory of authorship. For example, Peter Davids more than inclines to the view that the Lord's brother was the author of the original deposit of material, but that the final form of the letter as we have it ought to be attributed to a redactor who edited James' sermons. But surely this is all a debate about a non-question! Artistic skills and exceptional abilities owe nobody an explanation. Time and again they rise where least expected – though we might well ask whether they would be 'least expected' in the case of the children of such exceptional parents as Joseph and Mary, even if we take no account of the fact that the first and most dramatic gift of God to the church, the essential Pentecostal gift, was a gift of languages, the gift of intelligible communication (Acts 2:8, 11). We cannot affirm what James might have inherited from his parents, but we cannot overlook the fact that he shared the original Pentecostal outpouring (Acts 1:14) with its specifically linguistic focus. Furthermore, as Sophie Laws says

[5]Mt. 13:55; Acts 12:17; 15:13ff.; 1 Cor. 15:7; Gal. 1:19; 2:9. For the sake of variety we sometimes refer to this James as 'the Lord's brother', sometimes as 'son of Joseph and Mary' and sometimes as 'James of Jerusalem'.

(p.40), 'it is no longer possible to assert with complete confidence that James of Jerusalem could not have written the good Greek of the epistle, since the wide currency of that language in Palestine is increasingly appreciated'.

If there are no other grounds, then, for denying authorship to James the Lord's brother than the quality of his Greek, we ought rather to congratulate him for it and be thankful. There are, however, arguments which some think point away from this James. First, when we read between the lines of the letter, we seem to see the churches living in settled conditions and themselves to be well-established. J. H. Ropes, for example, thinks that this must refer to the middle period between AD 70 and 130, long enough after the fall of Jerusalem in AD 70 for things to have settled down and long enough before the Jewish rebellion under Bar-Kokhba in AD 130 for it not to cast its shadow before it. But this argument cannot stand by itself. There are far too many periods, early and late, when a letter to widespread but distinct communities could give the impression of settled conditions.

Secondly, there are arguments which depend on the relationship thought to exist between this letter and the writings of Paul. J. H. Ropes, again, contends that the letter must be later than Paul, 'of whose formulas he disapproves without understanding their real purpose'. The point of this most unfortunately worded contention is that 'James' did not agree with the Pauline doctrine of justification by faith and wrote his letter in a controversial spirit to put the church right. The traditional date, however, for the death of James of Jerusalem is AD 62. By that date both Galatians and Romans had been written and Paul had doubtless formulated and publicized his doctrine of justification well in advance of writing those letters – well within the lifetime of James. This aspect of their relationship cannot, then, require a late date for the authorship of the letter.

But J. H. Ropes' more than arrogant words cannot be allowed to pass without further comment. Are James and Paul at variance? The answer depends on the meaning of the key passage, 2:14–26, and we must not repeat here the details which will concern us later. The view taken in this present book is that disagreement between James and Paul is in fact artificially produced by wrenching James' words out of their context. Paul and James are no more in contradiction than are Articles 11 and 12 of the Thirty-nine Articles of Religion of the Church of England. Article 11 reads: 'We are accounted righteous before God, only for the merit of our Lord and Saviour Jesus Christ by Faith.' Article 12 reads: 'Good Works, which are the fruits of

19

Faith . . . are . . . pleasing and acceptable to God in Christ, and do spring out necessarily of a true and lively Faith.' Paul and James respectively could not be more succinctly expressed. To Paul the question was, 'How is salvation experienced?' and the answer, 'By faith alone.' To James the question was, 'How is this true and saving faith recognized?' and the answer, 'By its fruits.' The supposition that Paul and James are at variance is a false trail. Both actually faced the same problem: people were saying that, if salvation is all of grace on God's side and solely by faith on ours, then how can it matter what way we live so long as we have 'simple faith'?[6] To this both gave the same answer but in different words. Paul answered it by pointing out that saving faith brought us into union not only with the Jesus who died, but also with the Jesus who rose from the dead; if we truly died with him, then we must just as truly live with him.[7] James answered the question by examining the nature of faith itself, and showing that a true definition of faith must include the subsequent life, with those good works which 'do spring out necessarily of a true and lively Faith'.[8]

Thirdly, there are arguments against linking the letter with James the Lord's brother arising out of the relation between it and Acts 15. The Council of Jerusalem is generally dated AD 48. It was obviously an issue of enormous importance to the early church whether and on what terms Gentiles could come into membership, and James played his part in the conclusion reached. Yet there is no reference in the letter to either the Council, or the controversy, or the decision. John Robinson[9] is prepared to understand this as implying that the letter was written before the Council; J. H. Ropes understands it as requiring that a long enough time had passed since the Council for the dust of controversy to settle and cease to be an issue. Neither position carries any necessity about it.

Life is always stranger than theory. We read in Acts 16:1–3 that Paul came hotfoot from the Council, where he had toiled energetically and successfully against the requirement of circumcision for admission to the church, and circumcised Timothy out of regard for the Jews living around. Even as quickly as that did the dust of controversy settle! For Paul – and for James too, as we shall see – other factors could be more important. The non-mention of the Council, then, has

[6]*E.g.* Rom. 3:8; 6:1; Jas. 2:18–19.
[7]Rom. 6:2ff., 13ff.   [8]Jas. 2:20–22.
[9]J. A. T. Robinson, *Redating the New Testament* (SCM Press, 1976), pp. 118ff.

no bearing on the date at which the letter might have been written, and certainly constitutes no argument against authorship by James of Jerusalem.

There are two other items of evidence from Acts 15 which ought to be considered. First, there are verbal parallels between words used at and by the Council and wording in the letter. Some of these parallels concern commonplace matters and cannot be allowed significance,[10] but there are a few to which weight might be attached. James begins his submission to the Council with the words 'Brethren, listen to me' (Acts 15:13) and our memories flit to the identical call, *Listen, my beloved brethren* (Jas. 2:5). He quotes from Amos about 'the Gentiles upon whom my name has been called' and both thought and words are matched in 2:7. If James had a hand in the writing of the communiqué which the Council issued (as surely he must), then the reference to 'our beloved Barnabas and Paul' bears on it the mark of the loving ways of the author who uses again and again the words *brethren, my brethren, my beloved brethren* (*e.g.* 1:16, 19; 2:5). It is unfair of Sophie Laws to dismiss this evidence on the (unprovable) ground that 'the historical accuracy of Luke's report is debatable', for she proceeds to place absolute reliance on the portrait of James in Acts 15 and Acts 21 and on her own understanding of it. James, she believes, is a devotee of the old law: does not Luke portray him here as presiding over a Council concerned with observances, and succeeding in enforcing some? Does he not suggest to Paul (Acts 21:18ff.) the advisability of engaging in ritual purifications? Such an attitude to the law is not consistent with that of the author of the letter. It is difficult to see what the problem is. Let us suppose for a moment that the letter is by James of Jerusalem and indeed written in the immediate aftermath of the Council. James himself may very well have been devoted to many of the ways of the old law in which he had been nurtured, as tradition says he was, but as a signatory to the Council's communiqué what would he say to the church as a whole? He would certainly not represent as essential for them what the Council labelled as non-essential, nor would he urge on them practices which his proximity to the temple allowed him to enjoy, but which would have had no practical possibility in their case. He would have brought out, on the contrary, the abiding and central moral thrust of the law — which is just what the letter does, for it is a 'law book' in a deeper and more pervasive sense than any other single writing in the New Testament.

[10]*E.g.* the greeting in Acts 15:23; Jas. 1:1 is identical. See also Acts 15:29 with Jas. 1:27.

But was devotion to the law James' motivation in Acts 15 and 21? There is no need to think so. His behaviour at the Council is that of a great conciliator. His intervention in the debate aims to provide a common ground on which all may unite. Likewise in Acts 21 he does not take sides, but stands between two sides which, if nothing is done, might well pull apart from each other. His persuasive ways are evident in that Paul followed his advice, and if he fell foul of the Jews in doing so this was not germane to James' purpose, which was to provide common ground for different views and emphases among Christians.[11] Such a James is essential as author of this letter, with its central insistence on harmony and the composing of differences.

It can be urged[12] that if James were the Lord's brother then, surely, there would be more reference to the Lord Jesus than the letter contains. But who can tell? One might well reply that, if the letter were by an author wishing to pass himself off as James, he would have made it unambiguously clear which James he wished to personate. But, again, who can tell? Certainly there is nothing in the letter which speaks against authorship by the Lord's brother and, as we have suggested, much that speaks in its favour. If we ask another question it may help. What James do we know of in the New Testament, after the death of the son of Zebedee, the apostle James, who could simply sign his letter 'James' and expect everyone to know who was meant? None but James, son of Joseph and Mary, brother of the Lord.

The one thing on which the letter itself insists is that its author was named 'James'. This is as much part of the inspired testimony of the Word of God as anything else in the letter. It is inadmissible, therefore, to search for an anonymous writer, for the author's name has been revealed, and in so far as we have pointers to follow, they point to only one James.

---

[11]The legalists of Gal. 2:12 claimed to have come from James. Acts 15:24 shows in another setting how James might have disclaimed any link with such self-professed disciples.

[12]*E.g.* Laws, p.40.

1:1
1. Setting the scene

James, a servant of God and of the Lord Jesus Christ,
To the twelve tribes in the Dispersion:
Greeting.

If James were to post his letter today it would be marked 'Return to sender' on the ground of being insufficiently addressed. He names no names and specifies no place as destination: *twelve tribes* contain a lot of people and *the Dispersion*, in its special sense of the scattered people of God, was in principle world-wide.

Yet, at first sight, is any great problem really involved? *Twelve tribes* reminds us of the Old Testament people of God, the children of the twelve sons of Jacob (*e.g.* Ex. 1:2–5). Even in the New Testament Paul can still speak of 'our twelve tribes' (Acts 26:7), referring to those who can trace their descent back to the twelve patriarchs. *Dispersion*, too, is a term with a clear meaning. From the time of the return from exile in Babylon, the people of God were in two sections: those who had come back to live in the promised land (*e.g.* Ezr. 1: ; 2:1ff.) and those who remained living among the nations. The latter group were seen as 'dispersed' throughout the world, and the word 'dispersion' came to be used both of the scattered people and the world-wide area, outside Palestine, where they lived.

But no sooner do we feel our problem is clarifying than fresh difficulties arise. There are two. First, by the time of James, the physical descendants of the people of the Old Testament had long since become 'the Jews'. James, however, writes as a Christian to Christians. Both he, the writer, and they, the readers, acknowledge Jesus as Lord. James is *a servant of God and of the Lord Jesus Christ* (1:1); they are his 'brethren' (1:2) whom he further describes (2:1) as united

23

with himself in 'the faith of our Lord Jesus Christ'. Secondly, as James sees it, the whole of *the twelve tribes* are *in the Dispersion*. The words have lost their characteristic contemporary use among the Jews; they no longer contrast some who are 'abroad' with others who are 'at home'. Every one of the tribes addressed is away from the homeland, dispersed in the world.

We would seem, therefore, to be back in square one! Who are these *twelve tribes*? To answer this question we must follow another line – the straight line from the Old Testament into the New. Our Lord Jesus chose out twelve apostles (Mk. 3:13–14) and looked forward to the day of his own glory when they would sit on twelve thrones ruling the twelve tribes of Israel (Mt. 19:28). In doing this he was not creating a 'new' Israel (either alongside or replacing an 'old' Israel); he was leading the Israel of the Old Covenant on into its full, intended reality as the Israel of the New Covenant, the apostolic people of our Lord Jesus Christ, those whom Paul calls 'the Israel of God' (Gal. 6:16). In a word, 'Israel' is the name of the people of Jesus; it is the true and inalienable title of his church. Because of this Paul teaches that Christians are children of Abraham (Gal. 3:7) and that Abraham is our father (Rom. 4:11, 16). He does not qualify this relationship by saying, for example, that we can think of ourselves as if we were children of Abraham, or that we might find it helpful to draw an analogy between ourselves and those who are Abraham's children, or anything like that. He asserts a fact: those who have put their faith in Jesus for salvation are Abraham's children and the Israel of God.

Peter brings us a step even nearer to James. He writes his first letter (1:1) to 'the exiles of the Dispersion' and goes on (1:2) to define them as people who know God as the Holy Trinity, Father, Son and Holy Spirit, and who have experienced the sprinkling of the blood of Jesus Christ. Old Testament terms again describe New Testament people; they are God's exiles of the Dispersion. No adjustment of meaning is made, no compromise with truth, for they are God's Israel.

James brings these lines of Bible truth together and so sets the scene for his letter. Better than any other description could, *the twelve tribes* places the church firmly within the pressures and persecutions of this life. We can think of our ancestral tribes in the storm and stress of Egyptian slavery (Ex. 2:23), redeemed by the blood of the lamb (Ex. 12:13), on pilgrimage with God through 'the great and terrible wilderness' (Dt. 8:15; *cf.* Ex. 15:22), battling to enter into what the Lord had promised (Jos. 1:2) and struggling ever after to live in holiness amid the enticements of a pagan environment. These are the experiences through which James would have his readers understand their pilgrim path. They are the Lord's twelve tribes and they are dispersed throughout a menacing and testing world. Their homeland is elsewhere and they have not yet come to take up their abode there. Their present lot is to feel the weight of life's pressures, the lure of this world's temptations and an insidious, ever-present encouragement to conform to the standards of their pagan environment. They are the Lord's people indeed, redeemed by the blood of the Lamb himself – but not yet home.

First priority

James has a name for being the pre-eminently 'practical' man among the New Testament writers. It is a true reputation. The scene he has set in verse 1 demands that he address himself in a down-to-earth fashion to people whom he has so firmly placed right in the realities of this earth's life. So what will he put first? What is the first thing the Lord's people on earth need to be told?

To find the answer to this question we must, for a moment, stand back from the letter and look at it as a whole. James' practical letter finds its focus in one set of topics: it is a letter about relationships. He calls us, for example, to care for orphans and widows (1:27), to be impartial in our courtesy and care of others (2:1); he emphasizes the duty of love for our neighbour (2:8), speaking of it as 'the royal law'; he scorns a profession of faith which fails in love and compassion (2:15–16) and applauds the life that risks itself for the sake of those who are at risk (2:25); he warns against feelings which imperil fellowship (3:14) and words which denigrate a brother (4:11); we are to discharge our honourable debts (5:4), guard our reactions (5:9), minister to the sick (5:14), share with the distressed (5:16) and urgently pursue those who stray from Christ (5:19–20). His letter is quite a catalogue, quite a sustained emphasis on this single set of topics.

But this focus is absent from the whole of the first section of the letter (1:2–25) following upon the opening greeting (1:1), making a most marked contrast. The opening section is all about the individual: the one who lacks wisdom (5), who is not totally committed (7), the *brother*, poor or rich (9–10), the one who receives the crown (12). The terms of verses 13–14 could not be more individual and personal: *I, each, his own desire*; and the same is true of the birth described in verse 18. We could continue in the same vein through to verse 25: a self-ward, individual concentration.

25

James, in fact, puts first the duty of self-care in the things of God. Who would have thought it? The Christian looking after Number One! Yet Paul said the same thing to the elders of the Ephesian church: 'Take heed to yourselves and to all the flock' (Acts 20:28) – *yourselves* first, then *all the flock.* James writes in the same spirit and to the same point. Before we care for others we must look after ourselves. The ever practical James puts his finger right on the spot. It is all so personal, so self-ward, that it can be faced only in first person terms. In verse 4 he teaches about a path which leads to Christian maturity: before I can lead anyone else along that path or assist a brother or sister caught in life's toils, I must ask am I on that path myself? Am I holding fast through the testings of life and so growing to maturity? Verse 12 promises a crown to the one who loves God and walks the way of endurance: how can I hold another Christian to such demands unless I am accepting their discipline myself? In verse 18 James uses the illustration of first-fruits. In the agricultural community of Old Covenant days the first of the crop was the Lord's and specially holy: am I such, notably holy, something special for God? According to verse 25 there is a particular doorway into blessing, through hearing and doing God's word: is that my daily experience? Am I enjoying the blessing? For I cannot point others this way unless I am walking the road of obedience myself.

It is at these points of priority that James meets us: forget about others for a bit! What is your life with God like?

Jesus is Lord

Just suppose for a moment that this letter was written by James, the brother of the Lord Jesus – not, as we have seen, an extravagant supposition. James loves the word *brother.* He writes to *my brethren* (1:2; 2:1, 14; 3:1; 5:12, 19), to *brethren* (4:11; 5:7, 9, 10) and to *my beloved brethren* (1:16, 19; 2:5). He expects Christians to think of each other as brothers and sisters (1:9; 2:15; 4:11). But when he writes of one who was in fact a brother within his own family, he calls him *the Lord Jesus Christ* (1:1).

Seeing the verse this way sharpens our awareness of what early believers thought about the Lord Jesus, and this point can be made irrespective of the identity of the writer. Many agree that the Letter of James is a very early piece of Christian writing.[1] Sufficient time had

[1] J. A. T. Robinson (*Redating the New Testament*, p. 138) says 'early in 48 – not later,

not yet elapsed for that process, dear to some who write on the incarnation, by which the 'poetry' which hailed Jesus as son of God 'hardened into prose and escalated from a metaphorical son of God to a metaphysical God the Son'.[2] Early as it is, the Letter of James betrays no hesitation on this point, no sense of groping after a new theology or of expressing a doctrinal innovation about Jesus. The words have an assured ring and he uses them as stating something which his world-wide readers will endorse.

We have become accustomed to the standard English translation, *a servant of God and of the Lord Jesus Christ*. But the Greek could equally well sustain the rendering 'a servant of Jesus Christ who is God and Lord'. Commentators tend[3] to step back from this translation though without arguing a case, but we can put it this way: James was a master of the Greek language. James Adamson, for example, writes of his exercising 'the power of the expert craftsman in language' and again of 'the expert classic who wrote the Greek of the Epistle of James'.[4] Even, therefore, were it the case that he intended the meaning which the English Versions express — that God and the Lord Jesus are co-owners of their 'slaves' — yet it cannot have escaped his notice that his words were equally capable of ascribing deity to Jesus. But he did not alter them. Some, today, find themselves satisfied 'to say . . . *He is "as-if-*

---

and possibly a year or so earlier'. Paul's 'first extant letters, to the Thessalonians, date from AD 50 or 51' (M. Green (ed.), *The Truth of God Incarnate* (Hodder, 1977), p. 18).

[2]J. Hick (ed.), *The Myth of God Incarnate* (SCM Press, 1977), p. 176.

[3]*Cf.* Mitton, *in loc.* There is no exact New Testament parallel to the wording in James, where neither of the nouns 'God' and 'Lord' has a definite article (*theou kai kyriou Iēsou Christou*). There are examples which show how both the nouns joined by the conjunction can refer to the Lord Jesus: 2 Pet. 1:11; 2:20; 3:18 (*tou kyriō hēmōn kai sōtēros Iēsou Christou*), with which it is interesting to compare 2 Pet. 1:1 (*tou theou hēmōn kai sōtēros Iēsou Christou*) or 2 Thes. 1:12 (*tou theou hēmōn kai kyriou Iēsou Christou*). 2 Pet. 1:11 and its two companions require the translation 'Jesus Christ, our Lord and Saviour'; by parity of translation 2 Pet. 1:1 can be rendered 'Jesus Christ, our God and Lord'. Jude 4 (*ton monon despotēn kai kyrion hēmōn Iēsoun Christon*) is of interest as introducing an exegetical factor into the discussion, for out of four other examples where *despotēs* is a divine title only one explicitly refers to the Lord Jesus: some commentators therefore prefer 'the only Sovereign (God) and our Lord Jesus Christ'; yet it is hard to resist the strong impression that the Greek points to 'our only Sovereign and Lord . . .' like Tit. 2:13 (*tou megalou theou kai sōtēros hēmōn Iēsou Christou*), 'our great God and Saviour, Jesus Christ'. In James, therefore, 'Jesus Christ, God and Lord' can be resisted only if there are clear dogmatic grounds for saying that such an ascription of deity to the Lord Jesus is impossible. Such grounds do not exist.

[4]Adamson, pp. 19, 72.

God" for me.[5] But there is no 'as if' in James: Jesus Christ is *the Lord.*

The corollary of this divine Lordship is that James is his slave – 'not a term of special humility, nor . . . to be understood as involving a claim to the rank of a prophet or distinguished leader . . . simply . . . to belong to Christ as his worshipper'.[6]

To belong to Christ, to acknowledge him as Lord and God, to worship him – but surely, in addition, a slave is there to serve, to do his lord's bidding. Like James, Paul saw himself as the slave of Jesus (*e.g.* Rom. 1:1; Gal. 1:10; Phil. 1:1), but he became a slave the day he said, 'What shall I do, Lord?' (Acts 22:10). For though to be the slave of such a Master is a glorious and privileged relationship, it is far from being ornamental. We in turn look up to Jesus: What shall we do, Lord? If we see the letter of James as the inspired reply to this question, then we have the same practical and earthy approach to reading these five chapters that James had in writing them.

[5]F. Young in J. Hick (ed.), *The Myth of God Incarnate*, p.39.
[6]Ropes, *in loc.*

1:2–4
2. The life-giving trial

Count it all joy, my brethren, when you meet various trials, [3]for you know that the testing of your faith produces steadfastness. [4]And let steadfastness have its full effect, that you may be perfect and complete, lacking in nothing.

The all-too-dedicated mother, the seven-days-a-week parson, the workaholic tycoon can all justify their life-style by saying, 'My family needs me', 'My church needs me', 'My business needs me'. But what happens if the end of all this selfless wear and tear is breakdown? The needs of family, church and business remain unaltered, but the indispensable helper is no longer there.

These are not James' illustrations, but possibly he would not disapprove, for they do point up the balance of teaching which we have seen in his letter. The first priority for the church in the world, under the Lordship of Christ, is that Christians must look after themselves, for the life which issues in the caring ministries of 1:27 is the life which is itself moving forward to maturity.

On to maturity

This is the note which James strikes right away. There is a goal of maturity: *that you may be perfect and complete, lacking in nothing* (4b); there is a pathway to maturity: *testing . . . produces steadfastness. And let steadfastness have its full effect . . .* (3b–4a); and there is a terrain through which that pathway must go: *Count it all joy . . . when you meet various trials* (2). To us this may all sound quite amazing, but to James it is the clue to the meaning of life. He is nothing if not realistic: life is a tale of *various trials*. The Greek here is more vivid than the English word *various*. In classical Greek *poikilos* means 'many-coloured, variegated', and from this basic meaning it came to be used for 'diversified, complex, intricate'. Matthew (4:24) uses it to describe 'any and every kind' of sickness dealt with in the healing ministry of our Lord; Paul (2 Tim. 3:6) uses it of the limitless shapes which human desires take; and Peter (1 Pet. 4:10), of the endless ways in which the grace of God is proved to be sufficient for our needs. As he writes, James throws his main emphasis on *poikilos*: '. . . when you fall in with trials – no matter what form they may take.' What a true picture of life! The man who went from Jerusalem to Jericho and 'fell in with' (the same word) a band of robbers was neither expecting it nor prepared for it. It came to him as one of the 'changes and chances of this mortal life'. And any day, at any time of day, some experience of *trial* is, as it were, lying in wait ready to leap on us so that we cry out in surprise, 'What is this?', and in perplexity, 'Why has it happened to me?'

It may well be that we are sometimes guilty of saying to others, 'You must not worry so', while our hearts are telling us that the particular trial they are enduring contains every reason for anxiety. Too often there is this element of loving (or maybe cowardly) duplicity in our ministry to the distressed. It is not so with James. The *realism* with which he faces the fact that life brings trials of every shape is wedded to his *perception* of the inner meaning of all experience. Interestingly, however, he does not say 'I have discovered a secret'. The meaning of life is not a clue unveiled to James, but a truth common among Christians – at least as he sees it – for he says *you know* (3). He appeals, therefore, not for the adoption of a superficial gaiety in the face of life's adversities, but for a candid awareness of truth already known.

The clue to life: progress through trial

What is the clue, then, the vital truth, with which we are to face our trials? We shall follow through James' teaching in verses 3–4 with the help of three statements.

First, in the trials of life our Christian faith is being *tested for genuineness. The testing of your faith* means 'the experience of having your faith put to the test'. James takes it for granted that 'the natural effect of (trials) is to imperil persistence in faith' (Ropes), and how true this is. We have all met people who, though with different terms suited to their differing experiences, would concur with the sad words of one elderly man: 'I used to go to church, but five years ago my wife and my only daughter died within six months of each other, and after that it didn't seem worth the bother.' It is hard to use such a bitter experience as an illustration without seeming either to criticize the speaker for not being more resolute in the face of calamity, or to minimize the sharpness of his human sorrow. But no such criticism or insensitivity is meant: it is an only-too-often repeated fact that such faith as we possess collapses before the storm of sorrow, or pain, or disappointment, or whatever it may be. We say that we believe that God is our Father, but as long as we remain untested on the point our belief falls short of steady conviction. But suppose the day comes – as it does and will – when circumstances seem to mock our creed, when the cruelty of life denies his fatherliness, his silence calls in question his almightiness and the sheer, haphazard, meaningless jumble of events challenges the possibility of a Creator's ordering hand. It is in this way that life's trials test our faith for genuineness.

Secondly, James insists that we *know* (3) that the testing is *designed to result in strong consistency*: the experience of having your faith tested *produces steadfastness* (3). There is nothing unusual about this statement. It is just good observation of life. Young couples in the first excitement of their attraction to each other readily believe that theirs will be a life-long partnership: they are meant for each other. At this point in their relationship it is, of course, no more than a matter of opinion, and much more tentative than they are in a position to realize or willing to admit. Soon, however, their belief will face tests: the counter-attraction of other possible partners, a growing experience of individual likes and dislikes which will not harmonize without serious adjustment, maybe the cool or antagonistic reaction of one or both sets of parents, and so forth. It is as testings are endured that the relationship itself becomes more durable, and along the line of this process the incipient belief that they are meant to marry becomes a settled conviction. The same process goes on into their marriage. They have pledged themselves to forsake all other partnerships for life, and in the course of their life together – maybe by the experience of fighting off temptations or of gritty determination to save their marriage in a period of coolness, or just the shoulder-to-shoulder facing and bearing of the vicissitudes of life – their minds become irrevocably weaned away from the thought of infidelity. What began as a tentative belief ends as a fixed, unchangeable constancy of life.

The *steadfastness* of which James speaks (3–4) can thus be illustrated from life, but the reality to which he calls us is consistent living for Christ. He answers the cry of our hearts that we might be less fluctuating in our loyalty, less erratic in our conduct. His answer is this: the trials of life are God's testings. They may come from outside, through circumstances or people, or, as we shall see in the use of the same word in verses 13–14, they may be the inner promptings of our sinful natures. But they are God's designed way forward. It is only by meeting and passing its tests that faith grows into strong constancy.

We can now proceed to the third statement: *by persistent steadfastness we grow to full maturity*. Verses 3 and 4 are 'sewn together' by this word *steadfastness*. James uses it again in 5:11 and in doing so perfectly illustrates what it means – it expresses the characteristic of Job. We proverbially speak of the 'patience' of Job, and indeed the word is thus translated in 5:11 in the older English versions. But so much more is involved in the word, and in the life of Job, than the sort of passive acceptance of things which 'patience' tends to convey. James' word (*hypomonē*) is well summed up by Sophie Laws: 'active steadfastness in, rather than passive submission to, circumstances.' It is a word which means 'staying power', 'constancy' (or better, as it was put just above, 'strong constancy'), 'endurance' and 'stickability'. My wording of the 'third statement' as including 'persistent steadfastness' attempts to draw out the teaching which James adds in verse 4. Note that this verse begins with *and*; the word is of some importance. (NIV seeks to achieve the right stress by omitting 'and' and introducing the thought of 'must'.) James is bringing in a word of caution. A believer might endure for a while, and then tire of enduring. In this case the desired growth to maturity is halted mid-way. There has to be a persistency of enduring. *Steadfastness* must *have its full effect* (4) or, as the Greek might be rendered more literally, 'enjoy a mature work'.

The road is, therefore, hard and long, and the task is unremitting: to endure the first onset of the startling, unexpected trial, and to endure again while it persists, and then to go on enduring. It is like the Lord Jesus who 'endured the cross' (Heb. 12:2) right through to the point where the whole work of salvation was accomplished, and he himself entered upon the unbroken possession of eternal glory at the Father's right hand. We are thus called to a persistent endurance. But this hard road has a glorious destination for us too: *that you may be perfect and complete, lacking in nothing* (4). James allows word to build upon word until he has created an impression of total fullness.

Perfect is a word for both the ultimate and the near future. On the one hand it is the daunting word which the Lord Jesus used when he said that we are to be perfect as our heavenly Father is perfect (Mt. 5:48); and, while this is ever our present target, we know that it can be our experience only when we see Jesus, and shall be like him (1 Jn.

3:2). But also it is the word Paul uses when, having acknowledged that he is himself not yet perfect,[1] he at once addresses himself to 'those of us who are mature' (lit. 'perfect', Phil. 3:15). Without losing sight of the ultimate aim, here is our present target: maturity of personality – and to this, just as to the heavenly fulfilment, the path is the same, namely, testings, endurance and perseverance. But lest we should miss the magnitude of what awaits us at the end of the road, James allows our minds to dwell on the thought of perfection by first a positive and then a negative qualification. Positively, *perfect* means *complete* (*holoklēros*), that is, possessing every part which goes to making up the complete whole;[2] and negatively, it is *lacking in nothing*.

Prescription for health

A doctor who diagnosed but could not or would not prescribe would find his consulting rooms deserted. So far we have listened to James diagnosing. He has brought out the main lines of our condition: we suffer from *various trials*, whose nature and onset cannot be predicted in advance. He has also given in some detail the course of treatment appropriate to such a case: a course of testings, strong constancy and persistence. But, we might reasonably ask, 'Doctor, what are we to do?'

He replies, *Count it all joy*. Each word in the prescription is important. The verb, *count*, refers to the importance which we accord to something – the 'account' we would give of it. Paul, for example, 'counts' everything as loss in respect of the surpassing glory of knowing Christ (Phil. 3:7–8); Peter urges us to 'count' the seeming delay in the return of Christ as the Lord's forbearance (2 Pet. 3:15). James uses the form of the verb (aorist) which signifies being precise, definite or decisive about something: in a word, to 'have a settled conviction'. The small word *it* contains the whole of life. It sums up in its tiny compass every one of the *various trials* which the present may contain, the future may bring, or the past may keep stored in memory. Paul's experienced sailors did not plan to 'strike a shoal' (Acts 27:41), for they did not know it was there – but they did strike it, and the account in Acts uses the same verb as is here in James: 'falling upon or into'. Life is full of hidden rocks, sudden violent winds of circumstances

[1]The verb corresponding to the adjective (Phil. 3:12).
[2]The adjective, *holoklēros*, is excellently illustrated in the only other place it appears in the New Testament, 1 Thes. 5:23. See also the noun, *holoklēria*, Acts 3:16.

lying in wait for the believer. Every single one of them is embraced in James' word *it*. There is no trial, no great calamity or small pressure, no overwhelming sorrow or small rub of life outside that plan of God, whereby it is a stepping-stone to glory. And it for this reason that our settled conviction must be to appraise it as *all joy*, not because it is joyful in itself (for 'all discipline seems painful rather than pleasant' (Heb. 12:11) when it is in full flood), but because 'later it yields the peaceful fruit of righteousness' (Heb. 12:11). In James' words, it is the only way forward to become *perfect and complete, lacking in nothing*.

'Doctor,' we might say, 'does the medicine have to be so nasty? Does the treatment have to be so severe?' And he replies, 'Don't you want to be better?' So then, do we want to be like Jesus? Do we want to come to the full enjoyment of our full salvation? Do we want, when we reach heaven, to have our perceptions and faculties so sharpened and sensitized that we will be able to see the glory? Then there is no other way. If the tares are pulled out prematurely the wheat will come, damaged, to the harvest (Mt. 13:29–30) In this too we must be like our Lord: we must set the great *joy* before us and, in consequence, endure (Heb. 12:2).

Is it any wonder that, in setting this teaching out for us, James has attempted to breach the stronghold of our minds and to capture the way we think? Peter says we are not to think it strange when trials try us (1 Pet. 4:12), but generally speaking we find it very strange indeed and are greatly surprised at it. James says we are to *count it all joy*, but do we ever do so? If we are to line ourselves up with Scripture a whole revolution in thinking is called for. And this revolution touches not only our appraisal of life's experiences, but of our spiritual expectations also. So often we are encouraged to think of holiness, sanctification, perfection, victory over sin (or whatever way the ultimate glory of the likeness of Christ may be expressed) as the result of an inner transaction with God, a total commitment, a self-abandonment to him; sometimes even we hear those who promise these benefits as instantaneous results, open to us now. How very far this is from the teaching of James and the expectations he encourages! By comparison, James' road is both uphill and thorny; the benefits he promises are hard won, and progress painfully made can be consolidated only by repetition of the same costly effort.

But let us ask ourselves: is this what James teaches? For if it is – and, indeed, there can be no 'if' about it – then Scripture has spoken, and our duty (and privilege) is to reform our thinking in the light of God's Word. But even more deeply, and with a greater privilege, is not this the way our Saviour went forward to his glory? And if it is the way the Master went, shall not the servant tread it still? Furthermore, do we know anything that our hearts want more than to be made like the Son of God in all things?

3. The way of wisdom

If any of you lacks wisdom, let him ask God, who gives to all men generously and without reproaching, and it will be given him. ⁶But let him ask in faith, with no doubting, for he who doubts is like a wave of the sea that is driven and tossed by the wind. ⁷,⁸For that person must not suppose that a double-minded man, unstable in all his ways, will receive anything from the Lord.

⁹Let the lowly brother boast in his exaltation, ¹⁰and the rich in his humiliation, because like the flower of the grass he will pass away. ¹¹For the sun rises with its scorching heat and withers the grass; its flower falls, and its beauty perishes. So will the rich man fade away in the midst of his pursuits.

Sometimes after a meeting a preacher is asked, 'Had you thought of putting that in writing?' And when the preacher demurs, pleading lack of time to shape the material into written form, he is urged not to let this bother him – 'Even if you just copied out your notes, it would be such a help to so many.'

One is tempted to wonder if this is what happened to James! His letter so often has the appearance of a rather disjointed series of paragraphs. Were he to use them as preaching notes, he would, of course, build connections between them. But as things are, we, his readers, lacking the benefit of his personal exposition, often have to ask ourselves why this follows that, and where the exact line of thought flows.

In the present case, there is a clue to follow. James has linked verse 5 back to verse 4 by a word common to each: . . . *lacking in nothing. If any of you lacks.* . . This does seem to be the connecting idea, and we can open out the thought like this: Look forward, then, to the day when you will stand complete, lacking in nothing. But just at present I am pretty certain there is one thing you know yourself to lack. It may be that you cannot quite see life as I have portrayed it. You are in the thick of such a tangle of circumstances that there is no way in which it can seem other than a purposeless mess. There is no stretch of the imagination by which it even begins to look like a stepping-stone to maturity. In a word, you need wisdom: the wisdom that sees all life as serving the purposes of the Lord. Or your situation may be somewhat different: you accept that your circumstances are designed by the Lord to exert those pressures and impose those tests which, in due time, will bear the fruit of increasing maturity. But you find that seeing life like that does not make it either easy or plain which way to turn. There is more than one path opening ahead. Prepared as you are to persevere, you do not know which to choose as the divinely appointed way forward. Again, you need wisdom.[1]

Wisdom from God

The heart of verses 5–8 can be expressed in answer to three questions. What does the Bible mean by 'wisdom'? What does James say here about God? And what does he teach about prayer?

The Lord Jesus grew in wisdom (Lk. 2:52), and during his ministry people marvelled that he showed such wisdom, and wondered where he had got it (Mt. 13:54). Moses was educated in all the wisdom of the Egyptians (Acts 7:22). In these references 'wisdom' has a very general meaning. Moses was an 'educated man'; Jesus impressed people as being a learned person. But it is plain from many other passages that the word (*sophia*) has a much more specialized meaning than this. The 'wisdom of Solomon' (Mt. 12:42; *e.g.* 1 Ki. 3:16–28) was 'practical sagacity', the ability to apply what he knew to the problems of life. The Lord Jesus promised to his disciples that at times of trial they would be given 'a mouth and wisdom' (Lk. 21:15), *i.e.* an ability to speak appropriately to the situation. Stephen had this gift pre-eminently for the purposes of ministry (Acts 6:10). Another side of 'wisdom' is exemplified in 1 Corinthians 1:21, the wisdom which sees the meaning and significance of things. If we say about someone, 'He knows his Bible really well,' so far we have described a knowledgeable person. But if he also knows how to *use* his Bible to understand life and

[1]For these two aspects of the possible link between vv.2–4 and 5–11, see Calvin: 'All our feelings are averse to the thought that we can be happy in the midst of evils'...(hence)...'he bids us to ask wisdom...'; J. B. Phillips' translation takes account of the other need of wisdom: 'If any of you does not know how to meet any particular problem...'

the world around him, and to guide his own conduct and the conduct of others in the maze of life's problems, then knowledge has passed over into wisdom (*cf.* Jas. 3:13, 17).

Wisdom, then, is particularly related to the two ways in which we tried to link verses 5ff. back to verses 2–4. The wise person will be able to see life as James has pictured it in verses 2–4; able to make personal decisions and to shape life's pathway, so as to enjoy the progress towards maturity which he has promised. Such wisdom is a gift from God.

In conformity with his practical approach to things, there is a beautiful directness and simplicity about the teaching of James: whoever lacks wisdom can ask for it, and God will give it. Just like that! Such simplicity is either totally unrealistic, or else finds its justification in what is known about God. For James, it is the latter. His doctrine of God is such that he can afford to make large promises in his name, and to affirm that those promises will be honoured. He teaches us, first, that *God's nature is to give*. He writes (literally) '. . . let him ask from the giving God . . .'. The requirements of English make it impossible for us to leave the words just like that, because we have to accommodate the remainder of what James writes within the framework of English grammar. But this is, in fact, how he sees God in himself: he is 'the giving God'. No one attribute expresses all that is true about God, but each expresses something about him that is true all the time. If we speak of him as 'gracious' there are very many other things to say before the divine nature is fully described. Yet there is never a time when we could come to him and find that he was no longer gracious. So it is, also, when he is described as 'the giving God'. His attributes are as infinite as he himself is, but there is no war among them: they are as perfectly one as he himself is. When we come with our prayers, he never replies, 'Come back tomorrow. Perhaps I will then be able to be "the giving God" again, but today I must occupy myself with being something else.' 'Giving' is not the whole truth, but it is ceaselessly true. He is more than 'giving', but he is always 'giving'.

James now proceeds to teach us that *God's bounty is unrestricted*: he *gives to all . . . generously* (5). In these two expressions he directs our attention first to earth and the recipients of the giving, then to heaven and the manner of the giving. God's giving knows no earthly limitation; he *gives to all*. And it knows no heavenly limitation. *Generously* may be as close to the Greek as we can get, but the thought of the word itself is richer. We have here the adverb (*haplōs*) of the adjective (*haplous*) which the Lord used (Mt. 6:22) of a *sound* eye. Literally it means 'single', not plagued with double vision or any such thing as might diminish clarity of sight. The noun (*haplotēs*) is used of 'single-mindedness' – referring to our devotion to the Lord Jesus (2 Cor. 11:3), or of a slave's loyalty to a master (Eph. 6:5). The same word is used of giving, a ministry of generosity (Rom. 12:8; 2 Cor. 8:2). It is not easy to be certain along what path a word meaning 'singleness' came to mean 'generosity', but two possibilities suggest themselves: 'selflessness', *i.e.* with a single-minded concern for the other person; or 'exclusive preoccupation', *i.e.* with the mind set upon this one task as if there were nothing else to do. This is how the 'giving God' gives – with a selfless, total concern for us and with an exclusive preoccupation as if he had nothing else to do but to give and give again.

There is a third element in James' teaching – *God's welcome never fails: and without reproaching* (5). Some commentators introduce here the thought that human giving is often spoilt and made a burden to the recipient, because the giver cannot forget the gift and alludes to it again and again. This is hardly a suitable meaning for *reproaching*, which must surely refer, not to the conduct of the giver, but to some misdemeanour on the part of the recipient.[2] In other words, James here calls to mind everything which we know to stand in the way of a free asking and everything which we might imagine the Lord would hold against us. It is a true impulse which prompted the hymn-writer to plead, 'Look not on our misusings of thy grace.' Right though confession is in our prayers, however, our 'misusings' never call in question his generosity or make him other than the giving God.

Wanting God's gifts

In all this the generous, loving, forbearing nature of God is revealed to us, opening before us an exciting prospect of the possibilities of prayer – and a prospect which, as a matter of fact, is scripturally true. But there is also something else to take into account. It is humbling to ask why the teaching of verses 6–8 follows on from that of verse 5. The answer is this: verse 5 holds before us the unquestioned sincerity of God who desires our progress to maturity and who, therefore, as far as he is concerned, will not withhold from us the wisdom we need. But

---

[2] *Cf.* Mitton, '. . . continual reminders of it after the gift has been made . . .'; Ropes, '. . . the meanness which after a benefaction calls it unpleasantly to the mind of the one benefited . . .'.; Barnes is to the point, 'He does not reproach or chide us for our past conduct.'

verses 6–8 raise the question of our sincerity. Do we want to go forward with God? Are we whole-heartedly committed to his way of seeing things and his ambitions for our future? Or are we keeping a door open for the world? Are we trying to have a foot in each camp? God's mind is clear; but are we *double-minded*? *Faith* (6) is our absolute confidence that he will give what we ask; *doubting* (6) is our own inner uncertainty about whether we really want him to give or not.

The two key words which James uses both focus on this one point. He uses the verb which RSV represents as 'to doubt' (*diakrinomai*). In itself it does not necessarily have a bad meaning. It means 'to know how to decide as between alternative interpretations' (Mt. 16:3) or 'to argue/discuss the respective merits of two points of view' (Acts 11:2); or 'to be hesitant how to decide a matter' (Rom. 14:23). Basically the thought is that of making up one's mind between alternatives. But then the bad meaning comes in: it is to be a person in two minds, one whose allegiance is not committed either way. The other word comes in verse 8, *double-minded*, *dipsychos*, a word James may even have coined himself. He uses it again in 4:8. Literally, it means 'two-souled', 'with divided soul'. We must put on one side our English usage 'two-faced', for James' meaning is not that of duplicity. It is rather, as with his other word, to be in two minds: not two-faced, but facing both ways.

The Lord Jesus had his own thoughts about the person who would serve two masters (Mt. 6:24), pointing out that divided loyalties cannot be sustained but must finally settle one way or the other. But, as James' illustration shows, he is concerned not with the ultimate impossibility of the situation but with its sad, present consequences. The experience of *a wave* 'whipped up by the wind and blown about' would have been all too familiar to a Galilean James (*cf.* Mk. 4:37). All is in flux and motion; no sooner is the surge of the sea set in one direction than a fresh gust of wind whips it round. And such is the *doubting* (6) and *double-minded* (8).

Two results follow. We will take first the one that is directly related to James' immediate line of teaching: the power of prayer is vitiated. Comparison of English translations will show that there is some uncertainty as to how verse 8 ought to be punctuated. RSV represents one possibility; NIV (*cf.* RV) represents another: 'That man should not think he will receive anything from the Lord; he is a double-minded man . . .' Not a great deal is at stake either way, and in each case there is this common ground that prayer is tragically bereft of power. The Lord Jesus taught the same thing when, for example, he commented that those who forgive can confidently ask for forgiveness, but those who are unforgiving will go unforgiven (Mt. 6:14–15), or that the unmerciful will find no mercy (Mt. 18:23–35). It is the same issue of the double mind – as if our heavenly Father replies: How can I give you forgiveness when you are not in fact concerned for forgiveness? Why should you receive mercy when there is no place for mercy in your life? On the other hand, the Lord Jesus also taught that unanimity is a crucial factor in effective praying both on the corporate (Mt. 18:19) and on the individual level (Mt. 21:21). Indeed in this latter case the same word for 'doubt' occurs as in James. Equally in each case the problem is not intellectual doubt but moral and spiritual commitment, the devotion of our whole loyalty to the Lord.

The second result of the doubting and double mind is a widespread instability affecting the whole of a person's life: *unstable in all his ways* (8). James often turns aside like this to pass a general comment arising from particular teaching. Here he affirms that, if we are not secure with God, then we are not secure at all. We may relate the idea of instability to the trials and tribulations of life. Amid all the trials to which James has alluded, here is a person who 'never can keep a steady course' (NEB). On the other hand, the instability may refer to personal character, to an inner division and therefore insecurity which shows itself in all life's experience, smooth or rough. Either way, James is touching on very deep matters, at the core of today's problems.

One of the frightening features of the present day is the widespread dependence on sedatives to cope with situations which our grand-parents would not have seen as a problem – ordinary factors like bringing up children, facing a tomorrow which is essentially the same as today; problems of feeling trapped and bored; problems of having time and not knowing how to fill it. The cynic would say that the problem whether there is a life after death has been replaced with the problem whether there is a life before death. But essentially it is the problem of finding meaning: which James says can be answered by a gift of wisdom from God given to those whose personalities are integrated around him. Or again, widespread in society, there are breakdowns brought on by the really sharp problems of our day. People find themselves no longer able to face the grind of making ends meet, or they are dealt peculiarly savage blows by the onset of disease in themselves or their family, and they have no resource by which to find their way effectively through such hazards. But again, there is the wisdom of God, which, however, is granted to those whose hearts confess a sole loyalty to him. James' diagnosis does not find expression in many consulting rooms, but that does not affect its truth as an acute diagnosis. People astray from God are 'troubled'; they have no inner or outer restfulness.

The truth also bears upon those who do acknowledge God as Father, Jesus as Saviour and the Holy Spirit as Comforter. For we too know the pressures of the day; we too imbibe easily the spirit of the age and find ourselves 'fraying at the edges' in the changes and chances of life. James says that our first thought should be to look at our relationship to God. If 'life' is getting through to us, if the ability to cope, to absorb our own 'hassles' and those of others, is a diminishing quantity, then this is the crucial question. Is our heart *one* with God (not 'right with God', for that has been eternally secured for us by Christ), without any division of loyalty? And a second question follows: are we proving the reality of that sole allegiance to God in the place of prayer – not in the public place of confrontation with the world (that will come later), but in the secret place of prayer? For out of this will emerge that wisdom which unifies the personality and holds us on a steady course in the storm.

For instance

When we come to verses 9–11 with their unexpected advice to poor and rich Christians, we experience again that sense of slight bewilderment which overtakes the reader of James. By what connection of ideas or development of theme do we find ourselves here? But as we ponder, lines of connection begin to emerge. First, the verses are about contrasting circumstances of life: poverty (9) and wealth (10–11). This at once relates them to James' main theme as he has been developing it since verse 2: life is full of *various trials*. The poor man may say he would not mind swapping his problems for those of the rich, but the Bible is clear that the problems of prosperity are as keen as those of stringency. Indeed, they constitute, if anything, a more insidious threat to a committed life with God.[3] Secondly, the verses address both poor and rich with an exhortation to *boast* (9). The verb used here sometimes yields to the translation 'rejoice' (see Rom. 5:2–3, RSV) though really, when it has this good sense of boasting, it deserves something stronger, such as 'to exult' or 'glory'. It does mean, however, that in the present case we are, in principle, back to James' initial command to *count it all joy* when we *meet various trials* (2). And thirdly, we note the fact that the attitude commanded in relation to poverty and wealth is not that which is current in the world – either

[3]*Cf.* Mk. 4:19; 1 Tim. 6:9 (which uses the word *peirasmos*); etc.

the world James knew or ours. A new perspective is offered. In sum, therefore, we find in verses 9–11 James' chosen illustration of what he has been teaching in the previous seven verses: life is full of varying experiences and here is a typical contrast of lot, the poor man and the rich man. Each, within his circumstances, must rejoice, even glory, for this is the true response of the Christian. But each, too, must see his situation not through the eyes of this world's wisdom, but in the light of a wisdom sought from God.[4]

How, then, does the wisdom of God teach us to view our circumstances? James' illustration in verses 9–10a looks back to his foundation teaching in verses 2–4. The great goal of all life is Christian maturity. Towards this we are to bend all our efforts. Life's pleasant paths are made all the sweeter as we keep in mind that they lead to this great spiritual end; life's grim moments are to be endured patiently, remembering that patience and persistence turn sorrows into stepping-stones.

The illustrations of the poor and the rich do no more than drive this lesson home: each is exhorted to see his lot in the light of spiritual reality. To his financial adversities, the poor brother says, 'But how rich I am!' To his earthly glories, the rich brother says, 'But what a wretch I am!' Each keeps life in the perspective of eternity. James leaves it to our imagination to decide what each might mean, respec-

---

[4]In v. 10 James simply says 'and the rich in his humiliation'. Commentators differ over whether we should supply the noun 'brother' (*i.e.* assume that the rich man is a Christian) and what verb James intended to be understood in v. 10. The majority of commentators (*e.g.* Ropes, Mitton) urge that it is natural to supply 'brother' (and unnatural not to) and therefore they repeat in v. 10 the 'let . . . boast' of v. 9, understanding James to make a parallel appeal to the rich believer. Others (*e.g.* Alford, Laws) hold that James is describing rich people in v. 10 – and therefore understand an indicative mood of the verb: 'The rich, however, boasts in his humiliation.' They understand this statement in the same way as, for example, Phil. 3:19, 'They glory in their shame', *i.e.* in things they should be ashamed of; so, in James, the rich man boasts of something that is, in reality, his downfall. Neither interpretation is free of difficulty. If we assume James is addressing rich Christians, then we must also assume that he proceeds (from the word 'because' onwards in vv. 10–11) to speak of rich folk as such. If James is describing the rich as such in v. 10a, then he is, firstly, not expressing himself with his customary clarity, for the Greek is naturally suited by the insertion of 'brother' and of the hortatory form of the verb; secondly, the reference to the 'rich' becomes no more than an encouragement to the poor brother to endure his lot ('See what the Lord has spared you!') rather than (as the context leads us to expect) another example of the contrasting experiences of life. There is no ground for holding that James always sees the rich as outside the church: 2:1ff. is based on an example of a rich man coming into the assembly. We adopt, on balance, the view that James turns in v. 10 to address the rich brother.

tively, by *exaltation* and *humiliation*[5] (9–10), but imagination does not have far to run. The one, against whom life's tides seem to be running, and who is *lowly* as this world reckons things, seeks to live in a sustained awareness of the heights to which he has been lifted in Christ. The other, with his rich supply of this world's goods, looks rather to the depths from which Christ has rescued him, where, but for the grace of God, he would still languish, and to which, in his own heart, he knows he is still prone. To this extent the exhortations to the lowly and the wealthy run in parallel, and this is the main thrust of James' appeal. This is the way of wisdom, or one side of it – to see ourselves in the light of what is spiritually, and by revelation of God, true of us; to live by what is true as between us and God. In a word, it is to keep our eyes on the goal, and the pathway to the goal, as set out in verses 2–4, and to weigh life accordingly.

The heart of the matter

The other side of the wisdom which God will give is the ability to see things as they really are, to arrive at true definitions, to cease to live by what appears to be true and to live, instead, by what actually is the truth of the matter. We follow James as he turns, in the middle of verse 10, from the rich brother to the rich person. He shows us how the wisdom of God penetrates the façade of wealth to the distressing reality beneath. He offers a comparison (10, *like the flower*); then he proceeds to an explanation (11, *for the sun*), and finally he draws a conclusion (11, *So will*). The comparison is with fragility and evanescence; the explanation is dependence on favourable circumstances and helplessness in the face of adverse conditions; and the application is to the person (*so will the rich man*) and whole way of life (*pursuits*, lit. 'ways', *i.e.* characteristic life-style) of the person devoted to wealth. Thus, to the eye of man, riches may seem secure ('as safe as houses', 'like money in the bank') and seem to offer security (a 'secure investment'), but they are essentially perishable because they are at the mercy of circumstances ('not worth the paper they are printed on'). And those who worship wealth perish with their god. Paul touched the Achilles' heel of the world's wealth with his description of 'uncertain riches' (1 Tim. 6:17). James goes further: the transiency of riches is a malignant infection spreading to the rich person too.

[5]*Lowly (tapeinos)* and *humiliation (tapeinōsis)* are related words. They share the sense of 'lack of power/status', *etc.*, in this world (Lk. 1:48, 52). The adjective is used of a lowly spirit (Jas. 4:6) and the noun in the bad sense of humiliation (Acts 8:33).

The magnetism of riches is powerful and insistent, and we constantly need the wisdom of God to see through the façade. We do not have to be wealthy to desire money, and the desire is as threatening as the actuality (1 Tim. 6:9); we do not have to possess much in order to be snared by the delights of possession. But the Bible never teaches that wealth is wrong – did not the Lord give Solomon, as an intended blessing, riches as well as wisdom (1 Ki. 3:12–13)? Everything depends on how it has been acquired (*e.g.* Je. 17:11), how it is used (*e.g.* Lk. 12:19–20) and what place it holds in the heart of its possessor (*e.g.* 1 Jn. 2:15). Maybe James was thinking of Solomon. Do God's gifts ever come without God's testings, whereby we learn (or fail to learn) to enjoy his gifts? Was this why Solomon got money as well as wisdom? Is this why James illustrates the use of the gift of wisdom by displaying its ability to see to the heart of wealth? Or was James just following the teaching of the Lord Jesus and seeing that 'the love of mammon is the most common source of double-mindedness'[6], that fatal flaw (8) which holds us back alike from the gifts of God and from true stability of life?

Walking in wisdom

James chose to illustrate his theme (2–4) by reference to poverty and wealth. He could equally have chosen any of life's contrasts – loneliness and companionship, long married life and unexpected bereavement, hope fulfilled and hope disappointed, work and unemployment. These are the endlessly varied testings (2) which make the colours in the tapestry of each life: family life and childlessness, marriage and singleness, health and illness. There is no end to the lists to be made and the contrasts to be drawn. Life is like that. How, then, are we to steer a straight path to the goal of maturity? How are we to see what is of stable worth, and what a tinsel of disappointment and loss? Only by the wisdom God gives, a wisdom that makes us see earth in the light of heaven, life in the light of eternal life, the flickering pattern of experience in the light of the steady reality of salvation. And wisdom is sought from God in the place of prayer.

---

[6]Plumptre (*ad loc.*) uses the teaching of the Lord (Mt. 6:24) to make the link between Jas. 1:2–8 and 9–11, a significant link if we are reading the words of James, the Lord's brother.

1:12–19a
4. A battle of wills

Blessed is the man who endures trial, for when he has stood the test he will receive the crown of life which God has promised to those who love him. [13]*Let no one say when he is tempted, 'I am tempted by God'; for God cannot be tempted with evil and he himself tempts no one;* [14]*but each person is tempted when he is lured and enticed by his own desire.* [15]*Then desire when it has conceived gives birth to sin; and sin when it is full-grown brings forth death.*

[16]*Do not be deceived, my beloved brethren.* [17]*Every good endowment and every perfect gift is from above, coming down from the Father of lights with whom there is no variation or shadow due to change.* [18]*Of his own will he brought us forth by the word of truth that we should be a kind of first fruits of his creatures.*

[19]*Know this, my beloved brethren.*

We might well have entitled this chapter 'a peep behind the scenes', for that would accurately catch the contrast with what has gone before. We have been living among life's trials in verses 2–11, so much so that James was able to illustrate his theme by the contrasting outward circumstances of poverty and wealth. But now all is inward: he speaks of *love* (12); *God*, seen in his own nature (13); *desire* (14); the ultimate but at present unseen reality of eternal *death* (15); the nature of God again as *Father* (17); and the mystery of the new birth (18). The passage is a balanced presentation of three themes: what God gives (12, 17a), what he is (13, 17b), and what we are (14–15 and 18). The rebukes of verses 13–15, warning us away from false ways of thinking, are rounded off by the stern prohibition of verse 16, *Do not be deceived, my beloved brethren*; and the positive teaching of verses 17–18 is driven home by the command, *Know this, my beloved brethren* (19a). Lastly, in our review of the verses, 12 speaks of *life*, 15 of *death*, and 18 of birth.

In a nutshell, the triad of birth, life and death is what the verses are 'all about'. Behind the circumstances of life (2–11) there are the unseen factors of human nature (13–15) and of the divine nature (17) – and, above all, that basic unseen but potent factor, what God has done for us in the new birth (18). In this way James takes us 'behind the scenes': if we are to live for God, then we must understand how things are. Or, to put it another way, if verses 2–11 explore the way of wisdom, verses 12–19a explore the way of knowledge, with the necessity to reject the untruth (16) and to hold to the truth (19a).

James believes in setting goals before us. That is how he started out in verses 2–4 and it is what he does here again in verse 12. There, the goal could be expressed in the command 'Be an adult'; here, the command is 'Be blessed'. The former is the great goal of a truly fulfilled personality; that in verse 12 is the goal of God's final approval, *the crown of life*.

There is a true biblical psychology in all this. By the terms of our creation, the Lord intended us to guide our lives in the light of some foreseeable good: that is why (Gn. 2:16–17) he set before Adam the tree of life and the warning about the tree of the knowledge of good and evil. Adam was thus required to make his daily decisions in the light of a good to be attained and an evil to be rejected. James follows in the same pattern of things, as we shall now explore.

The target of life (1:12)

Blessed is the man who endures trial, for when he has stood the test he will receive the crown of life which God has promised to those who love him.

First sight of verse 12 is true sight: it recapitulates verses 2–4. James, as it were, brings us back to the beginning of things again, reminding us of our basic position – namely that we move forward, through and by means of trial and test, to maturity. It would, therefore, be possible to see verse 12 as concluding the section which opened at verse 2, rounding things off in a heart-warming repetition. But it is better to see James as returning to the same truth as an introduction to a new perspective on things. He writes, therefore, of a means of blessing (*Blessed . . . endures trial*), the end which is to be held in view (*the crown of life which God has promised*) and the clue to this great objective (*to those who love him*).

The word *blessed* contains two strands of meaning. It means 'happy' in a fairly general sense in Acts 26:2 or Romans 14:22, but in the more particular sense of 'fulfilled' in cases like Luke 12:37. Along this line, *blessed* picks up James' teaching in verses 2–4 that persistence through trial brings personal fulfilment and enrichment. In most cases of the word (*makarios*) in the New Testament, there is a plain hint, if not a clear assertion, of the activity of God in imparting blessing. In the Beatitudes (Mt. 5:3ff.) the Lord Jesus describes a life which is fulfilled and fulfilling because it is under the blessing of God. Luke 10:23 is a particularly good example of this meaning. While, therefore, James is in part looking back to the promise of adult maturity at the end of the process in verses 2–4, he is in the main underlining the fact that God is at work in all this business of trial and persistent endurance, God is imparting blessing all the while as well as guiding us towards the great, ultimate blessing of his total approval. As Sophie Laws puts it, 'the ideas of trial, probation and endurance' are 'now seen not in relation to the present perfecting of character, as in i.2–4, but to the prospect of a future reward'. This brings in a whole new range of motivations on the call to endure. If the former motivation was to see realized in ourselves all that was intended in Christ, the present motivation is to please him who holds out the crown – to envisage his approval and so to live as to delight him. But though the motivation can be phrased differently, the programme remains the same. The blessing is not in being delivered from the trial, but is something found within and through the trial by means of the practice of endurance. We might well say to God, 'Give me life and then I will be strong enough to endure trial.' And there is a biblical sense in which this is absolutely true and right. The Lord Jesus encouraged his disciples to pray so that they would not fall before the assault of the coming trial (Mk. 14:38, using the same word, *peirasmos*, as James). But James would have us learn a different, though parallel, lesson: the trial and test is a sort of divinely given 'homework' in which we work out the truths God has taught us in his Word – for it is through this exercise of working it out that we progress in knowledge and grow in spiritual stature. Thus, alongside the perfectly legitimate cry, 'Give me life and I will endure', James writes his (typical) command, 'Endure and God will give you life.' For it is equally true in the Scriptures that God gives his Holy Spirit to those who obey him (Acts 5:32).

The blessings God will give are summed up in the gift of *the crown of life*. In the Bible, the wearing of the crown speaks of dignity of position, royal or otherwise (Est. 8:15; Ps. 21:3). It speaks of gladness and rejoicing (Song 3:11; 1 Thes. 2:19); it is given to the victor (1 Cor.

9:25); it is the prize at the end of the race (2 Tim. 4:8), the chief Shepherd's reward to his undershepherds (1 Pet. 5:4). Specially, it is the reward of faithful endurance (Rev. 2:10). This last reference seems to be the only other place where a *crown of life* is mentioned, and the setting is the same as in James. Those who are prepared to use this life as an arena of endurance for Jesus' sake will find that an abundant life awaits them from the hand of God. In this world, the onlooker might see them as sacrificing life, as having a wretched time, as 'missing out on life'. They might be asked why they bother, why they do not opt out and enjoy themselves for a bit, and so on. But they have chosen to endure for Christ, and to live with their eyes on the life which he will give, crowning them with dignity, victory, happiness and reward in heaven.

But what attracts the reward is not their endurance, but the love for God which prompted it. *The crown of life* is his gift *to those who love him*. What a key truth for the whole of life! For in the light of it, all life becomes a trial (as James uses the word). Here, for example, is a person to whom the Lord accords an experience of deep happiness, whatever it may be. The Lord gives the happiness so that he may presently ask: Now do you love me more? And often we sadly answer that we have thoughtlessly enjoyed our happiness as though it were something we could demand as of right, and that easy days have blunted the sharp edge of our love for him. Many people have pondered the 'problem of pain'. Few pause to ponder the problem of happiness. Why should a holy God give restful days, a happy home, healthy and dear children to a sinner like me? How I should love him for his blessings! Likewise it is true that the Lord visits with hardships and sorrow so that he may draw near to us and ask, Do you love me still? An elderly man, bereaved of his wife, said: 'It must be that the Lord still has something for me to do, else why has he left me here?' And someone replied, 'He has not left you to do anything except to love him still.'

In the opening paragraph to this section we noted this reference to loving God as the clue James gives to making our way through life to the crown. It is a genuine clue, but it is a searching truth. Our progress to the crown is expedited not by our powers of endurance but by the depth and reality and pervasiveness of our love for him. We live by what we love; the shape of our lives is determined by the joys of our hearts.

Thereby hangs the whole tale, as we shall see, of verses 13–18.

The pathway of death (1:13–16)

*Let no one say when he is tempted, 'I am tempted by God'; for God cannot be
tempted with evil and he himself tempts no one;* [14]*but each person is tempted
when he is lured and enticed by his own desire.* [15]*Then desire when it has
conceived gives birth to sin; and sin when it is full-grown brings forth death.*

[16]*Do not be deceived, my beloved brethren.*

Between verses 12 and 13 James performs another of his lightning
changes of direction. In verse 12 he pronounces a blessing on the one
who *endures* (bears up under, perseveres through) *trial (peirasmos)*. But
when we come to the related verb *(peirazō)*, in verse 13, it refers no
longer to the outward, circumstantial trial, but to inner enticement to
sin: what we speak of as 'temptation'. Typical of his approach, he does
not warn us of this change of meaning; he plunges us into it. In other
words he writes to us in exactly the same way as experience comes to
us: the same circumstances which are, on the one hand, opportunities
to go forward are, on the other hand, temptations to go back. There is
no need to illustrate the point. We all know only too many people who
have ceased to walk with God under the pressure of trouble or tragedy;
the call to endure and mature was abandoned in favour of the suggestion
to give up. Every trial is also a temptation. James is not using any sort
of pun or linguistic trick, for throughout the New Testament the
peirasmos-group of words mean circumstantial trial or temptation to
sin, according to context.[1] Rather, he is making this shift in meaning
serve his own subtle purposes. He has been teaching us that trials are
blessings, in that they lead forward to maturity and the crown. But
they do not do this by some inherent power of their own. Everything
depends on our response and the use we make of our circumstances.
James is too down to earth not to make us face a flaw within ourselves,
a flaw whereby in time of trial it is always easier to slip back than to
step forward. Trial becomes temptation, and finds an answering chord
within us. Every circumstance we meet, therefore, requires a decision:
will we persevere and go on with God, or will we listen to the voice
which suggests the easy way of disobedience and disloyalty? But where
does that voice come from? James teaches us where the blame for
temptation does not lie (13) and where it does (14–15).

The command that, in the thick of temptation, no-one must say *I
am tempted by God* (13) is all too necessary. It is a short step from saying

[1]The verb *peirazō*: compare the use in Mt. 4:1 and 1 Cor. 10:13; the noun *peirasmos*,
compare Lk. 4:13 and 8:13.

that God uses our circumstances to saying that he ordains them – a step that the Bible would, in any event, encourage us to take, for this is its view of the power of God, and of the nature of our life and experiences in this world. But there is an additional and impermissible step. Suppose in any given experience of trial I give up trying, I listen to the tempting voice and come a spiritual cropper, is it not then all his fault? Did he not put me there? Was it not by his will that I found myself cornered by temptation which proved too strong? In reply to this James says two things. First, *God cannot be tempted with evil.* The divine nature is of such unmixed holiness that it is impossible for him to be enticed to plot to harm us. There is nothing within his whole nature to which that or any other temptation could appeal, or which would respond to that or any other base suggestion. Secondly (and consequently) *he himself tempts no one.* He is of such unmixed goodness in his attitudes and actions that there is no room in motive, will or deed for that which would bring disaster, great or small, on any of his people. To be sure, he places tests in our pathway. Indeed, it is even possible to say that he never gives any gift without, at the same time, providing some test regarding our use of his bounty. When he gave Solomon wisdom, he gave him also wealth and reputation, the very things which would put his wisdom to the test and reveal whether he would use it for God or for himself (1 Ki. 3:12–14). When he would give his people the blessing of their own land, he would give them also the perilous pathway leading to it, to reveal how their hearts stood with him (Dt. 8:1–2). But there is never an ulterior motive in all this, for his holiness offers no lodging-place for evil within his nature; neither is there the least impulse to trip us up, for his goodness forbids that he should seek our hurt. When he tests, it is so that we may pass the test and inherit the blessing. When the reverse happens, the blame lies elsewhere than in the God of all grace.

The source of the voice

The blame lies, in fact, in ourselves (14–15). The tempting voice is the voice of our own sinful nature. The upward path is demanding: it consists of a test, a response of endurance and persistence resulting in adult maturity. It is demanding, but it ends in fullness of life (2–4). By contrast, the downward path is easy. Desire arises within us (*his own desire*); it gives birth to *sin*; and sin produces *death* (14–15). Unlike the divine nature with its transparent goodness and holiness, human nature is centrally sinful, so that what emerges as a desire proves to be

51

an avenue into sin and death. The word James uses for *desire* (*epithymia*) does not necessarily have a bad meaning. The translation 'lust' in the older versions is unwarranted. The milder word, *desire*, is, if anything, more dramatic in its significance, for it suggests that, such is the pollution deep within us, at any moment something seemingly harmless may present itself to us. Yet, in that simple, even artless, desire there is both the reality and the power of sin and death. Thus we are *lured* and *enticed*. The latter word is well translated: it expresses the magnetism of desire, the hypnotic attraction of bait for a hungry beast (*deleazō*; *cf.* 2 Pet. 2:14, 18). But the former word (*exelkomai*) means 'to drag off' and points to a dominating and directive power within our desires.

We can dramatize this aspect of our natures by thinking of some of the more startling ways in which it manifests itself. The gentleness of the first impulse to experiment with drugs seems at such a far remove from the savage and destructive power of that same drug over the addict. Yet the difference is not one of fact – the drug was always like that, even at the start. The difference is only one of guise – that the subtle sinfulness of our nature made the death-dealing bait put on a face of innocence, and hold out a promise of liberating fulfilment. But there is no need to be dramatic: far more Christians are likely to be deceived, and to give house-room in their lives to the forces of death, by lingering in bed in the morning when they should be busy with their Bibles. This, too, makes its appearance as an enticing desire, wearing, more likely than not, a garment of self-justification – 'I need my eight hours' . . . 'I've got such a tiring day ahead.' The fact of the matter is that there is no way in which we can trust our own natures. There is within us a deep well of dominating and alluring desires; there is within us the fatal weakness which guarantees that we will fall short of God's glorious intentions for us. This latter, James describes by the word *sin*, the child of *desire* (15). The word (*hamartia*), in its classical Greek background, means 'a failing to hit the mark'. It is the most general New Testament word for sin, but it has not wholly left its roots behind, as Romans 3:23 shows. Our ability to produce deceptive desires is thus linked with our inability to live for the highest and to achieve the best. No wonder that the process thus begun and continued ends in *death*.

The meaning of death

James, that most succinct of New Testament writers, does not help us here by offering a definition of what he means by *death*, and his commentators are equally elusive. 'Death in all its forms' says A. Barnes; J. H. Ropes proffers '. . . the opposite of the blessed life with God'; and James Adamson cuts through to the ultimate significance: 'The "consummation" and the *death* are in the "next world".' Possibly James means us to pause for a moment and ponder a parallel. Twice over he has presented us with a sequence: testing, endurance, perseverance and maturity (2–4); testing, endurance, perseverance and life (12). Here, in verses 14–15, he introduces us to a sinister replica: desire, sin and death. In verse 4 there is one sort of maturity: 'that you may be perfect' (*teleios*); in verse 15 another, full-grown (*apoteleō*) sin. In verse 12 there is a crowning experience of *life*; in verse 15 a conclusion in *death*. In the light of the parallel with verse 12 we cannot refuse to follow James Adamson. The *crown of life* is bestowed (*cf.* 2 Tim. 4:8) at the End and so, too, is the eschatological death as revealed in 2 Thessalonians 1:8–9 or Revelation 20:14–15. But the parallel with verse 4 shows that the indulgence of desire, producing sin, triggers the forces of death in our experience even now. We might well say – and rightly – that as those redeemed and made eternally secure in Christ, the dread reality of eternal death cannot touch us. We are registered in the book of life (Rev. 20:15). But redemption does not make us immune from, or independent of, the processes which control our lives and which are there by the will of God the Creator. Just as James, therefore, would have us engage in that procedure which brings us to maturity of life, so also he would have us beware of that which engenders death.

We are now able to see that behind his single word *death* there lies a wealth of biblical understanding. In Scripture, 'death' signifies the continuation of personal life but in a changed state. Throughout the Old Testament, it would be true to say, the change was seen (on the whole) as a diminishing of life as known on earth. For though the dead live on in Sheol, the body has been left behind at death and therefore what survives is less than a whole person. It is true that the Old Testament also looked forward to a glory after death (Ps. 73:24), and that this has now become a life with Christ which is 'far better' (Phil. 1:23) than living on here on earth. Yet, even so, the full and final glory of the resurrection body (1 Cor. 15:51ff.; 2 Cor. 5:1ff.) is not the immediate experience of those who die in Christ. Death is, even for them, a sundering of true personal life. We need to speak hesitantly and carefully, for nothing must be diminished from the glory of the 'far better'. Yet God created man to be the personal unity of soul and body, and while the moment of death ushers us into the presence of Christ, with consequent glory and the expectation of a consummation of glory, the touch of death sunders the God-intended unity, and the body enters into corruption.

Such is the disintegrating force to which we expose ourselves when we allow desire to *give birth to sin,* and sin to *bring forth death.* James uses two verbs with indistinguishable meaning (*tiktō* and *apokyeō* respectively). It proves to be a pointless exercise trying to isolate a distinct meaning for either as compared with the other: they both mean 'to produce (children)', 'to bring forth (young)'. The point is not to be found by searching for differences but by heeding what they assert in common. The act of procreation leads to conception, conception to gestation, gestation to birth. Once the process is set in motion it takes over; it has an inevitability about it. The end is implicit in the beginning. Let us then but entertain the desire which conceives sin, and we have admitted death and disintegration into our experience. Through endurance and perseverance we come to the wholeness that is ours in Christ; through desire and sin we forfeit that wholeness and instead embrace death.

At this point comes the warning call of verse 16: *Do not be deceived, my beloved brethren.*[2] Note how the addition of *beloved* strikes the note of urgency. The rich love which links believer with believer prompts concern for spiritual welfare, and issues in a call to be clear-headed and open-eyed as to the realities of the situation. Present within is the great and inescapable foe of progress with God, the subtle and insinuating power of our sinful and fallen nature.

Where so much present-day Christian preaching and conversation would have introduced 'the devil' or 'Satan', James has no reference to this arch-enemy. And where so much contemporary analysis of the human condition would introduce external factors, such as amenities and facilities to keep people positively occupied, or circumstantial factors like boredom as a sufficient exculpation for delinquency, James says nothing of such matters. There is no need to introduce Satan here as an explanation; neither is there any excuse arising from circumstances or idleness. Were there no Satan there would still be wickedness; were every prospect pleasing, human nature would still be vile. The enemy is not only within the camp, within the heart; the enemy is the heart itself.

---

[2]See the outline on p.46, above.

The miracle of birth (1:17–18)

Every good endowment and every perfect gift is from above, coming down from the Father of lights with whom there is no variation or shadow due to change. [18]*Of his own will be brought us forth by the word of truth that we should be a kind of first fruits of his creatures.*

Verse 17 comes with an abruptness worthy of the abrupt James. We must resist the temptation to see it as an intended contrast with verse 13, as though James were countering the imputation that God sends temptation by insisting that God sends what is good and perfect. If this were his intention he would have had to include the word 'only', saying that God does not send temptation, for only the good and perfect gift is from above. But the word 'only' does not occur in this verse. Rather we must see it this way, that verse 17 comes as the solution of the problem.

According to verse 12, there is a way forward into life. It consists of making the right choices in the moment of trial and temptation, enduring and, since the crown comes to those who love God, keeping alive the glow of love for him in our hearts, come what may. It means making our decisions out of love for him; holding on through thick and thin for love's sake. But, according to verse 14, this is impossible. We have a nature (heart) which gives rise to desires, insistent and alluring, leading to sin and death. However are we to step forward to life when the whole thrust and pull of our nature is to sin and death? How are we to love and keep loving God when our hearts are springs of death-bearing wishes? To these questions verse 17 replies: Every good we need is in, and from, him.

James traces this basic position out in three steps. First, he explores the bounty of God (17a); next, his changeless nature (17b); and, thirdly, one particular and utterly basic way in which the bounty of the changeless God has operated towards us (18).

The bounty of God

The duplication, *endowment . . . gift*, leaves us in no doubt what verse 17a is about. It is most likely that the words are intended to be synonymous, and that the repeated idea is for the sake of emphasizing that God is a superb Giver (*cf.* v.5). If any difference of meaning is intended, then *endowment* (*dosis*) is the activity of 'giving', and *gift* (*dōrēma*) is the thing given. But once the point of the half-verse is established by the nouns, all attention swings to the adjectives. In giving, God is inexhaustible (*every . . . every . . .*): he gives everything that could possibly be needed; he gives everything, holding nothing back. In giving, he is simply beneficent, for in its character everything he gives is *good*. And in giving, he is exactly appropriate to what is required: his gifts are *perfect*. The word here (*teleios*) is the same as in verse 4 (*cf.* a related verb in v. 15), but now carries the significance of that which reaches its mark, matches its objective. Our need, then, is the objective; his gift is that which exactly meets it.

Thus we begin to climb out of our dilemma. We need loving hearts if we are to walk on into life. We can, of ourselves, only offer defiling hearts; but every need is fully underwritten by the endless and exactly appropriate gifts of God. Furthermore, in this giving, he is changeless. There is no way in which we might come to him in our need and find that he is unwilling, unable or unavailable. The gifts come from *the Father of lights with whom there is no variation or shadow due to change* (17). For reasons of his own, which will become clear to us in verse 18, James suddenly introduces the thought of God as *Father*, moves on to what we can learn of him by pondering the work of creation, *of lights*; and then, with the same *lights* as his background, shows how, by contrast, our Father is changeless.

The source of *every good endowment and every perfect gift* which comes to us to meet our needs is *the Father*. If we want to see something of his nature, we look at what he has done in creation. He said, '"Let there be light"; and there was light.' Furthermore, he 'made the two great lights, the greater light to rule the day, and the lesser light to rule the night' (Gn. 1:3, 16). The Creator God is thus committed to light. As he made his first move to order the meaninglessness of the initial creation (Gn. 1:2), he declared his priority by calling light into being; and when, on the fourth creative day, he turned to make his world habitable – with the creation of man in mind – he concentrated his created light in the great light-bearing bodies. John saw the same truth, the priority of light. He contemplated not what God had done in creation, but what God had done in revealing himself through the word of life: 'God is light and in him is no darkness at all' (1 Jn. 1:5). The counterpart of the truth that 'God cannot be tempted with evil and he himself tempts no one' (13) is that he is wholly light – pure, clear and luminous with goodness.

But his created lights also reveal him by contrast, for they are not always in the same place, nor does their light always shine with the same intensity. They are subject to *variation*, a word (*parallagē*) combining the senses of regularity and change,[3] movement and system; also, in their case, there is 'darkening which has its basis in change',[4] so that the light they give is by no means steady and persistent but at best variable, at worst fitful. The Creator is, in all this, unlike his creation. He never changes his position; he never alters either the fact or the intensity of his outshining goodness.

We now come (with v.18) to the heart of the matter. James' argument runs like this. A steady persistence is necessary if we are to make headway to maturity and life. Amongst other ways in which we are to show ourselves durable, there is the maintenance of a heart of love to God (12). But this very heart is itself a central foe of righteousness, because of its contagious sinfulness (13–15). About this we must see to it that we are in no doubt (16). But there is a solution to our dilemma: from heaven we may expect absolutely every needed good thing, coming to us by divine gift (17). And in particular there is one thing God has freely chosen to do for us: he has brought us to birth by his word with the intention that we should be specially his, and notably holy (18).

The new start

The idea of a divinely-given 'new start' is expressed in many ways in the Bible. Jeremiah, for example, stressing that obedience to the Lord's law is the leading characteristic of the new life, speaks of a heart on which the law of God is written (Je. 31:31–34), *i.e.* a heart tailor-made for obedience. Ezekiel too speaks to the gift of a new heart (Ezk. 36:26), a heart expressive of the true human nature which the Lord intended – therefore a 'heart of flesh' replacing the heart of stone which sin had produced. Paul speaks of a new creation (*e.g.* 2 Cor. 5:17; Eph. 4:22–24). James looks straight back to the teaching of the Lord Jesus, who spoke to a baffled Nicodemus about being 'born again' (Jn. 3:3–8) or 'born from above'. Here indeed is the new start presented in its most vivid terms. Earthly life originated with human

[3]The classical Greek background helps us to understand *parallagē* (*variation*). Liddell and Scott, *A Greek-English Lexicon* (Eighth Ed.) suggest 'a passing from hand to hand, transmission...alternation...alternate movements...interchange... variation'. The related adverb *parallax* means 'alternately' and the verb *parallassō*, 'to make things alternate...to change...alter a little...deviate from the straight course'. Jas. 1:17 is the only place *parallagē* occurs in the New Testament; none of the related words occur at all. In LXX *parallagē* occurs at 2 Ki. 9:20 (LXX, 4 Ki. 9:20), of the driving of Jehu, 'for he is in constant motion'.

[4]So AG.

parents, who bequeathed to us human nature in all its fallen hopeless-
ness and helplessness. But there is another birth, coming to us,
irrespective of the age we have reached in human life, and wholly apart
from our own or any other human agency: a birth of the Spirit (Jn.
3:5–8). With this new birth there comes new life, new energies, new
prospects and, above all, a new relationship with God, by whose will
the birth has come about.

We turn then to see what James teaches about this great topic. At
the heart of verse 18 lie the words, *he brought us forth*. This makes it
plain that James is not speaking of a natural birth, with human
parents, but of a supernatural birth, with a divine Parent, the Father.
Around this centre James groups three other truths: the *ground* of
this new and supernatural birth is the Father's will. The words *of his
own will* are given great emphasis in James' Greek; more literally, we
might translate 'having made his decision'. To this extent the new
birth and natural birth are analogous: the decision is that of the parent,
not of the child. Birth is something that happens to a child as a result
of decisions and actions made by others, the parents. Spiritually and
doctrinally, the 'new birth' (or 'birth from above') belongs with all
those passages of Scripture which unveil the secret story lying behind
our conversion. From the point of view of God's decision, the Lord
Jesus made the stark affirmation, 'You did not choose me, but I chose
you' (Jn. 15:16). Yet many of us remember with great clarity the day,
hour and even the approximate minute when we chose him! But since
we are taught that 'no one can come to me unless the Father who sent
me draws him' (Jn. 6:44), and that the very faith we exercise when we
believe in Jesus is the Father's gift to us (Eph. 2:8; Phil. 1:29), we
learn that behind our choice, making it possible and making it real, is
the wonder that he first chose us. This is what James refers to when he
says, *Of his own will he brought us forth*. The decision was his; so also, as
we shall see, was the action which implemented the decision. Our
conscious experience of conversion, of committing our lives to Christ,
of receiving him into our hearts – all this was consequent upon his
decision and action, and derivative from it, just as the love we give to
our human parents is a reflex of their parental love and care for us and
is, indeed, part and parcel of the life which they gave us.

Having made his decision, the Father, secondly, implements it.
James tells us that the *means* the Father used to bring about the new
birth was *the word of truth*. Typically, James does not elaborate what he
means by this, and we must appeal therefore to what other passages
teach in order to give ourselves a lead. As we have seen, there is a clear

link between James and Jesus, in that both speak of a supernatural birth and the start of new life in us. The Lord Jesus went beyond the need and the fact of the new birth to elaborate on the means: he spoke of the mysterious and powerful action of the Holy Spirit. Using the illustration of the wind, Jesus noted how, to the eye of the ordinary observer, the wind comes (so to speak) from nowhere and gives no indication where it is heading (Jn. 3:8). Its power and its effects are seen, but its origin and aims are not. How very well this suits a situation where the Father has kept so many secrets locked up within himself! The Holy Spirit proceeds on a mission from the Father to those whom the Father has willed to bring to the 'birth from above'. It is in a way parallel to this that James refers to *the word of truth*: it is his way of describing the life-giving agent used by the Father to impart new life and bring about the new birth.

A central truth of the Bible

For clarity's sake, it helps to link this with two other passages. In 2 Corinthians 4:1–6 Paul contrasts those who know the gospel and know Jesus Christ as Lord with those whose eyes have been blinded by 'the god of this world'. He explains the fundamental difference in verse 6: 'For it is the God who said, "Let light shine out of darkness," who has shone in our hearts to give the light of the knowledge of the glory of God in the face of Jesus Christ.' In other words, he draws a parallel between the word of God acting as his agent in creation, and God's use of his word in bringing new life through the gospel. We might put it this way. Just as God said, 'Let there be light' (Gn. 1:3),[5] so also he said, 'Let there be life', thus bringing us to the new birth. Turning to 1 Peter 1:23, we read that 'you have been born anew . . . through the living and abiding word of God'. Peter thus matches what James says: the word is the agent in the new birth. But he also takes us a little further in our understanding of James, for he defines the life-giving word: 'that word is the good news which was preached to you' (1 Pet. 1:25). James' *word of truth* must therefore be 'the word of truth, the gospel of your salvation' (Eph. 1:13). If this is so, then the Father uses the powerful word of the gospel in two ways: first, he speaks it, inwardly, to our dead souls, imparting life, bringing us to new birth; secondly, he presents the same word of truth to us as a preached gospel, to which the new life within us makes a personal and believing response.

[5]*Cf.* Ps. 33:6a.

This is one of the most glorious truths in the whole Bible. It teaches us that salvation is truly all of God: for until new life is imparted we are 'dead in trespasses and sins' (Eph. 2:1), and as totally unable as anything that is dead to respond to God in repentance and faith. If anything is to be done, he must do it; if any blessing or change is to come to us, it must come from outside; if any agency is to be at work, it must be other than ours, for we are dead, and our only activity is to increase in corruption. Here is the greatness of the divine mercy, the sufficiency of the divine strength and the depth of the divine condescension. He has come right down to us in our death; he has raised us up into life; and it is all due to a rich mercy prompted by a great love (Eph. 2:1, 4–5). It is no more possible for us to be agents or contributors to our new birth than it was for us to be so in our natural birth. All the work, from initial choice to completed deed, is his – and so is all the glory. But there is something else as well: inherent in this great truth of the new birth is the security of our salvation. Were salvation to depend on my choice, it would be as uncertain as my will which fluctuates, blows hot and cold, and reflects my divided, fallen nature. But it is his choice: *of his own will he brought us forth by the word of truth.* And until his will changes, his word alters or his truth is proved false, my salvation cannot be threatened or forfeited.

We move on, now, to the third truth which James links with the fact of the new birth. Just as natural birth looks forward to life, so the new birth has a forward look to the fulfilment of a *purpose* our Father has in mind: *that we should be a kind of first fruits of his creatures* (18).

James is here drawing on an Old Testament regulation which required the presentation to the Lord of the first of the crop. Three ideas found their focus in this offering: (i) out of all that belonged to the Lord, this was *specially* his; the rest remained to be used in the ordinary purposes of life; (ii) the first-fruits had to be the best, and were set apart as holy to the Lord; (iii) the offering of the first-fruits was an annual reminder that the Lord keeps his promises to his people, bringing them from slavery, giving them a homeland, providing for them in it. We can now easily see why James can speak of the church as the Lord's first-fruits. The Lord brings people to the new birth to be a demonstration to all that he keeps his promises (in this case, the covenant promise to take and keep a world-wide people for himself); the people who are the first-fruits are *specially for him*, and *notably holy.*[6]

---

[6]The bringing of the first-fruits was an obligatory annual appearance before the Lord (Ex. 23:16, 19; 34:22–26). Nothing of the new season's crop was available for

Caught in cross-fire (1:19a)

Know this, my beloved brethren.

As we now stand back from this absolutely key section (1:12–18) in James, we see in particular the two things that are true of every Christian. In verses 14–15 James sees *each* person subject to a process of sin and death which has its headquarters within the individual concerned. But in verse 18 James sees something else that is true of the same individual: a new life from God specifically designed to issue in the fulfilment of a purpose of holiness. He drives home the teaching about our death-bound, sinful nature with the cry *Do not be deceived, my beloved brethren* (16); he drives home the teaching about the new birth with the cry *Know this, my beloved brethren* (19a). We are to be equally open-eyed about what we are in ourselves, letting nothing deceive us in this regard, and about what God has done for us, holding firmly to it as to a great and vital truth.

Looking back, we can see that in verses 5–11 James was calling us to walk in the way of wisdom. Here (12–19a) he calls us to walk in the way of knowledge: knowledge about ourselves, knowledge about the work of God in us, knowledge of our old nature *and of our new nature*. This path of knowledge is not easy. We find ourselves constantly pressed from both sides. At one and the same time the old nature lures us to follow its desires and so to walk the path of sin and death, while at the same time we are being summoned to live out our true nature. This is the new nature given in the new birth, filled with new life, bound for new destinations of holiness. This is the battle of the wills – the will of the old nature, and the will of God expressed in the new nature. This clash of wills is the very heart of the life-giving conflict of which James has been teaching.

---

ordinary consumption until the first-fruit had been presented (Lv. 23:10–14). The first-fruits were the best of the crop (Nu. 18:12) and 'holiness to the Lord' (Lv. 23:15–20; Je. 2:3; Ezk. 48:14). It is in token of thus belonging specially to the Lord that the use of the first-fruits was confined to the priests (Nu. 18:12; Dt. 18:4). The offering of the first-fruits was proof that the Lord keeps his promises (Dt. 26:2–10). None of these references invites any comparison between the first-fruits and the remainder of the crops – except that the remainder was free to be used once the first-fruits had been offered. The central truth about the first-fruits is positive: *this is specially the Lord's.*

1:19b–25
5. The life-giving Word

Let every man be quick to hear, slow to speak, slow to anger, ²⁰*for the anger of man does not work the righteousness of God.* ²¹*Therefore put away all filthiness and rank growth of wickedness and receive with meekness the implanted word, which is able to save your souls.*

²²*But be doers of the word, and not hearers only, deceiving yourselves.* ²³*For if any one is a hearer of the word and not a doer, he is like a man who observes his natural face in a mirror;* ²⁴*for he observes himself and goes away and at once forgets what he was like.* ²⁵*But he who looks into the perfect law, the law of liberty, and perseveres, being no hearer that forgets but a doer that acts, he shall be blessed in his doing.*

The ever-practical James would never face us with conflict and not go on to point the way forward. He has just been speaking of the word of God as the seed in the womb (18) issuing in birth. Now he speaks of the word of God as the seed in the soil (21) growing to the (full) salvation of the soul. He has held before us the stimulating prospect of the future crown (12). Now he wants to help us to enter into a present *salvation* (21) and a blessing here and now (25). He has made us aware that our position as Christians is one of conflict, the battle of the two natures within us. But the word is *able to save* (21), and God's law is a *law of liberty* (25). Along these lines, this section grows out of, and develops, the theme of the preceding verses. Though the conflict lasts while earthly life continues, it may be hard but it is not fruitless. The key to this desired productivity is the word of God.

The Word

Even a survey as brief as this allows us to see that the connection between verses 19b–25 and what has preceded is forged by the idea of the word of God: *the word of truth* (18) . . . *the implanted word* (21) . . . *the word* (22) . . . *the word* (23) . . . *the perfect law, the law of liberty* (25). James does not pause to define his terms and we are left to ask what this word could be which is available for us to hear and do, and which lies before us as a perfect law for us to obey. Does the rest of the letter of James offer any clues?

The *law of liberty* (25) reappears at 2:12, summing up the teaching of the preceding verses. James will there lay particular stress on one command by calling it 'the royal law' (2:8); he affirms its authority in the words 'according to the scripture'. It would seem natural, therefore, to understand the broad description, *the law of liberty*, as the whole scriptural law, or the whole Scripture considered as a divinely authorized way of life. In 2:8–11, then, there is no doubt what *word* it is that James wants us to hear and heed. The same is true throughout his letter: the stories of Abraham and Isaac are scriptures to be heard (2:21–23); he calls attention to Rahab (2:25), the prophets (5:10), Job (5:11) and Elijah (5:17–18). The word which James would help his readers to hear is the word of Scripture. In this he is acting in accordance with the established view and practice of the early church, as seen in the sermons in Acts.[1] Furthermore, given the sense of authority which pervades his own letter, it is inconceivable that he would disagree with the position Paul reached in his final letter. This position is that the church lives under the authority alike of the apostolic teaching (2 Tim. 3:10, 14) and of the inherited sacred writings (2 Tim. 3:15), and that these *together* are to be recognized as God-breathed[2] scripture (2 Tim. 3:16).

As we study the present passage (1:19b–25) we shall note how (19b) James calls us to be *quick to hear*. The key word is *hear*, and the context (as we shall see) requires us to understand that he is commanding us to hear the word which God speaks. As we come to verse 21 we note the words *receive . . . the implanted word*. James here commands something beyond 'hearing': there is a distinct response to God's word whereby we *receive* it. And finally, with verse 22, he brings us to a final stage in our response to God's word: we are to hear and do. Thus the passage falls into three sections, each with a distinct response to the word God speaks: hearing (19b–20), receiving (21) and obeying (22–25).

[1] Peter's Pentecost sermon falls into three sections (Acts 2:14–21, 22–28, 29–35), each ending with an appeal to Scripture to validate what he has said. Stephen's defence (Acts 7) and Paul's sermon at Antioch (Acts 13:16–41) do little more than re-tell the scriptural story.   [2] NIV offers this accurate translation of 2 Tim. 3:16.

Hearing God's Word (1:19b–20)

Let every man be quick to hear, slow to speak, slow to anger, [20]*for the anger of man does not work the righteousness of God.*

Both verses 19b and 22 have the same particle linking them with what has gone before. In verse 22, RSV rightly translates it *but*. There is no justification for omitting it in verse 19b, for this whole section really hinges on these two great 'buts'. Having called us to keep the truth of the new birth in the forefront of our minds (19a), James wants to guard us against becoming stuck in infancy as Christians. We must learn how to capitalize on the birth which has come to us from our Father. Therefore he says, 'But let everyone be swift to hear.' The link between verses 21 and 22 is identical: we must *receive the . . . word* (21), *but* (22) there is one essential factor in fruitful reception: *doers . . . and not hearers only.*

How we move on from the new birth into the new life, then, is the question James is raising, and a key question it is. The old nature (14–15) and the new nature (18) are locked in conflict. As James sees it, this is not meant to issue in stalemate, for 'every good . . . and . . . perfect gift' is available to us. The preponderance of resource is thus on the side of the new nature. But how is this resource to be mobilized and the heavenly forces brought up to engage the enemy?

The short answer is this: *he brought us forth by the word of truth* (18) . . . *Let every man be quick to hear* (19). By the experience of conversion we discovered an important truth about ourselves – that the word of the gospel matches the new nature which God had secretly created within us, so that we were able to hear, understand and respond. The truth triggered the response. Conversion itself needs no repetition. It is a once-for-all, eternal transaction with God (*e.g.* Eph. 1:13–14). But the same pattern remains as the key to an on-going experience: we must go on hearing that word which corresponds to the God-given new nature and in this way progressively enter into new life.

By hearing the life-giving word, the energies of the new nature are stimulated into action. Therefore, we must be *quick to hear*. We might wonder why the ever-practical James does not proceed to outline schemes of daily Bible reading or the like, for surely these are the ways in which we offer a willing ear to the voice of God. But he does not help us in this way. Rather, he goes deeper, for there is little point in schemes and times if we have not got an attentive spirit. It is possible to be unfailingly regular in Bible reading, but to achieve no more than to have moved the book-mark forward: this is reading unrelated to an attentive spirit. The word is read but not heard. On the other hand, if we can develop an attentive spirit, this will spur us to create those conditions – a proper method in Bible-reading, a discipline of time, and so on – by which the spirit will find itself satisfied in hearing the Word of God.

In what he actually says in verses 19b–20 James seems to mix together the two ideas of getting on with people, and going on with God. It is surely correct to see (as we have done) the command to be *quick to hear* as looking back to the reference to *the word of truth* (18). But corresponding to this positive command about spiritual progress, there is also the negative command to be *slow to anger, for the anger of man does not work the righteousness of God* (20). The word *righteousness* has here the same concentrated meaning as, for example, in Matthew 3:15. It means all that God in his righteousness purposes to be done. The growth of the new nature from babyhood to adult spiritual maturity is the righteous purpose of God for us; this is what will happen if we go on with the blessed task of hearing the word of truth. This is how James develops the idea of going on with God. But the prohibition against *anger* must have to do with getting on with people – and surely this is the context also of the command to be *slow to speak*.

The blunt fact is that our life with God is not something segregated, to be restricted to 'quiet times', and insulated from our life with people. If we do not have an attentive ear in the ordinary circumstances of life, we do not become different people when we shut the door and open the Bible. We must cultivate over the whole area of life those virtues and practices which will pay dividends when we turn our minds to God and to his Word. In particular, we must use the relationships and situations of the market-place of life as a training-ground for a readiness to hear, a control of speech and a cautious abhorrence of anger. The great talker is rarely a great listener, and never is the ear more firmly closed than when anger takes over.

There is some ambivalence in James' teaching about *anger*. On the one hand, just as *slow to speak* does not mean 'never speak', but 'speak with due thought and care', so *slow to anger* is not the same as 'never be angry'. On the other hand, to say that human anger does not forward God's righteous purposes is pretty unequivocal. Paul evidences the same duality when he says, 'Be angry but do not sin; do not let the sun go down on your anger' (Eph. 4:26). Both writers imply the possibility of a righteous anger; both give a straight warning that anger and sin

65

are never far apart; both counsel great watchfulness. It is an aspect of James' style to say things bluntly and not to pause to spell out details or make refinements. He contents himself, therefore, with the general truth about human anger. It is not a pure emotion; it is usually heavily impregnated with sin – self-importance, self-assertion, intolerance, stubbornness. Most of us would have to confess that holy anger belongs in a state of sanctification to which we have not attained. James is writing of us and to us: your anger does not bring about the righteous plans of God. It is a salutary reminder and a merited rebuke. At any rate, an angry spirit is never an attentive one. When anger comes in, listening flies out. The courts of men are our drill-ground for the courts of the Lord. Those who would listen to him must train themselves to be listeners and, to that end, they must covet and cultivate a reticent tongue and a calm temper. For nothing must militate against – rather, everything must be made an adjunct to – that great, fundamental practice, hearing God's Word.

Receiving God's Word (1:21)

Therefore put away all filthiness and rank growth of wickedness and receive with meekness the implanted word, which is able to save your souls.

We are to expose ourselves to God's Word by hearing it; we are to make our first response by receiving it. In opening up this topic, James touches on four aspects of this 'receiving': first, the proper preparation for receiving the word (*put away all filthiness and rank growth of wickedness*); secondly, the required attitude (*with meekness*); thirdly, the thing to be received (*the implanted word*); and finally, the expected result (*able to save your souls*).

We shall consider first those two elements in verse 21 which make a connection with the teaching James has already imparted (*the implanted word...able to save...*) and then move to the other two elements which describe what it is that makes our reception of the word productive.

Able to save your souls is James' third description of the objective at which the new birth is aimed. The first was 'that we should be a kind of first fruits' (18), the objective of being wholly and specially for the Lord; the second was 'the righteousness of God' (20), the realization in our conduct of the righteous life which he purposed; and now here is a third description, the salvation of our souls. In the healing miracles of the Lord Jesus, people are 'saved' from disease and death and brought into a state of personal 'wholeness'.[3] This provides us with a pattern for that total salvation which Jesus came to accomplish.[4] It can be spoken of as past,[5] because the work of salvation was completed by Jesus when he died for us. It can also be spoken of as future, because the full experience of salvation will not be ours till Jesus comes again.[6] But it is also present in that day by day we can experience a greater and greater measure of what has been done for us by our Lord.[7] In this passage in James the tense of verb used (aorist) underlines the power of *the implanted word* actually to make salvation a positive reality in daily experience.

Every day, then, should provide us with some fresh evidence that we are saved, that new powers are at work within us, and that the Lord is progressively 'making us whole'. The energy behind all this is *the implanted word. Implanted* is used only here in the New Testament, but in other Greek literature, according to J. H. Ropes, it refers to what is 'natural' as contrasted with what is 'taught' or 'acquired'; it is the 'deep-rooted' as contrasted with the 'superficial'. Sophie Laws suggests 'implanted from birth', and while she does not herself develop the thought in the following way, it is surely suitable both to the word (*emphytos*) and to the present passage to think of God's word as the 'implanted' agent of the new birth (18), and also as the agent in daily growth. Just as at conversion we were presented outwardly with the gospel message which was already secretly lodging in our hearts, so, throughout our life of Christian development, we promote the growth of the new nature by facing it with the same message which is the inner secret of its life. Growth follows as we *receive* more fully the word which has made us children of our Father, the 'word of truth' (18) which, as we have seen, James would identify with the word of Scripture.

As at so many other points, James shows himself to be deeply imbued with the teaching of Jesus. In the 'parable of the sower' there is both the planting of the seed and the reception of the seed that has been planted, so that, as Mark (4:20) records it, fruitfulness follows in the good soil as people 'hear the word and accept it'.[8] As the soil 'identifies' with the seed sown, growth and fruit take place. Our daily embracing of the word of truth creates the conditions in which the

---

[3]Lk. 7:50; 8:48.   [4]Mt. 1:21; Acts 4:12.
[5]Jn. 19:30; Tit. 3:4–7.   [6]*E.g.* Rom. 5:9; 1 Pet. 1:5.
[7]*E.g.* 1 Cor. 15:2 (lit. 'by which you are being saved'); 2 Cor. 2:15.
[8]Of receiving the word, James uses the simple verb *dechomai* and Mark the compound *paradechomai*. The compound may intensify but does not alter the meaning.

implanted word germinates, grows and becomes fruitful in *salvation*.

But what makes the soil good so that growth is guaranteed? First, the soil must be cleared by putting away *all filthiness and rank growth of wickedness*. Then the cleared soil must be furnished (as with a rooting hormone) with one special ingredient, that is, *with meekness*.

The noun *filthiness* (*rhyparia*) appears as an adjective (*rhyparos*) in 2:2, referring to 'shabby' clothing. The adjective and the verb (*rhypareuomai*) occur in Revelation 22:11 as moral 'shabbiness' — everything that taints, soils or devalues our lives. *Wickedness* is a very general word. It is rooted in the idea of 'badness' and covers, in a broad way, everything that might be 'wrong' in character or conduct. The word which RSV represents as *rank growth* is a bit more difficult to pinpoint. The central idea is 'excess', 'overplus', 'remainder'. Thus it refers to the way the Corinthians' joy exceeded their affliction (2 Cor. 8:2), or the way Paul looked forward to future endeavours for the gospel exceeding anything already done (2 Cor. 10:15). We come very near the meaning of the present passage in Romans 5:17 where our word (*perisseia*) expresses the way in which grace not only redresses the damage done by sin, but goes far and away beyond. James thus thinks of the wickedness we find in ourselves and in our lives as 'ever abounding' and therefore, adopting the metaphors of the context, RSV *rank growth* is not at all bad. We dig out the weeds of wickedness in one place to find them growing in another, and then reappearing with vigour where we thought we had eradicated them. It is a word which spells doom to any theory of sinless perfection in this life. Rather our experience is to be one of constantly working, hoe in hand, against the fertility of the old nature. James is the realist supreme.

Many a gardener sighs over the 'losing battle' against his weeds. We may sigh at the thought of the battle we have on our hands, but James does not represent it as one that is lost before it is joined. *The implanted word* is *able to save*; it is undergirded by the vitality of the new nature and backed up by 'every good endowment and every perfect gift' (17). It just needs *meekness* (*prautēs*) to activate its immense powers. It is a Christlike quality, for he said 'I am meek' (*praus*, Mt. 11:29). As exercised towards people, meekness is 'self-subduing gentleness' (Adamson). But here the direction is Godward, or rather towards the word of God, and it is 'that temper of spirit in which we accept his dealings with us as good, ... without disputing'.[9] It is the spirit which says a simple 'yes' to what the word teaches and commands, it is

[9]R. C. Trench, *New Testament Synonyms* (Macmillan, 1894), p.152.

'the mind disposed to learn' (Calvin) – and to do so with prompt readiness.

Obeying God's Word (1:22–25)

But be doers of the word, and not hearers only, deceiving yourselves. [23]*For if any one is a hearer of the word and not a doer, he is like a man who observes his natural face in a mirror;* [24]*for he observes himself and goes away and at once forgets what he was like.* [25]*But he who looks into the perfect law, the law of liberty, and perseveres, being no hearer that forgets but a doer that acts, he shall be blessed in his doing.*

James now turns to something else in our fruitful relationship with God's Word. We listen (19) and take it in (21). But we must also express it, carry it out (22–23, 25); we must be *doers*. And we must take care not to deceive ourselves (22) about this. We shall see what James means by this warning against self-deception if we set out, side by side, the key verbs in the illustration of the man with the mirror (23–24) and in what it is intended to illustrate (25):

the man with the mirror	the believer with the word
observes (23–24)	(25) looks into
goes away (24)	(25) perseveres
forgets (24)	(25) acts

This way of setting out the words shows that the comparison is not (as some commentators hold) between a hasty glance (the man with the mirror) and a sustained gaze (the believer with the word). Both are, as a matter of fact, equally intent on what they see: *observes* (*katanoeō*) means 'to look at, with reflection; to consider'[10]; *looks into* means literally 'to bend over',[11] therefore, in relation to God's Word, 'to pore over'. Each is equally serious in his gaze. It is what happens next which makes the difference. As for the man with the mirror, 'off he goes', but his friends meeting him on his way could tell him that the mirror is not the comb or the face-flannel, and that without these aids to gracious living his devotion to the mirror is, in itself, without value.

It is in connection with all this that James says we have a choice: we

[10]AG offer this as the basic meaning of the verb, but add 'also simply "look at" *to prosōpon* (the face), Js 1:23 . . .', *i.e.* contrary to its real meaning they think this context requires a 'superficial' meaning. So also, *e.g.*, Adamson, but mistakenly.

[11]See, *e.g.*, Jn. 20:5, where the beloved disciple 'stoops down' to look into the tomb.

can either deceive ourselves (22) or bless ourselves (25). We deceive ourselves when we mistake the part for the whole. It is only part of our fruitful use of the Word of God to hear it and receive it, but it is a part on which we might unduly preen ourselves: 'I spent fifty minutes this morning reading the Bible – and I can remember what I read. It was a super, uninterrupted time.' And James would say, 'Well done! But now, what about obeying the word you read? Have you actually changed your mind so that you now hold to be true what you learnt in the word? Have you (and are you) re-directing your imagination and your eyes and your thoughts so as to live according to the standards of the world? Are your relationships different, as the word instructed you they should be?' – and so he could go on. We must be *doers of the word*. Where the man with the mirror *goes away* (24), the believer with the Bible *perseveres* (25) – more literally, 'continues (in its company)'. This can happen any day and every day. There can be a continuing enjoyment of a relationship with God's truth and God's law begun in the early morning – but it is the work of a lifetime. It is like the deep and pervasive matching of lives, personalities and thoughts which emerges in the course of a happy marriage.

It is to this sort of 'companionship of the word' that James encourages us when he speaks of *the perfect law, the law of liberty* (25). As *law,* the Word of God is designed for obedience, though there is more to it than just that. Against its Old Testament background, *law* means 'teaching'. It is what happens in the home, between caring parents and beloved children (*e.g.* Pr. 4:1–4; 7:1–3), but they do it as imitating the loving way in which the Lord has instructed his sons and daughters. Of course, his instruction contains rules for living and he intends his commands to be obeyed (*e.g.* Dt. 6:2), but even his sharpest and most demanding laws are not a stern imposition by external authority, but a paternal directive arising from love.

James describes God's law as *perfect* and as *the law of liberty*. This way of linking law and liberty at once excites our interest and challenges so much modern thinking which makes law and liberty antagonists. Once more, there is a long Old Testament background. The law of God is perfect, first, because it perfectly expresses his nature and, secondly, because it perfectly matches ours. These two sides of the law belong together. In his commandments, the Lord has taken what is true about himself and has expressed that truth in a rule for us to obey.[12] Take, for example, the seventh commandment, which, at first

---

[12]It would be a long study in its own right to work out this thought fully, but it is seen, for example, in Lv. 19. This collection of widely varying laws finds common

sight, seems to have no bearing on the God of the Bible in whom earthly sexual distinctions have no place. As he reveals himself to us, we learn that he is totally and eternally faithful to his covenanted promises. It is this aspect of his nature which the seventh commandment enshrines: we enter into marriage with its covenanted promises, and in it we are commanded to be like our God who never breaks his pledged word. This example brings into the picture the way in which God's law matches our human nature, for we were created in the image of God (Gn. 1:26–28). We live the truly *human* life when we express his likeness in our conduct. In this way the seventh commandment (and all the commandments of God in his Word, whether expressed as precepts, or by way of principle or example) brings out what we truly are, and expresses our true humanity when we obey it. The law which is the *perfect* expression of the divine nature is also the *perfect* vehicle of expression for human nature.

We shall begin to understand the link between law and liberty if we go back to the very moment of the law-giving at Mount Sinai. The Lord is speaking (Ex. 20:2a) to those whom he has brought out of Egypt. They have been redeemed (Ex. 6:6) and the means of their redemption was the blood of the lamb (Ex. 12:13). We see, then, that the Lord gives his law not as a means of salvation, but as a life-style for those who have been already saved. It is the way he wants his redeemed ones to live. But then he goes on to say that he is speaking to those whom he has brought out of bondage (Ex. 20:2b): not to those whom he is bringing into bondage by imposing his law upon them, but to those who are now (for the first time) enjoying liberty, and to whom he gives his perfect law in order to safeguard the freedom he has secured for them. True freedom is the opportunity and the ability to give expression to what we truly are. We are truly free when we live the life appropriate to those who are created in the image of God. The law of God safeguards that liberty for us. But it does even more, for obedience brings life and power (Lv. 18:5; Dt. 4:1a; Acts 5:32). The law of God is *the law of liberty* because it safeguards, expresses and enables the life of true freedom into which Christ has brought us. This is the blessing of which James speaks (25), the blessing of a full life, a true humanity. Obedience is the key factor in our enjoyment of it.

---

ground in the recurring assertion, 'I am the LORD' (vv. 10, 12, 14, 16, *etc.*), *i.e.* 'I am Yahweh', 'I am what I am'. Each law or group of laws, therefore, is saying, 'You are to be like this because I am what I am.' The divine nature determines what shall be commanded. Lv. 19:2 provides the purpose animating God's law: 'You shall be holy; for I . . . am holy' – the law is given so that we may be like the Lord who gives it.

1:26–27
6. Transition: the Father's children

If any one thinks he is religious, and does not bridle his tongue but deceives his heart, this man's religion is vain. ²⁷*Religion that is pure and undefiled before God and the Father is this: to visit orphans and widows in their affliction, and to keep oneself unstained from the world.*

'Like father, like son' is a well-worn earthly maxim – not least when the more regrettable attributes of the older generation show themselves in the young! But it is also full of biblical truth, for the Lord Jesus commanded us to 'be perfect, as your heavenly Father is perfect' (Mt. 5:48). He reminded us that, when we love others as our Father loves us, then we prove ourselves to be his children (Mt. 5:44–45).

In his letter so far James has brought us into dynamic touch with our heavenly Father at two points: first (5), that he is ready to give his wisdom to us, and secondly, that he shared his nature with us (18) when he brought us forth as his children. So then, we may ask, what will life be like if it is controlled by the Father's wisdom? And what will it be like if it is the outworking of our new nature?

The threefold likeness

With his customary abruptness James simply faces us with verses 26 and 27. He has been talking about our obedience to the perfect law (25), and without preparation or warning we find ourselves reading about three marks of genuine religion: a controlled tongue (26), a caring ministry to the needy (specified as orphans and widows in 27a), and personal holiness *unstained from the world* (27b). How are we to explain this leap from broad exhortations to obey the word of God to specific areas of Christian living?

72

The first answer to this question is obvious. In verses 5–8, as we saw, James dealt with God's gift of wisdom, and then plunged headlong into two case-studies (9–11). In the same way we could hold that in verses 19–25 he has been dealing with hearing, receiving and obeying God's word, and he follows this by turning to key areas of our obedience. So far so good: but why these areas? After all, verses 2–8 were concerned with the need for wisdom in the face of life's diverse circumstances. The contrast between poverty and wealth easily suggests itself as a typical illustration. But why should the tongue, care for the needy and personal holiness be chosen to illustrate our obedience to God's law?

To answer this question we must note again the pathway by which James has brought us to the present point in his letter. In the passage immediately before verses 26–27, he was dealing with the topic of hearing, receiving and doing God's word (19b–25). Great and important as this is in its own right, James came to it as the necessary consequence of something else: it is the way the new birth develops into the new life. The cry 'Know this' (19) summons us to a clear understanding of what God has done for us (18): making up his own mind to bring us to new birth, doing so by means of his word of truth and purposing that we should be his first-fruits, specially his and notably holy. If we now take the whole passage from verse 18 to verse 27, there is a natural sequence about it: (i) the new birth (18–19a); (ii) the growth of the new life (19b–25); and (iii) the characteristics that the new life displays (26–27). This sequence is bound together by the fact that the same three features are central to the acts of God the Father (18) and the acts of his new-born children (26–27): he first reached out to us through the life-giving word he spoke, that is, 'the word of truth' (18), and we, on our part, should be marked by a bridled tongue (26). Behind his spoken word lay that act of his will whereby he determined what he would do for us (18), depraved in nature and death-bound though we were (14–15). In a word, our Father cares about the needy, and so should we (27a). But his life-giving work for us had a purpose, 'the first fruits' (18), namely that we should be specially his and notably holy. Therefore we ought to bear the mark of a personal holiness *unstained from the world* (27b).

The picture enlarged

The three Christian characteristics of verses 26–27 are thus not an arbitrary choice. They say to us 'Like Father, like child'. It is right that the life which he has given to us should bear the same fruits in us as in him. James is so convinced of this that it is to these three topics he devotes the whole central substance of his letter (2:1 – 5:6). We can set it out as a diagram:

	(i)	(ii)	(iii)
Three Truths about our Father	His spontaneous care for the helpless (18a)	His word of truth (18b)	His purpose of holiness (18c)
Three marks of the child of God	(i) A controlled tongue (26)	(ii) A caring ministry (27a)	(iii) A holy life (27b)
The three topics developed	(i) A caring ministry (2:1–26)	(ii) A controlled tongue (3:1–12)	(iii) A holy life (3:13 – 5:6)

This overview makes it clear that James' teaching about how we should live rests on what he discerns to be true about our Father. The spontaneous outreach of his will to bring us the new birth (18a) is taken up by the question in 2:5, 'Has not God chosen those who are poor . . .?' The implication is drawn out that we should have the same spontaneous and caring ministry for all the needy. In the same way, the perfect word which the Father spoke to bring us to new birth (18b) finds its counterpart (3:1–12) in the Christian's determination to bring the tongue into subjection. The Father's word was his potent instrument for our good and, in our natures (3:2–5), the tongue is a master-key for either blessing or bane. Finally, at 3:13, James announces the topic, 'his good life', which takes up and develops the first-fruits theme of 1:18c.

But this identity between 1:18 and 2:1 – 5:6 throws into strong relief the other feature which emerges from the diagram, namely, that James follows a different order in 1:26–27, putting the tongue first and, indeed, imposing a great weight of emphasis upon it. Is there any reason for this?

True religion

The words which unite verses 26 and 27 are *religious... religion*. Of these, the adjective (*thrēskos*) occurs only here in the New Testament. The noun (*thrēskeia*) is used characteristically in Acts 26:5.[1] Outside the Bible, the words have a general reference to the outward forms of religion, but as far as James is concerned, H. Alford sets us on the right track when he writes that religion (*thrēskeia*) is 'the external manifestation of *eusebeia*', for *eusebeia* means something like 'spirituality', *i.e.* a relationship to God rooted in the heart and shaping the life.[2] *Religion* is thus a comprehensive word for the specific ways in which a heart-relationship to God is expressed in our lives.

If our lives, then, are to express what we think about God, in what sense does James define pure religion in the three areas of behaviour mentioned in these verses? He does not, of course, intend them as a comprehensive list of religious activities, so that if we do these things we can count ourselves religious, even if we never pray, read the Scriptures, meet in a worshipping fellowship, receive baptism and share the Lord's Supper. But he does offer them as a sufficient test whether or not all that we do under the heading of religion has validity in the sight of God. The first test case is the *tongue* (26), which James links with the *heart*; the second and third tests (27) are both linked with *God... the Father*. In itself, this connection confirms the relationship we have already outlined between verse 18 and verses 26–27: the Father looks to see the lineaments of his own life in the lives of those who claim to be his children. But, under this general relationship to the Father, the second test (27b) is exemplified in the care of needy *orphans and widows*, and the third test (27c) is stated negatively, as keeping free from the world's stain.

The index of the heart

James does not call us to a silenced tongue, but to a bridled one. The picture is vivid – and realistic in the light of experience. As we shall yet hear James say in greater detail (3:7–8), our tongues possess in themselves all the untamed vigour of a wild beast and, left to themselves, all their savage instincts will be given full play. They need, like wild horses, to be broken in and harnessed.

[1]It occurs elsewhere only in Col. 2:18.
[2]*eusebeia* is a favourite New Testament word. It is well exemplified in 2 Tim. 3:5 (RSV 'religion') and in the adverb (*eusebōs*) in 2 Tim. 3:12 (RSV 'a godly life').

There is something else, too, which James will presently elaborate (3:2–6). There is a very special nexus between the tongue and the central forces of the personality. We must not anticipate here the discussion which properly belongs to chapter 3. But in essence James makes his point when he says that, if we profess religion, but leave our tongues unbridled, we are practising a central deception on ourselves: *deceives his heart* (26). We are telling ourselves things about our inner state which are simply not true. We may have all the religion of the famous Pharisee of Luke 18:11–12 but, like him, we profess a religion that is *vain* (*mataios*, failing in its essential purpose). The tongue and the heart are linked so that the tongue is an accurate index of what we are at the core of our persons. Was James, we may ask, quietly recalling and accepting the words of the Lord Jesus: 'How can you speak good, when you are evil? For out of the abundance of the heart the mouth speaks' (Mt. 12:34).

The whole passage in which these words of the Lord Jesus occur would repay study here, but we have possibly noted enough to recognize what James is teaching. We see now that his first statement of the three marks of the child of God (26–27) is devised for self-examination, and he puts the tongue first as it gives an immediate answer to the question: What are you? Are you a child of God? Are you sure you are? Is that mark of the child evident which is the index of an inner reality? For if the heart is right, the tongue will show it.

Whose are you?

The fact that (as our Bibles are arranged for us) James devoted a whole verse to the tongue (26) underlines the importance which he always attaches to this aspect of Christian living. But this does not diminish the importance of the other two hallmarks, even if they have to be content to share a verse (27) between them.

The two aspects of conduct in verse 27 are linked equally emphatically to *God and the Father*. Religion is pointless unless it corresponds to the mind and will of God. Once more, it is hardly extravagant to think of James recalling the teaching of Jesus, that commandments proceeding merely from man 'make void the word of God' and issue in vain worship (Mt. 15:6–9). James, however, would have our religion to be *pure and undefiled*[3] in the Father's sight. When he taught us about the

---

[3]The words can be treated as synonyms, with positive and negative aspects both stated to give emphasis. Each word has its background in Old Testament ritual law with its demand for cleanness and spotlessness as the absolute divine requirement.

tongue, he bade us look inward to examine our hearts. Now he bids us look upward to see if we really belong to the Father and, in particular, to see if his life is at work in us and if our life belongs to him.

Does his life pulse in our veins? How are we to know? The ever-practical James proposes a practical test. The Word of God reveals the outworking of the divine Fatherhood: 'Father of the father-less and protector of widows is God in his holy habitation' (Ps. 68:5).[4] For this reason, James does not here speak in general but in specific terms about the caring ministry, for he wants us to test ourselves. He speaks not about our general kindliness, such as anyone might show, but about whether our actual display of concern for others bears the characteristics of our Father's concern. The larger development of this theme belongs, as we have seen, in chapter 2, but the illustration of care for orphans and widows sketches in some main ideas – a concern which is moved only by the need of others and looks for no return (for what could orphans and widows repay?). It is a costly concern, seeking to shoulder the other's whole need (like taking the place of a lost parent): a concern which takes the part of the needy in the face of a threatening world (defending the cause of the widow). The Deuteronomy references given below (in footnote 4) link our concern for orphans and widows with the Lord's concern to redeem us from our Egyptian slavery. They therefore call to our minds the redeeming, Calvary-love of Jesus as the model for the caring Christian.

But there is also another side to things. If our care for others in their need bears the marks of God's care for the fatherless and widows, then we have proof that his life is at work in us. Matching this, is our life wholly devoted to him? After all, he brought us to the new birth with the purpose that we should be 'a kind of first fruits' (18), a thought which we summarized above as meaning 'specially his and notably holy'. Correspondingly, then, James summons us to be *unstained from the world* (27b). 'The world' (see, especially, 4:4) has the same meaning for James as for Paul and John.[5] It is the whole human scheme of things organized in terms of human wisdom to attain a human goal, without reference to God, his laws, his values or his ultimate judg-ment. The world is, in fact, anything and everything that is at odds with the Lordship of Jesus over our lives. If we are to live for him in the world, there is a constant issue of commitment, loyalty, to be faced: are we his or are we not? Are we his, not by virtue of a past decision

---

[4]*Cf.* Dt. 10:17f.; 24:17f., 20f.; Pss. 10:14; 146:9; Ho. 14:3; *etc.*
[5]*E.g.* Rom. 12:2; 1 Cor. 2:12; and Jn. 1:10; 15:18–19; 16:33; 1 Jn. 2:15–17; *etc.*

allowed to grow stale, but in the daily pressure of the often small things by which our lives are besmirched? For it is more than likely true that, if life were all large decisions, few of us would go far wrong. Yet, faced with the world's ceaseless bombardment of our eyes, ears, thoughts and imaginations, the world's insidious erosion of values and standards, and clamour for our time, money and energy, it is easy to adopt a general way of life which, though it avoids the open pitfalls of sin, yet is not discernibly different from the style of one who does not know Christ. We may well decide to belong to Jesus, yet fail to carry that decision through with the rigour which alone proves that it was a real decision. It is one thing to yield our lives to him, but it is another to live each moment of the day on his side of the great divide from the world.

A moment of truth

Within the structure of James, then, 1:26–27 forms a most important transition: these two verses look back to the foundational verse of the whole book (1:18) and spell out in general terms how a real experience of new birth will display itself in a characteristic development of life. And, as we have seen, in doing this, verses 26–27 provide the 'chapter headings' for the rest of the letter: care, speech and holiness.

But in these two verses James has done more than build a bridge; he has provided us with space to reflect. His words are so sharp, so 'black and white', that he leaves no middle ground for a 'moderate' religion, or a spirit of self-excuse. It is possible for us to assume that we are 'religious' when we are not; to profess and practise a vain religion or one which (whatever it may mean to us) is impure and defiled in the estimation of the Father. We need to examine ourselves; we need to know, we must be sure. A thing as potent as the new birth, if it has taken place, cannot be hidden; it cannot fail to make its presence felt. To have the life of God in us and to remain unchanged is unthinkable.

Well, then, have we the evidence to prove it? If the question, put just like that, sounds sharp, even threatening, we need to remind ourselves that it is no sharper than the verses from which it arises.

2:1-7
7. Denying our faith

My brethren, show no partiality as you hold the faith of our Lord Jesus Christ, the Lord of glory. ²For if a man with gold rings and in fine clothing comes into your assembly, and a poor man in shabby clothing also comes in, ³and you pay attention to the one who wears the fine clothing and say, 'Have a seat here, please,' while you say to the poor man, 'Stand there,' or, 'Sit at my feet,' ⁴have you not made distinctions among yourselves, and become judges with evil thoughts? ⁵Listen, my beloved brethren. Has not God chosen those who are poor in the world to be rich in faith and heirs of the kingdom which he has promised to those who love him? ⁶But you have dishonoured the poor man. Is it not the rich who oppress you, is it not they who drag you into court? ⁷Is it not they who blaspheme the honourable name which was invoked over you?

We have lived in James' company long enough to know that he is a master of surprise. The one word for which the closing verses of chapter 1 have prepared us is conspicuously absent at the beginning of chapter 2 (indeed, James never uses it again): the word is 'religion'. Yet, surely, nothing would be easier than for him now to write, 'Now then, the first aspect of true religion we want to think about is . . .', for, as we have seen, this is in fact the link between chapters 1 and 2. Instead, however, a new thought is presented, *the faith of our Lord Jesus Christ* (2:1). In this way James sets the scene for the whole central, teaching section of his letter. Being a Christian is not conforming one's outward behaviour to a 'religious' pattern, for, as we saw (p.75, above), 'religion' is a comprehensive word for the specific ways in which a heart-relationsip to God is given outward expression. For James, this heart-relationship to God is simply faith in our Lord Jesus Christ.[1] He does not write to us about 'religion' but about 'faith', for

[1] RSV is a literal translation, *hold the fath of*; NIV, though paraphrastic, catches the

79

he desires to lead us from the external display to the internal reality.

In this way James alerts us to the importance of the subject he is about to tackle: *partiality* or 'favouritism' (NIV), or treating 'people in different ways according to their outward appearance' (GNB) or their worldly advantages. To do so is not simply to fail to conform to a desired 'religious' pattern of behaviour. It is to deny our faith in the Lord Jesus Christ.

Looking on for a moment into the whole of chapter 2, we discover that we have already stated its entire subject-matter. In verses 1–7 James argues out his case against *partiality* or 'respect of persons'. Verse 8 makes a link with verse 7. The connecting word is presumably represented in RSV (also NIV) by *really*, but, throughout its New Testament uses, it invariably means 'however', correcting or qualifying what has preceded.[2] This is how verse 8 relates to verses 1–7. The occurrence of the key-word, *partiality*, in verse 9 shows that James is still pursuing the same basic topic. In the same way, 'faith' is the leading idea in verses 14–26, failing to appear only in verses 15, 21 and 25. Each of the three sections, however, has its distinctive purpose. Verses 1–7 urge that, by falling into the sin of *partiality*, we deny our faith in the Lord Jesus; in verses 8–13 the major topic is God's law, which is mentioned in every verse, and the thrust of the section is to show that *partiality* is a departure from the way of obedience; and finally, verses 14–26 raise the more positive question, What is it that proves faith to be genuine? We shall, therefore, study James 2 under the headings 'Denying our faith', 'Obedient faith' and 'The proving of faith'.

Two sorts of glory (2:1–4)

In verses 1–7 the topic of 'Denying our faith' falls into three parts. In

---

heart of the matter, 'believers in'. The verb 'to have/hold' is frequently used along with 'faith' in the sense 'to have and exercise faith' (*e.g.* Mt. 17:20; 1 Tim. 1:19; *etc.*). The noun 'faith' is also frequently used with a following genitive case, 'faith of', meaning 'faith in' (*e.g.* Mk. 11:22; Rom. 3:22, 26; Eph. 3:12; *etc.*). Peter Davids is mistaken in saying that 'the genitive qualifier of *pistin* (faith) is quite unusual'. R. J. Knowling rightly opens the expression out as 'the faith which has our Lord for its object'. Eph. 3:12 and many other places show that the definite article 'the faith' cannot automatically be taken to imply 'credal faith', *i.e.* 'the faith which we hold about our Lord Jesus Christ'. We must understand the words 'the faith' in context and here in James the reference has to be to personal trust in Christ.

[2]Gk. *mentoi*; *cf.* RV 'howbeit'. Peter Davids: 'Only "however" will fit the other NT uses. . . .' (see Jn. 4:27; 7:13; 12:42; 20:5; 21:4; 2 Tim. 2:19; Jude 8).

verses 1-4 James puts before us two sorts of glory and invites a decision as to where our loyalty lies, seeing that they are mutually incompatible. In 5-7 he argues first from spiritual experience (5-6a) and then from earthly experience (6b-7) against the sin of partiality where it involves siding with the rich and neglecting the poor.

The heart of verses 1-4 is a homely, down-to-earth illustration such as James loves.[3] Into the church meeting come two strangers. That they are strangers is evident from the fact that they do not know where to sit and need one of the members of find them a place. One stranger has all the outward trappings of wealth and gets ushered into a seat,[4] while the other, *a poor man*,[5] has to stand or, at best, to squat on a stool. And when we ask why this is, it comes down to appearance: the one looks important, the other negligible.

It is this matter of 'looks' which must be stressed if we are to be faithful to James' teaching and at the same time keep within the balance of Scripture. The Bible is too courteous a book to allow us to lack proper respect for people to whom respect is due. It does not

[3] There is no need to be over-subtle about James' illustration. It is plain that the newcomers are strangers; there is nothing to show — and no need to show —whether they are believers or unbelievers. 1 Cor. 14:23-25 shows the possibility of the latter. In v.2, *assembly* translates *synagōgē*, 'synagogue'. James Adamson holds that this posits an early date for the writing of James, *i.e.* a date before it would be considered improper or misleading to use Jewish terms regarding the church; but Peter Davids lists Christian writers, outside the Bible, in the first and second centuries who referred to the church as a synagogue, so that the word is no help in fixing a date. But there is no ground for Davids' own suggestion that the word suggests, not the church gathered for worship, but as a church court such as is implied in 1 Cor. 6:1-11. He asks whether in a meeting for worship some would sit and some stand. But surely it all depends. We would not have expected that in a worship-meeting someone would sit on a window sill (not to mention subsequently falling out, Acts 20:9ff.). He doubts if Christians would need to be directed to their seats: but, if they were visitors, yes, they would. It happens all the time. Again, would a wealthy non-Christian attend a worship-service? Why not? Finally he wants to know, were people admitted to the Christian congregation before making a personal profession of faith? Evidently so in 1 Cor. 14:23ff. It is one thing to use a sledge-hammer to crack a nut; it is another to start by inventing the nut. Let us be as homely as James: the church gathers and, praise the Lord, there are visitors.

[4] In v.3 RSV '*Have a seat here, please*' and NIV 'Here's a good seat for you' represent the two usually proposed understandings of James' Greek, 'Do sit here well'. J. H. Ropes would contest an NIV-type rendering, urging some 'polite idiom' in the sense of 'please'. J. B. Phillips gets the best of both worlds: 'Please sit here — it's an excellent seat.'

[5] In v.2, *a poor man*, *ptōchos*. Laws, 'in classical usage ... a beggar.' This meaning is 'not strictly maintained in the ... NT' but 'the full force of *ptōchos* is no doubt intended by James in this context'.

reduce all to a common level in all things or refuse to take note of
worldly distinctions; certainly it does not sanction rudeness or uncon-
cern for what people are. It would not be showing *partiality*, for
example, to offer the last remaining seat to an elderly person and to
invite a younger person arriving simultaneously to stand or to sit on
the floor. The elderly command respect and considerate attention (Lv.
19:32). Or again, were Her Majesty the Queen or the President of our
country to come to worship, we would consider it both right and
indeed our privilege to stand when they entered and to have the best
seat held in readiness. Again, we would be obeying Scripture (*e.g.* Pr.
24:21a; 1 Pet. 2:17). But it is one thing thus to acknowledge inherent
dignity, whether of age or position; it is another thing altogether to be
swayed by the mere chance that one possesses worldly advantages such
as money and the other does not.

James' illustration is timeless. It speaks as loudly today as when he
penned it. It is still not always easy to know how to accommodate a
tramp in a worship-service and it still is easy to assume that wealth
gives a commanding voice in church affairs. The sin of *partiality*[6] is the
sin of judging by accidentals and externals and, as James noted, it
always bears down on the poor and disadvantaged.

But why is it a sin? This question brings us to the very curious piece
of Greek with which James begins what we call chapter 2. English
versions smooth it out in one way or another, but literally it says: 'My
brothers, not with partiality of any sort[7] must you hold the faith of our
Lord Jesus Christ, of the glory.' There are almost as many ways of

---

[6] *Partiality, prosōpolēmpsia*, is found in Rom. 2:11; Eph. 6:9; Col. 3:25, all denying
any such 'favouritism' or 'respect of persons' in God. The verb, *prosōpolēmpteō*, occurs
only in Jas. 2:9. It has a long pre-history in Old Testament usage where the Hebrew
nās'ā pānîm, literally 'to lift up a face', is sometimes used to express what James
condemns – favouring people on other than just, legal and worthy grounds (*e.g.* Lv.
19:15; Dt. 1:17; 10:17; 16:19; Jb. 34:19). The absence of any such reprehensible
favouritism in the Lord is not only the reason why his people should shun it, but is also
an important theological truth in its own right: it was not for this reason that he
rescued his people from Egypt, but for sound reasons within his own nature and in
accord with his absolute justice. In this way it stresses the righteousness or justice
which pervades the divine activity of salvation and which both Isaiah (45:21) and Paul
(Rom. 3:26) saw to be essential. The Greek *prosōpolēmpsia* is a compound word
meaning 'acceptance of the face' and in itself is not unlike our colloquialism about
'liking the shape of a person's face', *i.e.* to favour someone on grounds other than the
true merits of the case.

[7] In v. 1 *partiality* is, lit., 'partialities', the plural embracing every possible form and
occasion of the fault in question.

understanding this as there are commentators on James,[8] but two deserve consideration as more likely than the others. The first, as RSV, understands the abrupt 'of the glory' as an abbreviation meaning *the Lord of glory*, though, within the same general mode of interpretation, some would prefer to amplify it, with NEB, as 'who reigns in glory' or, with J. H. Ropes, 'our glorious Lord'. It seems a well-nigh fatal objection to this view that a master of words like James should make such a complication of saying a simple thing, if indeed all he wanted to do was to exalt our Lord Jesus as 'the Lord of glory'. As we noted in the introduction, one of the marked features of James is his stylish and accomplished Greek: how could he fall down at such an elementary hurdle? But if James was indeed such a fine linguist, then if there is an abruptness – and there is no ground for questioning the authenticity of the text – the author intended it to be so. To take this possibility seriously is the great merit of understanding 'of the glory' as descriptive of the Lord Jesus, equivalent to 'the faith of our Lord Jesus Christ, (who is) the Glory'. This is at once striking, scriptural and, more than any other interpretation, suited to the context of verses 1–4.

In one sense, of course, it does not really matter how we translate this verse. What matters is that James deliberately introduces the idea of the glory of Jesus and compels us to ask why he does so. This would be the case if we followed RSV in interpolating the words *the Lord* so as to read *the Lord of glory*; it would be so if we followed NIV with 'our glorious Lord' or even if we took the desperate course of following

---

[8]Amongst the commentaries readily available, Adamson resorts to altering the Greek text by moving the pronoun 'our' from its present position qualifying 'Lord' to the end of the verse where it would qualify 'glory', *i.e.* 'the Lord Jesus Christ, our Glory'. In its interpretation, this is indistinguishable from that advanced above, for Adamson explains that 'those who have the Lord Jesus Christ as their Glory cannot have "discrimination" in their brotherhood'. It is ironic that he dismisses the translation 'our Lord Jesus Christ, the Glory' as lacking evidence for, as Davids notes, 'Adamson's emendation . . . appears without basis either in the manuscript evidence or in the given word order. It simply conveniently rearranges the text'. Alford accepts '. . . (the Lord) of glory' while acknowledging that (from the point of view of James' Greek) this is 'harsh and unusual'. Ropes and Davids concur in taking 'of the glory' as referring back to the whole preceding phrase: 'our Lord Jesus Christ of glory' means 'our glorious Lord Jesus Christ' – though why James should express such a simple thing so tortuously they do not help us to understand. Knowling appears to favour the view which he traces to Bengel and which was supported by Mayer and Hort and is now advocated by Laws: that 'of the Glory' is an appended description of 'our Lord Jesus Christ'. It is not impossible that the Lord Jesus is referred to as 'the Glory' in Eph. 1:17 ('the Father of the Glory'); 1 Pet. 4:14 ('the Spirit of the Glory and of God'); *cf.* Lk. 2:32; Rom. 9:4.

James Adamson's alteration of the Greek text to read 'the Lord Jesus Christ, our Glory'. But it is inescapably so if we take the text as it stands with its assertion that Jesus is 'the Glory'. Why is the notion of glory so important?

In Exodus 33:18 we find Moses downcast over the history of Israel to date and desperately anxious about the future, if the LORD indeed insists that he continue to lead the people. In his need for encouragement and uplifting he begs: 'I pray thee, show me thy glory.' In reply, the LORD, ever prompt to meet the needs of those he loves, promises: 'I will make all my goodness pass before you, and will proclaim before you my name.' And this is exactly what he does in Exodus 34:5–8. The LORD's 'name' is a statement not just of *who* he is, but much more of *what* he is: it summarizes the LORD's character and attributes. In this way, when Moses asked to see the LORD's glory, the LORD in effect answered by saying: 'You will certainly see my glory, for I will come to you myself, reveal my essential goodness and spell out my very nature to you.' Glory, then, is 'shorthand' for the personal presence of the Lord in all his goodness and in the fullness of his revealed character. The Lord Jesus Christ is God's Glory: God himself come among us in all his goodness and in the full revelation of his person.

The meaning of glory

But we still have not answered the question why it is important for James to introduce the thought of *glory* at this point in his letter. Verse 4 supplies the answer. In the structure of the verses, the illustration begins with an *if* in verse 2. Verse 4 is, therefore, a 'then'-clause drawing out the conclusion: this is what follows *if* the wealthy are favoured and *if* there is discrimination against the poor merely on grounds of worldly advantage. James casts the conclusion, for emphasis, into the form of a question: *Have you not made distinctions among yourselves, and become judges with evil thoughts?*

With this translation, RSV pins one meaning on the text, and probably not the most suitable. *Among yourselves* demands the supposition that the two newcomers are Christian believers. The choice of the wealthy man simply on the grounds of his wealth, and the scorning of the poor man simply on the grounds of his shabbiness, constitute a false distinction. Those who made it first set themselves up as *judges* and then based their judgment on wrong reasons (*evil thoughts*). But in order to arrive at this understanding we have had to treat *made distinctions* as though it meant – and as though James intended it to mean – 'false distinctions'. We have no right to do this any more than James gives us ground for assuming that the newcomers are Christians. Now, there is no doubt that the verb can mean 'to distinguish' or 'to make distinctions', but also, and rather more commonly, it means 'to waver/be inconsistent'.[9] Likewise, the words which RSV renders *among yourselves* are more likely, on the ground of general usage, to mean 'in yourselves' in the sense 'in your hearts'.[10] The combined meaning would then be: 'Are you not inconsistent within yourselves...?' This fits in with the only other place where James uses this verb (1:6) and where the same notion of divided loyalty was expressed. There, the question was whether we are wholly devoted to the Lord in life's trials; here, it is whether we put the Lord's glory first in our scale of values or whether, all the time or from time to time, we allow ourselves rather to be led by the standards of this world as to what is worthy and worth-while. James Adamson catches the needs of the passage exactly when he says that the verb 'indicates their "facing both ways"'... nominally to Christ and actually to worldly snobbery'. James will presently tell us in some detail how the glory of God as revealed in Jesus touches on the situation which he has sketched, but in principle we have no need to wait to be told. We know the glory of God in the face of Jesus Christ only because, though he was rich, yet for our sake he became poor (2 Cor. 8:9) and because when we were wretched, pitiable, poor, blind and naked, he counselled us to buy gold from him that we might become rich, white garments for our nakedness and salve for our eyes that we might see (Rev. 3:17–18). He came right down to where we were, taking our nature upon him (Heb. 2:14), taking our sin upon him (1 Pet. 2:24), taking our curse upon him (Gal. 3:13), bringing to our blinded minds the light of the gospel of the glory of Christ (2 Cor. 4:4). In a word, it was in Christ that God the Father shone in our hearts to give the light of the knowledge of the glory of God in the face of Jesus Christ (2 Cor. 4:6).

To depart from this definition of what constitutes true glory is first to set ourselves up as *judges*, and in passing judgment to allow ourselves to be governed by 'wrong reasonings'. We have, in fact,

[9]Gk. *diakrinomai*. For 'make distinctions', *e.g.* 1 Cor. 6:5; for 'waver', *e.g.* Mk. 11:23; Acts 10:20; Rom. 4:20. The meaning 'to waver' is more favoured, and rightly so, by the commentators: *e.g.* Tasker, '...a divided allegiance, a hypocritical desire to serve God and mammon...'; Alford, 'You are not whole in your faith.'

[10]Gk. *en heautois*. Davids insists the newcomers are believers and translates 'among yourselves', a meaning supported, *e.g.*, by Acts 28:29; 1 Thes. 5:13; but the meaning 'in yourselves', *i.e.* 'in your hearts/minds', is more common, *e.g.* Mk. 4:17; Jn. 6:53; Rom. 1:27 and especially Mt. 9:3, where v.4 has the parallel 'in your hearts'.

committed a double fault. We have misunderstood our status – as if it were our position to sit in judgment on others; and we have trusted our own judgment – as if, by ourselves, we could make a true and accurate assessment. On the contrary, James teaches by a clear implication that in both status and judgment the Lord Jesus Christ, who is himself the Glory, must reign supreme. As to how we accept others, we must ask how he would accept them (*cf.* Rom. 14:1, 3; 15:7). As to how we appraise others, we must ask how he appraises them. As to how we act towards others, we must ask how he would act towards them.[11] Our values, priorities and activities must ever be governed by the definition of true glory displayed in the person, conduct and work of the Lord Jesus Christ.

Experience on two levels (2:5–7)

Listen, my beloved brethren. Has not God chosen those who are poor in the world to be rich in faith and heirs of the kingdom which he has promised to those who love him? ⁶*But you have dishonoured the poor man. Is it not the rich who oppress you, is it not they who drag you into court?* ⁷*Is it not they who blaspheme the honourable name which was invoked over you?*

There was no way in which we could come to grips with James' message in verses 1–4 without stealing his thunder. We had to pause to dwell on the striking, abrupt reference to the Lord Jesus as 'the Glory'. But it is in verses 5–7 that James makes his own applications and draws his own conclusions. In doing so he appeals to the experience of his readers on two distinct levels.

First, in verses 5–6a (. . . *the poor man*), he reminds them of *spiritual experience*. New life in Christ may trace its conscious and public history back to the moment of decision, of commitment, of accepting the Lord Jesus Christ as one's personal Saviour. But every conversion has a secret history which the Bible reveals and which owes its origin to God's choice. As James considers God's mind as revealed in the way he has exercised his choice, it is clear, he points out, that God has *chosen those who are poor in the world* (5). The words *in the world* are vitally important to James' meaning. They refer not to the sphere in which God's choice operates (*i.e.* he chooses people, here and now, in the course of earthly life in this world), but to the nature of the poverty experienced by those on whom the divine choice falls. It is poverty as

---

[11]*Cf.* Mt. 11:29 with Mt. 5:5; 2 Cor. 10:1; Gal. 6:1; Eph. 4:2; 2 Tim. 2:25; see also 1 Thes. 2:7 and 2 Tim. 2:24; 2 Cor. 10:1 with Phil. 4:5.

the world understands poverty. Again, the words *in the world* show that James is not making the same reference as Jesus did in Matthew 5:3, when he pronounced those blessed and happy who are 'poor in spirit', *i.e.* who 'acknowledge spiritual poverty . . . spiritual bankruptcy . . . before God'.[12] James follows here the words of Jesus in Luke 6:20 – those who are actually poor, as this world reckons poverty. These are the ones whom God has chosen. And if this is the case, then to dishonour the poor (6), as illustrated in verses 2–3, is to contradict the mind of God. Or, in terms of verse 1, to choose another glory as exceeding the glory of Jesus.

Secondly, verses 6b–7, James calls to mind *earthly experience*. He points out that it is in fact the rich who persecute believers (*oppress you*), using the forms and façade of legality to do so (*drag you into court*) and, in particular, defame the (lit.) 'lovely name', that is, the name of the Lord Jesus, by which they are called. Where, then, is the common sense of singling out the rich for preferential treatment?

Rich and poor

Such a blunt espousal of the cause of the poor and such an unqualified exposure of the rich are very much the cast of James' mind on the matter. In 1:9–11 there was no doubt where his sympathies lay in the contrasting human experiences of poverty and wealth. He was quick to use his chosen illustration to lift up the poor brother with a word of reassuring comfort and to take the rich brother down a peg or two. His treatment of the money-maker (4:13–17) and the money-abuser (5:1–6) is sharp to the point of becoming savage. No doubt his own growing years in the household of Joseph and Mary had sharpened his awareness of the inequality of social fortune and of the way the scales tip against the poor and in favour of the rich. For us the questions must be asked: how are we to understand the words he uses? Is the Lord unconditionally on the side of the poor? Are the rich by nature persecutors and inevitably such? And how are we to understand the mind that lies behind James' words? Is he calling us to take sides on every social issue on the assumption that the poor man must be right and the rich man wrong?

If it is only the poor who are privileged to receive the divine choice, then the rich brother of 1:10 is a considerable embarrassment! So also

[12]J. R. W. Stott, *The Keswick Week 1972*, p.46. See further John Stott's fuller study, *The Message of the Sermon on the Mount: Christian Counter-Culture* (IVP, 1978), pp.30ff.

are Abraham and Job, whom James quotes with approval (2:21–23; 5:11) and who were exceedingly wealthy men (Gn. 13:2; Jb. 1:3; 42:12). Furthermore, of course, the evidence of the rest of the Bible is by no means as unqualified as James' words, taken at face value, seem. The wealthy Joseph of Arimathea (Mt. 27:57), the proconsul, Sergius Paulus (Acts 13:7–12), Levi the tax-collector (Lk. 5:27) and his colleague Zacchaeus (Lk. 19:2) are sufficient to prove that the Lord has no animus against the rich as such. At the same time, since we have to search out such men among the many we meet in the pages of the New Testament, surely Paul gets the balance right when he says that 'not many . . . powerful, not many . . . of noble birth' were chosen by God (1 Cor. 1:26). We see, then, from this evidence inside James and more widely in the Bible, that James has learnt a teaching technique from the Lord Jesus himself. In some situations there are indeed two sides to the truth, but one so far outclasses the other that it merits stating as if it alone were the truth. This is what Jesus did when he affirmed that a real love for himself demanded hating our parents (Lk. 14:26). Does he really call us to hate our parents? Of course not! Yet in saying that the two loves are mutually exclusive he does no violence to the *practical* truth that our devotion to him, when it is real, is of necessity in a class by itself.

When we apply this formula to what James writes, we see that he is expressing a general rather than an invariable truth. The Lord does not choose only the poor; it is not only the rich who persecute believers and blaspheme the name of Jesus. Yet, in general, this is not only true but overwhelmingly true. The preponderance of the Lord's concern is shown for those who are towards the bottom of the world's heap. This appeared in the Old Testament's fundamental historical event, the Exodus. In Egypt the Lord chose out for himself the slave people. Marvellously, this act was not prompted by their misery as such, but by the Lord's inner heart of love (Dt. 7:7–8). In other words, love of the poor, downtrodden and helpless is written into the divine nature. Or again, we read that in taking the initiative to save Israel the Lord 'made a name for himself' (2 Sa. 7:23), *i.e.* revealed what he is really like. It is for this reason that an Old Testament word like 'needy'[13] can

---

[13]For example, the word *'ebyon*, translated either 'poor' (*e.g.* Ex. 23:6) or 'needy' (*e.g.* Ps. 9:18). Rooted in the verb 'to be willing, pliant', it means at its highest those who are willing to go the Lord's way and, on its darker side, those who must bend to the will of man and are therefore subject to being 'pushed around' by the more affluent and influential. They are an easy prey and can easily be deprived of their rights (*e.g.* Pss. 9:18; 12:5), yet the Lord is on their side (Ps. 35:10).

move in its meaning from the sense of financial poverty to social deprivation and oppression and then on to godliness, taking a spiritual stand against the prevailing social tide. Here, indeed, we find the proper background for both James' thoughts and his words. It has always been the case that the Lord's true people are predominantly less well off, the prey for stronger, more ruthless forces, and subject to less than justice from those who know how to manipulate the system. And, of course, finally, when we come to the Lord Jesus Christ himself, here is the Lord's true and only Glory: the one who for the sake of the poor became poor himself.

We can so easily excuse ourselves from facing the bluntness of James' words by allowing that (after all!) he is expressing a general rather than an exclusive truth. Yet the infrequency with which the Bible makes comparisons in this way — by allowing one side of the comparison to swamp the other — should alert us to the fact that we are not permitted to find an escape-hatch for ourselves. If we would follow the Lord Jesus then it must be our glory, as it was his, to be incessantly and preponderantly on the side of the poor, the underprivileged, the disadvantaged and the oppressed. To do this is to identify ourselves with the very heart of God and to live obediently to the main line of his revealed will. In fact there are three things which Scripture holds together in unity: what the Lord is in himself, how his nature leads him to identify with the needy and helpless, and how what he has done for us (the needy and helpless) should constitute a model for us to follow. Deuteronomy 10:17-19 expresses all this perfectly: 'The LORD your God is God of gods and Lord of lords, the great, the mighty, and the terrible[14] God, who is not partial[15] and takes no bribe.[16] He executes justice[17] for the fatherless and the widow, and loves the sojourner,[18] giving him food and clothing. Love the sojourner

---

[14]*Terrible, i.e.* awe-inspiring, worthy to be feared.

[15]The words translated *partial* are the Hebrew equivalent of *partiality* in Jas. 2:1.

[16]Refusal to take bribes is refusal to be impressed by wealth and the advantages the wealthy can confer. In this regard also Deuteronomy coincides with the teaching of Jas. 2.

[17]*Executes justice, i.e.* puts things right for.

[18]*The sojourner,* more literally 'temporary resident', 'resident alien'. The person who, for whatever reason, left his own land and came as a stranger among the people of God. Such stateless persons were frequently destitute — as indeed Israel became in Egypt. The orphan, the widow and the 'stranger' are frequently grouped as the characteristically helpless, who can so easily be exploited and who, simply because they are helpless, ought to be the objects of care and protection. *Cf.* Ex. 22:22; Dt. 16:11, 14; Jb. 31:17, 21; Pss. 10:14; 68:5; Is. 1:17, 23; *etc.*

therefore; for you were sojourners in the land of Egypt.'

If James calls us to live out the life of God by caring for the poor, he is equally determined that we should not be dazzled by the rich, and this too must be borne in mind. It is not all that long ago, indeed, when the wealthy paid an annual rent to secure a well-placed seat in our parish churches, while those who could not raise the financial wind had to be content with seats in the far-off corners bearing the (actual) label 'Free'. Even if such blatant inequality is now a thing of the past, it is by no means unusual for a person to have a voice in church affairs related not to his wisdom but to his wealth. In the same way it is common for well-heeled congregations to assume that they ought to have (and to get) the most gifted pastors, while fellowships in less promising or attractive areas cannot expect more than the average. Money still does the talking far too loudly in Christian circles, and where and when it does, the glory of Christ departs.

True riches

There is one further line of teaching in verses 5–7 which we must try to follow through. It is often the case in the Bible that, in dealing with one topic, something else comes in by implication or incidentally. So here: James' main contention is that God chooses the poor, but (within the terms of his illustration) it is easy for us Christians to give the poor less than their proper honour. Had James said no more than that, he would have made his point. But we may be thankful that he went further: the divine choice brings with it great spiritual riches, and the poor person becomes *rich in faith* and a heir *of the kingdom* which God *has promised to those who love him* (5). In the same way, when James pursues the other side of his illustration – the honour accorded to the wealthy merely because of his wealth – he not only alludes to opposition from the affluent but he analyses their opposition. They oppose believers, taking them to court (6); they also *blaspheme that honourable name by which you are called* (7). This is well exemplified in the persecution of the church organized by the then Saul of Tarsus, who 'dragged off men and women and committed them to prison' (Acts 8:3) and, according to his own later testimony, 'punished them often in all the synagogues and tried to make them blaspheme' (Acts 26:11). The forms of law were observed, no doubt, in the production of some charge meriting imprisonment, but behind this hatred of the Lord's people was a hatred of the Lord himself (*cf.* Jn. 15:18–24). We must assume that, at the time James wrote, this state of affairs was common enough to be used as a matter-of-fact illustration. But again, he does not simply say that the rich oppressors hate believers and hate the Lord, or even that they hate believers because they hate the Lord, but that, specifically, they *blaspheme* the name and that the name they blaspheme is the lovely *name by which you are called.*

In this as it were accidental way, worldly poverty serves to throw into relief the glory of our riches in Christ, and worldly wealth pales before what we gain when we are joined to him. There is, first, the wealth that is ours at the foundation of our Christian experience: faith and love.[19] In his teaching here James identifies himself with the main-line New Testament position. He agrees with Paul[20] that faith is God's gift to us and is the point at which conscious Christian experience begins as we respond to the Lord Jesus Christ by placing our faith in him.[21] He agrees with John and Paul that it is as our love arises from and responds to God's love for us[22] that we enter into his promised blessings, present and future. Secondly, James speaks of the rich sphere of blessing into which we have been brought, for we are *heirs of the kingdom* (5). The idea of the kingdom of God figures most prominently in the teaching of Jesus. James shows his faithfulness to the Lord's point of view in using *kingdom* as a summary word for the eternal sphere of blessing into which we have already entered. As the Lord Jesus used and developed the idea of his kingdom it lost all trace of territorial meaning. Entering into the kingdom is entering into the life which Jesus imparts (Mk. 9:45, 47); to be in the kingdom is to be saved (Lk. 18:25–26). The kingdom is not of this world (Jn. 18:36). It is not modelled on the earthly notion of a kingdom, nor does it arise

[19]Commenting on the phrase (lit.) 'poor in the world rich in faith', James Adamson says that it refers to 'those who are (*not* "those who are to be") rich in faith' and urges that 'the poor, in general, are much more likely and eager to believe in a celestial heaven to come'. Whether he is right in his understanding of the spirituality of the poor as such is not the point. Scripturally it is impossible to justify the interpretation that people are chosen *because* they are rich in faith. Eph. 2:8 defines faith as God's gift; *cf.* Phil. 1:29. Acts 15:7 makes this saving faith the product of God's previous choice. RSV is therefore correct in interpreting James as intending 'chosen those who are poor . . . to be rich . . .'.

[20]We shall note, in connection with Jas. 2:14–26, that some interpreters argue that James differs from Paul or even contradicts Paul on the foundational place to be given to faith in the Christian doctrine of salvation. Before ever we come to vv.14–16 we know from the present passage that this cannot be the case. The basic Christian wealth is God's gift of (saving) faith.

[21]*Cf.* Jn. 1:12; Acts 16:31; Gal. 2:16.

[22]*Cf.* Jn. 14:21, 23; 16:27; 1 Jn. 4:19; Rom. 5:5 with Gal. 5:22; Rom. 8:28; 2 Tim. 4:8.

from an earthly source, nor does it, or will it, find expression in an earthly, territorial expanse. It is the rule of Christ in and over believing hearts and brings the present kingdom benefits of righteousness, joy and peace, enjoyed through the Holy Spirit (Rom. 14:17).[23] It is also – and probably in the present passage in James even predominantly – the heavenly kingdom, the great and sure hope of every believer.

Thirdly, there is a personal blessing of high dignity accorded to every believer: we have each been called by that *honourable name* (7). The common marriage custom, whereby a wife takes her husband's surname, begins to illustrate what has happened. The taking of the name speaks of an intimate, personal and permanent relationship. Within the Bible, when Jacob gave the two sons of Joseph the status of being reckoned as though they were his own sons, he said (lit.) 'Let my name be named upon them' (Gn. 48:16, not as RSV): the name marks a new relationship – and indeed in this case secures a direct inheritance. Or again, when Amos foresees the gathering of Gentile nations into the kingdom of the expected David (Am. 9:12; *cf.* Acts 15:13–18), he speaks of 'all the nations who are called by my name'.[24] Many commentators see in James' words a reference to the ordinance of baptism, and while it is impossible to prove this, it certainly matches the practice of baptizing 'into the name'[25] and suits the meaning of the baptism as symbolizing our union with Christ in his death and resurrection.[26] But James does not in fact mention baptism and we ought, with him, to concentrate on the actual fact that we belong to Jesus and that by grace he shares his name and nature with us.

Held on course

The more we think of the illustration in verses 2–3, the more it gives really practical focus to a constant problem in Christian living. Imagine being on duty at the church door and being suddenly faced with both a well-dressed stranger and an unkempt, maybe smelly, tramp! It is so often in just such a way that experience tests our grasp of Christian principles of behaviour. James offers us three pointers to

[23]Note how, in Rom. 14:15ff., Paul uses, as parallel ideas, benefiting from the death of Christ (15), enjoying the life of the kingdom and the presence of the Holy Spirit (17), honouring what God has done in Christ (20) and living the life of faith (23).

[24]*Cf.* Dt. 28:10; 2 Ch. 7:14; Is. 4:1; Je. 14:9.

[25]*Cf.* Mt. 28:19; Acts 8:16; 19:5.   [26]*Cf.* Rom. 6:3–4.

correct reactions: first, think of Jesus as the (true) glory: he came right down to the poorest level, identifying himself with the least and worst. If our faith rests in him who is the glory (1), then how shall we behave? Secondly, James urges us to think of the mind of God (5): what choice did he make and, in consequence, how would he choose now? And thirdly, James reminds us of our own new position – that we (the least and the worst) have been enriched in faith and hope; it has been granted to us to believe in God and to love him; we are his heirs and have been called by his name. In what way, then, will the family likeness of such a Father show itself in us? And what should be our assessment of earthly wealth and position, who have been brought to see and to share true and eternal riches?

2:8–13
8. Obedient faith

If you really fulfil the royal law, according to the scripture, 'You shall love your neighbour as yourself,' you do well. ⁹But if you show partiality, you commit sin, and are convicted by the law as transgressors. ¹⁰For whoever keeps the whole law but fails in one point has become guilty of all of it. ¹¹For he who said, 'Do not commit adultery,' said also, 'Do not kill.' If you do not commit adultery but do kill, you have become a transgressor of the law. ¹²So speak and so act as those who are to be judged under the law of liberty. ¹³For judgment is without mercy to one who has shown no mercy; yet mercy triumphs over judgment.

The gospel is naturally on the side of the down and out. But what, then, about the 'up and out'?

The teaching of the first seven verses of chapter 2 has been pretty unequivocal. If we seek to set our priorities by the glory of Jesus (1) and to fashion our thinking according to the mind of God (5), then we shall go all out for the importance of the poor. But what, then, about the rich?

Illustrations need to be handled with great care. Like pebbles thrown into a pool, the ripples of an illustration can go far beyond the intention of the preacher. James began with an illustration (2–4) and its negative meaning was quite plain: we ought not to behave like that, giving honour to the rich simply because he is rich, discounting the poor simply because he is poor. But, positively, what ought we to do? Are we to take James' illustration on to its logical conclusion – that we should devote ourselves wholly to the poor and forget the rich?

Realizing that what he has said so far is capable of being pushed to this extreme, James, having made his point, turns to provide the needed corrective. This is why he links verse 8 to verse 7 by the word 'however'. He is turning our attention away from the illustration and directing our attention to a principle: 'If, however, you fulfil the royal law . . . you do well.'[1]

Another word which links verses 1–7 and 8–13 is *partiality*. In verse 1 it occurs in the plural in order to express the thought 'partiality in any shape or form'. This ought to have warned us that the illustration of the poor man (2–4) was not meant to be an exhaustive account of sinful favouritism, but only one example. When the word comes again (this time in the singular) in verse 9 it follows a reference to *your neighbour* in verse 8. According to the teaching of Jesus a neighbour is anyone who needs my care and attention (Lk. 10:25–37), and it would be just as sinful to refuse neighbourly concern to the rich simply because he is rich as to dismiss the poor because he is poor. Consequently the 'however' of verse 8 is a real clue to the understanding of the whole section. We might paraphrase: 'What it all comes to is this: keep the royal law.'

Law and the Christian

The principle on which James now rests his teaching is this: we have a law to obey. It is a very special law, for it is called *the royal law*. Also, it is *according to the scripture* (8), which means that it carries scriptural authority. This raises a whole series of questions: how can it be scriptural to say that Christians are under the law? Is James bringing us back into a bondage from which Christ liberated us? What place has 'law' in the life of the Christian?

The first twenty chapters of Exodus are a huge, God-given, visual aid on this subject. When the story begins, our ancestors were slaves in Egypt; at the end (Ex. 19 – 20) they are a free people, camped at the mount of God, Mount Sinai. It was not by accident that they arrived there – notwithstanding that the Lord brought them out of Egypt in order to bring them into Canaan. When he sent Moses on his mission of liberation, the Lord gave him this assurance, 'This shall be the sign for you, that I have sent you: when you have brought forth the people out of Egypt, you shall serve God upon this mountain' (Ex. 3:12). From the start, then, the Lord intended Mount Sinai as a primary destination. He took the wonderful step of acting as his people's guide, in the pillar of cloud and fire (Ex. 13:17–22), in order to guarantee that they would arrive there.

[1] We need to change RSV *If you really fulfil . . .* to 'Really, if you fulfil . . .'. See above, p.80, n.2.

Here, then, is our visual aid, drawn in the vivid colours of history. The first act of God is to redeem his people (Ex. 6:6). Then he brings his people to the place where he reveals his law to them (Ex. 20:1ff.). To put the matter another way: those who have experienced the benefit of the blood of the lamb (Ex. 12:13, 21–23) must come under obedience to the law. God the Redeemer and God the Lawgiver are the same. Grace comes first, then Law follows. This is biblical logic and, when we think about it, even we can see that it 'stands to reason'. For when people have received the wonders of God's grace in redemption, will they not, in gratitude, want to know how to live so as to please the God who has poured his grace upon them? The point is of such importance that it is worth stating it over again. In the Bible, the obedience we render to his law is not meritorious obedience but responsive obedience. We obey, not as those who are trying to merit salvation, but as those who have already received salvation and wish to respond by giving their whole lives up to God their Saviour.

There is a pattern, then, in the ways of God. Redemption by the blood of the lamb leads to responsive obedience – the life-style of the redeemed framed according to the law of the Redeemer. This is the message of the historical visual aid in the Scripture of the Old Covenant. There is no problem transferring it into terminology expressive of the New Covenant. Those who have been redeemed by the precious blood of Jesus, the Lamb of God, long to grow like him, to be made like unto the Son of God in all things. This is simply saying that his example comes to us with the force of divine law. In prediction, the New Covenant in fact involves the writing of God's law upon our hearts (Je. 31:31–34). This was fulfilled in Jesus (Heb. 10:15–17) and it is in this spirit that James can call us to make Jesus our standard of *glory* (1) and also to obey *the royal law* (8).

The royal law (2:8–9)

The use of the adjective *royal* must point to the importance of this law, but beyond that it is not certain quite what James intends. More is meant than that the law comes to us with authority, for that is covered by saying that the law is *according to the scripture.* [2] Some understand James to mean that this law is 'the king of all laws',[3] but this is unlikely, because the adjective *royal* (*basilikos*) is not used in the New

[2]The passage in question is Lv. 19:18. See the whole section, 19:9–18, as background to the present passage in James.

[3]*E.g.* Alford; *cf.* Tasker.

Testament with the meaning 'ruling' or 'governing'. But it does consistently have the meaning 'belonging to the king'.[4] If we accept this meaning here, then *the royal law* is that which comes to us with some special imprimatur from the King.[5] The case for this is strengthened when we recall that the Lord Jesus himself took this law and gave it a special dignity within the whole body of biblical law.[6] Furthermore, this is the sense which best suits the context in James. He has just said that God has made us *heirs of the kingdom* (*basileia*, 5), and now he enunciates the *basilikon*-law, the kingdom-law, the law which in a very special sense belongs to the king within whose realm we are privileged to live.

Here, then, is a law which comes to us with all the weight of scriptural authority, but which in particular is marked out as being a special concern of our King, something that is specially suited to him and which comes to us bearing the royal arms upon it: *You shall love your neighbour as yourself* (8). How very important the last two words are! They are the key to the whole meaning. If we want to know how we are to love our neighbours, then we must ask a prior question: how do we love ourselves? Never (it is to be hoped!) with an emotional thrill; rarely, as a matter of fact, with much sense of satisfaction; mostly with pretty wholesale disapproval; often with complete loathing – but always with concern, care and attention. When we catch sight of our faces in the mirror first thing in the morning, the word 'Ugh' comes spontaneously to the lips; yet at once we take that revolting face to the bathroom, we wash it and tend it and make it as presentable as nature will allow. And so it goes on through the day: loving ourselves means providing loving care and attention. This is the model on which we are to base our relationships to all to whom we owe neighbourly duty. Everything conspires today to define 'love' primarily in emotional terms. Scripturally, love is to be defined in caring terms, for the love that is owed to our neighbour is the love we expend on ourselves.

The opposite of *the royal law* (8) is *partiality* (9). They are contrasted as 'doing well' and 'committing sin'. The essence of the royal law is that wherever there is need there is an obligation to extend the sort of love we lavish on ourselves; the essence of partiality is to select the recipients of our care on some ground other than that they are in need. When the people of God of old entered the land of Canaan they were

---

[4]Jn. 4:46 (RSV 'official', lit. 'king's man'); Acts 12:20 ('king's country'), 21 ('royal robes'). *Cf.* Nu. 20:17 (LXX), 'the king's way'.

[5]*E.g.* Adamson, Laws.   [6]*E.g.* Mk. 12:28–31.

commanded to go to two mountains in the middle of the land, Mount Ebal and Mount Gerizim, and to identify them with the law of God. The blessings promised to the obedient were recited on Mount Gerizim and the curses threatened against the disobedient were recited on Mount Ebal.[7] As long as the people lived in the land they could no more escape the obligation to obey God's law than they could remove those two mountains, and they could no more forget the way of blessing and the way of cursing than they could fail to see the mountains before their eyes. In the same way there is, here in James, an Ebal and a Gerizim for Christians, a way of well-doing (8) and a way of sin (9). On Gerizim stands the royal law; and on Ebal, the sin of partiality.

But all this is very much more easily said than done. The world is full of the needy; we have far more neighbours than we could ever hope to care for. Three things may be offered as guide-lines. First, we must each discover from God what is our calling. The world is indeed full of our neighbours, in the sense of people requiring our aid, but the Lord of the harvest is the only one who can direct his work-force, some here, some there, according to his perfect will.[8] While all are still our neighbours, there is some particular concern which is our calling. Secondly, we must respect each other's callings. A man living in an area of tough housing estates stood on the steps of a thronged church in a well-to-do suburb and thought aloud: 'I wonder how this vicar would get on if he was down among real people.' This attitude is not uncommon. We have a great concern – and rightly – for those who are disadvantaged by living in the inner city, but sometimes those called to the hard graft of inner city ministry might wonder if God could in fact call anyone to suburbia. To our own Lord we stand or fall;[9] we must respect each other's callings. Thirdly, we must enter into each other's calling. There is a convenient phrase which runs, 'It's not my scene.' At best it is a statement of self-knowledge and it is far from a bad thing to know one's limitations. Some can work, unperturbed, in areas where mugging is rife; others know before God that this is 'not their scene'. But how easy it is to allow this to become indifference: it is not my scene – let them deal with it whose scene it is. Or, as someone once put it: 'Lord, here am I – send my sister.' There can be a middle-class assumption in the church which prefers to look the other way rather than face up to the realities of the urban wilderness. We must learn rather to rejoice in each other's callings; to marvel at the

[7]Dt. 27; Jos. 8:30–35.   [8]Mt. 9:35 – 10:5.   [9]Rom. 14:4, 10–12.

obedience which takes our brothers and sisters into grim areas at home and overseas, or into the hard graft of bringing the gospel to the comfortable. Where we cannot go ourselves, and where we are not called to go, we must stand behind those who are so called, for we are members one of another and all alike trustees of the King's commission to the whole creation. The needs which others are actually meeting are needs for which I have an obligation under the terms of the royal law: my brothers and sisters are due my loving prayers, concern and support. 'Partiality', says Leslie Mitton, 'is an affront to God, not an amiable weakness.'

God's law and God's character (2:10–11)

The argument so far is that there is one law which in a special way belongs to the King whom we serve. It is his *royal law*. It commands that we devote to our neighbour the same sort of concerned care which we automatically lavish on ourselves. But we might ask whether it is equally obligatory on all of us. Can we not side-step this particular on the ground that our bent is in other directions? Some find ministry to needy people congenial; to others it is pain and grief from first to last.

James might have replied to this by drawing out the significance of the word *royal*. He might have stressed that this law can be called *royal* because it has a special place in the heart and wishes of the King; in a special way it reflects what he is and what he wants. Therefore it carries a special obligation for any who desire so to live as to please the King. But it would seem from what he actually does say that this approach would not be strong enough. James wants to go beyond a special obligation to obey the royal law to establish a universal obligation, an obligation which no-one can avoid. He does it in this way: first (10) he insists that the law is one indivisible whole. There is no way in which we can pick and choose between the commandments, because to break one is to break 'the law'. When we see the crescent moon we say, 'There's the moon' because the whole is there even though we can see only a part. In the same way the whole law of God is represented in every individual precept. Or, to put it another way, the law is not like a heap of stones but like a sheet of glass. We could take one stone from a heap and leave the heap itself still intact; but when we throw a brick through a window, it strikes only one place but it fragments the whole. The law of God is like the glass: a break at one point cannot be contained; the cracking and crazing spreads over the entire area.

Why is this? James goes on (11) to explain. He does so by turning from the law to the Lawgiver: *He who said . . . said also . . .* The thing which gives the law its indivisible nature is the character of the God who spoke it. This means that there is nothing abitrary about the commandments of the law: each one reflects some facet of the divine nature.[10] Neither is there anything unnecessary: if the law is to express the whole nature of the Lawgiver, then each single precept has its place. To take away a precept from the law is to damage the revelation of God which he has given us in his law. To say that one of the commands does not apply to me is to say that there is some aspect of the nature of God which does not matter, as far as I am concerned. I can get on without it; it is of no particular value.

When Moses looked back on the experience at Mount Sinai he was adamant on this point. He reminded the people that the Lord had not shown them a 'form' which they might subsequently copy and say that God is like that (Dt. 4:12, 15). If, therefore, Israel should ever attempt some visible portrayal of God, it could only be a corruption of what God actually is. They would have to take a model from some part of creation (Dt. 4:16ff.) and, far from truly representing what God is, this could only diminish and damage his true nature. On the contrary, at Mount Sinai, the Lord revealed himself by what he said. Deuteronomy 4:15 puts it very sharply: 'You saw no *form* on the day that the Lord *spoke.*' Specifically what he said was his law: 'You saw no form; there was only a voice . . . the ten commandments' (Dt. 4:12–13). The Lord expressed himself in his words; the law of God reveals the nature of God. The brilliance of the diamond is the perfection of the holy God himself: the whole diamond is the law; the individual facets are the commandments.

The law of liberty (2:12–13)

James has so far taught us two truths about the command to love our neighbour as ourselves. First, because it is *the royal law,* the law that in a special sense belongs to the king, we would *wish* to obey it – simply because he would specially desire us to do so. Secondly, because it is a command of the law of God, we *must* obey it. To dismiss it is to dismiss the facet of the Glory of God which it represents; to leave it to others is to say that it is immaterial whether this part of the Lord's likeness is seen in me. It comes to us as a revelation of God, and with his authority, therefore we must obey it. But, thirdly, it is part of *the*

---

[10]See the discussion of this point, p.70, above.

law of liberty, and therefore we *can* obey it.'[11]

We have already noted (p.71, above) that the Lord gave his law to his people in order to safeguard the liberty which he had achieved for them by bringing them out of Egypt (Ex. 20:2). The law of God is not a new bondage, but is given to mark the end of the old bondage and the beginning of true freedom. We must now seek to understand how this is so.

All around us today we see the social rules and conventions, which used to be respected, being broken or discarded. It is very easy to lament over the spirit of rebelliousness which this seems to represent, but the true explanation lies deeper. What people are really seeking is freedom. We look around us at a whole array of inherited laws and customs, find them a real restriction and bondage, and cast them on one side, saying that we want to be ourselves, free of the cramping restrictions of former people and earlier days. The easiest and in many ways the best illustration is marriage and sex. Why should something as hopefully exciting and satisfying as sexual intercourse be reserved for marriage and restricted to the married? The adult generation replied: It has always been so; that is the way we were brought up. The young replied: But we are not yesterday; we are today; we don't see it like that; we want to be ourselves. The church said: It has always been church teaching and tradition; and the young replied: But we don't belong to your church; we want to be ourselves. And since neither Christian nor non-Christian marriages seemed to be a great commendation for the adult and church viewpoint, a generation of experimenters grew up, trying to find a life-style which would 'enable us to be ourselves' – in other words, to be free.

But what does it mean to 'be ourselves'? What is true human nature? What seems to enable us to 'be ourselves' so often leads only to a new bondage. We see it in the sex-scene and the drugs-scene all around us. Liberty was promised; bondage followed. We must first know what we are before we can arrive at 'being ourselves' and truly free. The Bible has the answer: Man is made in the image of God. Our true freedom depends on discovering how we can give expression to our true nature. How can we live so as to be like him? James answers this crucial question by his startling expression, *the law of liberty,* bringing together the two things which people think of as opposites, *law* and *liberty!* But, as we have seen, the law is the nature of God expressed in commandments. When we obey his commands, then we

[11]See the discussion of this point, p.71, above.

are living like him. We are in the image of God; the law is in the image of God. When we bring these two together, we are 'being ourselves'; we are truly free. God's law describes the life of true freedom; obedience opens the door into the free life.

It is for this reason that we as Christians never need hesitate to point anyone to the law of God as the true way of life, for it spells out the image of God for the benefit of those who were created in the image of God. It is the true way of life for all. We shall be accused, of course, of seeking to impose 'our standards' on those who do not share our convictions, but this is not so. The patient does not refuse the doctor's prescription, saying, 'I am not a doctor; he has no right to force his ideas on me.' With the Bible in our hands we happen to know what human nature truly is, and also the way of life that brings true human nature to full development. In a word, we have on offer what the world wants: real freedom. But for ourselves there is another whole dimension. Acts 5:32 says that God gives his Holy Spirit to those who obey him. In other words, the very act of obeying is a key to power. The law of God does more than describe the life of liberty; obedience liberates. Hebrews 10:16–17 (quoting Je. 31:33) explains this by saying that through the saving work of Christ we have been given by God a heart that matches the requirements of his law. James might put it in his own way: we were brought to new birth by the word our Father spoke (1:18). His word of truth in all its aspects resides in our new nature, and waits to be triggered off by the precepts of his law. We are called to obey and, because the law corresponds to the wishes and capacities of the new heart, we can.

Mercy and judgment (2:13)

Sadly we fail, over and over again, to live the life of obedience, and we are very blameworthy, for at one and the same time we have to admit that 'Yes, I did disobey' and 'No, I did not have to'. It is good for us that James goes on now to speak of *mercy*. We are in constant need of the mercy of God, and he shows us on what terms we may have it: *judgment is without mercy to one who has shown no mercy* (13).

The Lord Jesus taught that it is the merciful who obtain mercy (Mt. 5:7), and amplified his teaching in the story of the unforgiving servant (Mt. 18:21–35). Forgiveness was extended in relation to an impossible debt, but when the merciful king discovered that he was offering mercy to one who had no mercy in his own spirit the offer was withdrawn – and, said Jesus, 'so also my heavenly Father will do to every one of you, if you do not forgive' (35). It is not that our mercy has purchasing power, but that it has evidential value. Neither Jesus nor James would see our merciful deeds as meritorious acts by which we make ourselves worthy of God's mercy. If we could make ourselves worthy we would not need mercy! Both teach that, if we are not merciful, we can neither credibly seek nor effectively receive the mercy he offers.

The word which links verses 12 and 13 is *judged . . . judgment*. Since (12) the law of God is itself a liberating agent, disobedience is without excuse and we have much need of divine mercy. But (13) instead of simply saying that mercy is available, James states the truth about mercy in a way that rounds off his whole argument. The essence of the illustration in verses 2–4 is that a merciful spirit was replaced, on spurious, superficial grounds, by a spirit of partiality, favouring the wealthy. In verse 13 the mercy we need is conditional upon showing mercy, for only the merciful obtain mercy. We need to be careful about the words *without mercy* (13). James Adamson is quite wrong in saying that a person lacking mercy 'will come under the old ruthlessness of the "law" '. Ruthlessness is an inappropriate description of Old Testament law, which had as its basis an insistence on absolute equality between crime and punishment.[12] *Without mercy* is not the same as what we mean by merciless. If we fail to find shelter under divine mercy, then the law takes its absolutely just and equitable course; we get what we deserve. But the presence of a merciful spirit assures us that we can sue for and shelter under mercy.

RSV tries to help James by smoothing over the abruptness with which he ends his paragraph. We read, *yet mercy triumphs over judgment*. There is no *yet* in James' Greek. NIV makes the words an independent exclamation, and this is correct. But what do they mean? The words are not a command or an invitation, but an unqualified statement. We need to ask when and about whom such an assertion can be made, and A. Barnes gives us the lead we need: 'In the plan of salvation . . . respect is done to justice, but mercy triumphs. Justice *demands*, as what is

[12]The Old Testament expressed its basic legal principle in the *lex talionis*, the law of exactness (Ex. 21:23–25; Lv. 24:19–20; Dt. 19:21). The punishment must exactly fit the crime, no more, no less. There is no evidence in the Old Testament that punishment was actually carried out according to a literal understanding of the *lex talionis*. The Old Testament admitted the principle of commuting punishments; it provided for 'degrees' of murder, *etc*. The point of the *lex talionis* is not that it directs *how* offenders should be punished, but states the principle on which punishment should be assessed.

due, that the sinner should be condemned; mercy *pleads* that he may be saved – and mercy prevails.' In this way, at the end of a very searching section, James brings us a real word of comfort and assurance. To be sure, if we show ourselves to be merciful, we can reckon on God's mercy, but there is no way in which anything about ourselves is a sufficient ground of confidence in prospect of the judgment-seat of Christ. In fact, is our capacity for showing mercy worth talking about? Are we always as truly merciful as we ought? Even at its best is our mercy a pure, good, perfect mercy? Is it not a tawdry and inadequate thing, just as much shot through with the taint of our selfishness as is anything else we sinners do? Such questions flood the mind – and we know the answers only too well. Practical and loving James directs us, at the end, away from self-questioning to the one thing that is eternally certain. In the cross of Christ justice was fully done, its claims were fully met and God's mercy to sinners triumphed in the provision of a complete forgiveness and a full salvation. Maybe the very abruptness of his words as he (so to speak) blurts out this great truth shows how James' own heart was moved at the thought of Jesus, Calvary and the great, eternal acquittal. Thus even before the judgment-seat mercy wins the day. It 'crows over judgment'.[13] This is our position before God. Judgment looks at our deserts; mercy at our needs. And God himself looks at the cross of his Son.

But there is another application. In verse 4 James rebuked us for 'becoming judges'. This is not only wrong in itself, but makes us unlike our God. Should not we too be those in whose every act mercy has the last laugh?

[13]The verb is *katakauchaomai*, a strengthened form of the ordinary verb 'to boast'. It occurs elsewhere only in Rom. 11:18, where its 'crowing' sense is well (even if regrettably) illustrated.

2:14–26
9. The proving of faith

What does it profit, my brethren, if a man says he has faith but has not works?
Can his faith save him? [15]*If a brother or sister is ill-clad and in lack of daily*
food, [16]*and one of you says to them, 'Go in peace, be warmed and filled,'*
without giving them the things needed for the body, what does it profit? [17]*So*
faith by itself, if it has no works, is dead.

[18]*But some one will say, 'You have faith and I have works.' Show me your*
faith apart from your works, and I by my works will show you my faith.
[19]*You believe that God is one; you do well. Even the demons believe — and*
shudder. [20]*Do you want to be shown, you shallow man, that faith apart from*
works is barren? [21]*Was not Abraham our father justified by works, when he*
offered his son Isaac upon the altar? [22]*You see that faith was active along with*
his works, and faith was completed by works, [23]*and the scripture was fulfilled*
which says, 'Abraham believed God, and it was reckoned to him as righteous-
ness'; and he was called the friend of God. [24]*You see that a man is justified by*
works and not by faith alone. [25]*And in the same way was not also Rahab the*
harlot justified by works when she received the messengers and sent them out
another way? [26]*For as the body apart from the spirit is dead, so faith apart*
from works is dead.

Maybe we should give James credit for having a very impish sense of
humour. He certainly loves to take us by surprise, to catch our
attention, for example, by apparently darting off in some irrelevant
direction (*e.g.*, who could have foreseen 1:19 as a sequel to 1:18?), to
coin the startling expression (*e.g.* 'the law of liberty', 1:25; 2:12) – or
to be simply outrageous. And it is at this last point that we find him in
2:14.

We can just see his hearers sit bolt upright (if, indeed, it might be
true that his 'letter' first saw the light of day as a sermon). We can (or

ought to) feel the shock waves of disbelief running through his first readers: *can his faith save him?* What next!

James, of course, knows that he is being impish and provocative. This is what he intends. For behind his seemingly scandalous questioning about the truth of salvation by faith there lies his own clear teaching that faith is the primary thing, the hallmark of the Christian, the irreplaceable priority. The present chapter began by addressing *my brethren* as those who 'have faith in our Lord Jesus Christ'. It is the common characteristic of all Christians; it is the thing which binds them into a brotherhood. In verse 5, faith is the first way in which God enriches those whom he has chosen. Looking forward into the passage lying before us, verse 17 sees faith as 'having', *i.e.* possessing as part of its reality, works; in verse 20 faith is, as it were, a central core which should have works attached to it; in verse 22 faith is the dominant partner with works as its colleague (see below). If we look right back to the beginning of the letter, 1:2–3 pictures life as an arena in which faith faces the tests of experience; and if we look on to the end, 5:15 teaches us about the prayer which proceeds from faith. It is undeniably true that if we snatch some phrases from their context in the present passage we can make James fall out with Paul – but then the error is ours in forcing a meaning which the context disallows. But if we ask what place James accords to faith, then he and Paul are at one. Faith is God's foundational gift (Jas. 2:5; Eph. 2:8). It is the common mark of all Christians (Jas. 2:1; Gal. 3:26). It is the continuing reality, running like a story-line through all the length and all the experiences of Christian life (Jas. 2:22; 1 Tim. 6:12). It is the root from which good works (Jas. 2:22; Tit. 3:8) grow.

But if James basically gives to faith its proper biblical position, why does he face us with a question which seems to point in quite another direction: *Can his faith save him?*

There are four links between verses 14–26 and 1–13. First, there is what we may call a 'domino' link: *mercy* is a Christian essential (13) and an essential product of faith (14–15). Secondly, there is a verbal link: in verse 1 faith is the common characteristic of all Christians; and verse 14 begins to raise the question what faith is. Thirdly, there is a doctrinal link: verses 8–13 introduced and laid heavy stress on the place of *law* in the experience of the Christian. But are not 'law' and faith opposites and (so to speak) mutually exclusive (*e.g.* Phil. 3:9; Rom. 3:20–22)? How can James' teaching about law possibly match a Christian understanding of salvation by faith? And fourthly – and most directly – there is a topical link: along with the emphasis on law

(8–13) came the topic of judgment to come (12–13). Now, what is a Christian's ultimate security in the day of judgment? It is this, that we appear before the judgment-seat as those who are already saved. When the books are opened, there is also opened the Lamb's book of life and those whose names are recorded there cannot be touched by adverse judgment (Rev. 20:12–15). This great and eternal salvation is by faith in the Lord Jesus Christ (*e.g.* Jn. 3:16; Eph. 2:8). How very important, then, it is to know what a true and saving faith is! So much rests on it.

Making sure about faith

That, then, is the function that verses 14–26 have to fulfil in James' teaching. What makes faith real? Can we be sure that our faith is a saving faith? Faith can be such a vague word. Many people would say: 'Oh, I'm a great believer' – but all it amounts to is a wishful thought that in fact everything turns out for the best and that it will do so if only one believes it! James is far too practical – and far too concerned for us – to leave things like that.

To arrive at a correct definition of faith, James introduces four illustrations: the ill-clad and hungry brother or sister Christian (15–17), the believing but troubled demons (18–20), Abraham, the friend of God (21–24), and Rahab who welcomed Joshua's spies (25–26). Before tackling these illustrations in detail, notice three things: first, each illustration ends with a summary statement of what James wants us to learn (17, 20, 24, 26). Secondly, the first two illustrations are negative (what faith is not); the second two are positive (what faith is). Thirdly, the first and last illustrations deal with the manward evidence of a true faith (hungry people fed; endangered spies received); the second and third illustrations deal with the godward evidence of a true faith (peace with God – not terror, and a life of obedience to God's will).

It may help us to see the section as a whole if we set it out as a diagram (see next page):

107

A¹ (verses 15–17)
   (a) Spurious faith is ineffectual manward: the hungry are sent away unfed (15–16).
   (b) Summary statement (17): faith, lacking evidential work, is dead.

  B¹ (18–20)
     (a) Spurious faith is ineffectual godward: it gives no peace with God, for demons have faith of a sort but it leaves them in terror (18–19).
     (b) Summary statement (20): faith, separated from the works which validate it, is barren.

  B² (21–24)
     (a) Genuine faith is effectual godward: like Abraham's faith, it shows itself in works of obedience to the will of God (21–23).
     (b) Summary statement: works of obedience provide evidence that faith is true, justifying faith (24).

A² (25–26)
   (a) Genuine faith reaches out in costly compassion to people at risk (25).
   (b) Summary statement (26): it is the activity of 'works' that reveals faith as a living entity.

The opening verse (14) sets the scene for this four-step definition of saving faith. Imagine a person who professes faith. We must not emphasize the verb *says* as though from the outset to cast doubt on the testimony. As far as that goes, we may and must assume that the unnamed person offers an impeccable account of placing faith in Christ. But the observer can add to the spoken testimony something that the speaker left unsaid: 'Works, however, he does not have.' There is a claim to faith unsupported by any concrete evidence in the life of the man concerned. This, then, is our starting-point. As C. L. Mitton puts it: '. . . the claim a man makes to have faith, and the test by which the truth of his claim can be gauged.' The idea of 'claim' is important. R. V. G. Tasker is helpful here: James 'does not say "though a man has faith" but "though a man say...".' James offers something of a definition of the faith which he is examining. It is a mere matter of claim, a formally correct statement, but its doctrinal credibility does not issue in a new direction of life. The question which

James therefore asks expects the answer 'no': 'That faith cannot save him, can it?'[1]

It is very important to ask what James is assuming about his readers. Unless they are accustomed to say 'Salvation is by faith' there is no point in James approaching them in this way. But he approaches them with his challenging question, not because he would propose a different way of salvation, but because he would have them understand what 'by faith alone' really means. On his own part, the assumption he is making is common to him and all Bible writers: saving faith results in a distinctive life. Hebrews (6:9) speaks of 'things that belong to salvation' when it refers to the way of life which validates a claim to faith. James just says *works*, and into that one word he packs all that should be distinctive about the person who believes and is saved. Look again at the outline of the passage given above. The two B-sections lie at the centre of a circle; they are the heart of the matter – what we are in relation to God. The two A-sections are the circumference of the circle, the interface where our life with God meets with the watching world and interacts with it. In this way James sets out the totality of faith-with-works and at the same time keeps the two distinct realities in their proper balance. For it is only broadly correct to say (with Peter Davids) that 'James does not argue for faith instead of works or works instead of faith or even works above faith but for faith and works'. Put like this, the priority and centrality of faith in the teaching of James is not safeguarded. After all, in verse 17 it is faith which possesses (*has*) works; in verse 22 (see further, below) it is faith which is the dominant partner in its colleague-relationship with works. We must say, therefore, not 'faith and works', but faith productive of works.

Around the circumference (2:15–17, 25–26)

In the two A-sections James contrasts the armchair philanthropist of verse 16 with the active and personally risky compassion of Rahab. In each case James is starting at home. The needy in verses 15–16 are Christian brothers and sisters. In verse 25 the situation is that Rahab, though a Canaanite woman, had already identified herself through

---

[1]Literally, 'The faith cannot save him, can it?' This follows a regular use of the definite article 'the' in Greek: it points back to a definition of the noun in question given or implied by whatever has immediately preceded. AV is, therefore, wrong in context to say 'Can faith save him?' RSV is correct; *his faith*, i.e. 'the faith' just exemplified in the man of whom we have been speaking; or RV, NEB, 'Can that faith . . . ?' i.e. 'the faith' seen in such a person.

personal faith with the people of God (*cf.* Jos. 2:8–11). In consequence of this she can not only legitimately claim for herself the protected status that her faith affords (Jos. 2:12–13), but she recognizes the obligation to meet the needs of God's people as they present themselves to her (Jos. 2:12a). We must, of course, understand that James is here being practical rather than restrictive. He is illustrating his meaning from the situation which we are most likely and most often to face – the needs within our own fellowship. He is not suggesting that these are the only needs for which our faith should drive us to find a remedy.

The concluding summary statement with each illustration includes the uncompromising word *dead* (17, 26). When faced with human need there is a 'remedy' which restricts itself to kindly hopes and good advice: Off you go now; try not to worry. Do keep warm and eat plenty (16). This, to James, speaks not of a half faith or a sort of faith or a limited faith: it is *dead*. Rahab's sort of faith, by contrast, puts all life under contribution: her house, her resources, her ingenuity and her personal safety. This is living faith, *for as the body apart from the spirit is dead, so faith apart from works is dead* (26). We will confuse ourselves in seeking to understand what James means by this comparison if we introduce words describing the relationship between body and spirit: if we say, for example, that the spirit animates the body, and then try to discover how *works* might be thought to animate *faith*. We ought to start rather with the fact that unity of body and spirit is required for life, and so also there must be a unity of faith and works. They must belong together in a living Christian experience. A. Barnes puts it exactly: 'There is as much necessity that faith and works should be united to constitute true religion, as there is that body and soul should be united to constitute a living man.'

Whatever would James say to the situation we are in today? The ease with which information circles our globe and the way in which the media bring all life into our lives sets before us not *a brother or sister . . . ill-clad and in lack of daily food*, but thousands upon thousands of them (if we confine ourselves to our relatives in the Lord's family) and doubtless millions (if we think of the family of man). The presence of this need is the touchstone as to whether our faith is alive or *dead*. James is only echoing the Lord Jesus: we cannot claim a valid and eternally significant relationship with him if we sit loose to the needs of 'one of the least of these' (Mt. 25:45). If our faith is living, it will be seen in the pressure we try to exert on those agencies which have it in their power to meet the needs of the whole world virtually at a stroke.

We should be relentless in pushing governments – and pushing church leaders who have the opportunity to address world-governments in a significant way – to throw both economic and military caution to the winds in the face of the prior claims of human need. Meat mountains, butter mountains and powdered milk mountains are an offence to God and man if there is a hungry mouth in the world that can be filled through them. The pre-empting of the world's wealth for weapons of mass-destruction (whether 'conventional' or nuclear) is blasphemy against the living God while those to whom he has given life die for want of food or medical care. Even the millions of money that go out through voluntary relief organizations pale into insignificance beside what governments could do. Can we not hear James say: Unless your faith issues in pressure, *what does it profit* (16)? Unless your faith is willing to take personal risks, it does not come up to the test afforded by the faith of *Rahab* (25). Again, if our faith is living, it will be seen in giving and in other more direct exercises in personal involvement, in meeting needs. Amongst many other things that he is supposed to have said, C. H. Spurgeon is credited with the view that 'If you want to give a hungry man a tract, wrap it up in a sandwich'. With great respect, he might better have said, 'If you want to give a hungry man a sandwich, wrap it up in a tract.' For the eye of faith sees forward into the endless reaches of eternity, and is aware that the need to be right with God far outstrips the need for earthly amelioration. Plainly our giving must have 'the cause of the gospel' in this narrower sense well to the fore. But we are rarely caught by this dichotomy; the limitations on our giving are those imposed by our own cramped affections and concerns.

There are also needs all around us – including, very likely, undiscerned needs within our own church fellowship. In many areas the need among elderly brothers and sisters is not that they are ill-clad or unfed, but that they are lonely and long for a visit or an invitation out. In every area there is some opportunity to experience the great Christian truth that the abundance of the one is designed for the need of the other (2 Cor. 8:12–15). So much nonsense is talked about the early church of Acts 2 – 4 as practising an early form of communism. Nothing of the sort! Those who speak like this view it as an experiment which failed and from which, therefore, we can distance ourselves. What we find in Acts 2:44–45 and 4:32–35 was simply an intolerant attitude towards want. Private ownership was neither denied nor even criticized (*e.g.* Acts 5:4), but no piece of private good was held back if by its disposal some need of a brother or sister might be met. That is what James calls a true and living faith.

The heart of the matter (2:18–24)

We turn now to the two B-sections of the outline given on p. 108 and the contrast they offer between a spurious and a true faith godward. On the one hand, *the demons believe – and shudder* (19); on the other hand, *Abraham believed . . . and he was called the friend of God* (23). There is a faith productive only of fear; there is a faith productive of friendship.

The most straightforward understanding of verse 18 is offered by the punctuation given in RSV.[2] An imaginary interrupter is brought forward. He is not hostile to James' teaching but desires clarification.[3] Addressing (not James but) some other person he says, '*You have faith and I have works*' (18). His implication is that, just as God gives different people different gifts, so one person's gift is a spirit of unshakeable trust (*cf.* 1 Cor. 12:9) while another has a God-given aptitude for works of mercy (*cf.* Rom. 12:6a with 8b). Should not each then get on with the exercise of his gift without any implied criticism of the other whose gift is different? With this, no-one could disagree – not even James! The problem is that the interrupter has raised a quite different question, for, as James goes on to show in the illustration of the demons, the faith which he is speaking of is not the *special* gift which *some* possess, but the *general* gift of faith by which alone *all* become Christians. As verse 14 has made clear, it is 'saving faith' of which he is speaking.

This becomes very clear in the allusion to the *demons*, for demons are, as a matter of fact, unusually well placed to believe certain orthodox affirmations with all their hearts. James selects the truth that there is only one God. Yet, holding this, they continue as demons; they are not saved; they know nothing of peace with God; and they do not love the only God whom they confess. Their fear, says J. H.

---

[2] We need to recall that there are no quotation marks in Greek, and James gives no indication (other than what gives the best sense) whether the words of the new speaker end (as RSV) with '. . . *I have works*' or whether the quotation goes on to the end of v. 18. Neither does James make it clear who the 'you' is whom the interrupter addresses. Is it James himself? The view taken above is that (i) an imaginary interrupter addresses an imaginary partner. This would be better expressed in Greek (not by *some one . . . you*, but) by 'one . . . another', but James does something that is familiar to any preacher. Tone of voice and accompanying gestures often take the place of grammatical propriety! (ii) James himself intrudes on this conversation with his own challenge, *Show me your faith.*

[3] The words *But some one will say* can be hostile (*e.g.* Rom. 9:19), but they can also seek clarification (*e.g.* 1 Cor. 15:35).

Ropes, 'stands in contrast to the peace of salvation', and Sophie Laws perceptively notes that the affirmation (Dt. 6:4) that 'the LORD our God is one LORD' is followed by an immediate consequence (Dt. 6:5): 'and you shall love the LORD your God'. A. Barnes is frighteningly plain: 'If (demons) might hold such faith and *remain* in perdition, men might hold it and *go* to perdition . . . .'

How, then, can we be sure that ours is a true faith — that we really do have peace with God? There must be some way of certainty: for this is the implication of James' own claim, that *I by my works will show you my faith* (18). The answer comes in the illustrative use of the story of Abraham (21–24).

These verses are crucial to our understanding of what James is saying, and we will start by a broad review of their content:

(a) Verse 21. The proposition stated:
  1. Abraham was justified by works (21a).
  2. The particular work in question (21b).
(b) Verses 22–23. Explanation: *You see* (22).
  1. Faith promotes works (22a): works are not an exercise by themselves. Faith co-operates with them as a senior partner with a junior.[4]
  2. Faith needs works (22b): by engaging in the activity of 'works' faith grows to maturity.[5]
  3. Faith precedes works (23). Faith is the first and basic reality in Abraham's relationship with God.
(c) Verse 24. The proposition re-stated: *You see.*
  It is in this sense that works have their essential part to play. A faith with no results is a demonic and bare affirmation. Results (*works*) prove the living reality of faith and bring assurance that the believer has entered into the benefits (righteousness, friendship) promised.

The sequence of events of which James is speaking began in Genesis

---

[4] James says that *faith was active along with his works* (22), lit. 'was working with', 'was a fellow-worker with'. The verb is *synergeō*, Rom. 8:28; 1 Cor. 16:16; 2 Cor. 6:1; cf. *synergos*, 'fellow-worker', Rom. 16:3, 9, 21; 1 Cor. 3:9; *etc.* The relationship never assumes equality of co-working. A superior today often refers to his subordinates as colleagues: they are together in the work but not equal in the work.

[5] *Faith was completed.* Cf. E. H. Plumptre, '. . . the very form of the statement implies that faith existed prior to the works by which it was made perfect.' The verb (*teleioō*) means 'to complete' (a period of time, Lk. 2:43; a task, Jn. 4:34), to 'come to maturity/perfection', *e.g.* Phil. 3:12; Heb. 2:10; 10:1; *etc.*

15:6 and concluded in Genesis 22:12. Genesis 15:6 is a divine response to Abram's faith; Genesis 22:12 is a divine comment on Abraham's faith. Regarding Genesis 15:6, James would concur with Paul's understanding of what happened. God promised Abram an abundance of descendants. Abraham, on his part, took full cognizance of the total human impossibility of this ever happening; but 'no distrust made him waver concerning the promise of God . . . he grew strong in his faith . . . gave glory to God, fully convinced that God was able to do what he had promised. That is why his faith was "reckoned to him as righteousness"' (Rom. 4:20–22). In the earthly course of events, Abram was tested by a twenty-five-year wait (Gn. 12:4; 17:1; 18:10, 14) until the promised child was born. Under pressure of this testing delay, Abram was distracted from a position of patient trust and fell into the sin of a seeking a son and heir along human lines (Gn. 16), making use of a provision of the laws of his day. But some time after the birth of Isaac (Gn. 22) Abraham was called by God to the severest test of all, and this time there was no shadow of doubt. Isaac alone was the promised heir. Humanly speaking, the promises of God, that Abraham would have an abundance of descendants and be a blessing to the whole world, depended on this one boy – and now Abraham is commanded to use Isaac as a burnt offering! Genesis 22:5 shows the way Abraham's faith is running. Having arrived near the scene of the frightful sacrifice, Abraham proposes to leave his attendants behind and take Isaac alone with him. His words to his servants are: 'Stay here . . . As for me and the boy, we will go over there and we will worship and we will come back to you.' Three times the first person plural is used: 'we . . . we . . . we . . .'; yet between the second and the third, Isaac would not only have been killed with the sacrificial knife but his body would have been committed to the flames as a total offering to the Lord. Hebrews (11:19) reveals the mind of Abraham: 'He considered that God was able to raise men even from the dead . . . .'[6]

Alone of the New Testament writers James makes use of a very curious feature of the Genesis account of Abraham's faith. According to Genesis 15:6 the Lord is already convinced that the faith which has

[6]Paul (Rom. 4:18ff.; Gal. 3:6) uses Abraham to illustrate faith as meaning unqualified trust in God's promises – *i.e.* he focuses attention on the initial relationship of true and whole-hearted trust. Hebrews (11:17ff.) uses Abraham's experience to begin a section dealing with the perseverance of faith in the face of great odds and contrary circumstances. James makes the fullest use of Abraham: his initial trust confirmed by God as real and valid (23), and that perseverance of trust in the face of odds which demonstrates that faith is real (21b).

been exercised is 'the real thing' and so, at once, 'he reckoned it to him as righteousness'. He pronounced Abram to be righteous in his sight, on the ground of the faith which he had placed in the divine promises. Yet, in Genesis 22:12, as Abraham stands with the knife upraised, the Lord stops him with the words, '. . . now I know that you fear God'. But had not the Lord, who knows all things, known that from the start? Here, as so often, the Bible lets us into the mind of God by portraying God as if he were man. It brings divine mysteries down to our level so that we may appreciate truly the meaning and significance of a thing – for if we can see clearly what God thinks about something, then we have come to real certainty. So then, if God were human, he would register Abram's profession of faith (Gn. 15:6) and would say, 'So far, so good; it all seems correct.' Then he would wait: what will follow? Will there be results – or to use James' word, *works*? To the human eye, the episode of Hagar and Ishmael (Gn. 16) would make one wonder: Abram is not now really trusting God and the promises, is he? Has he not abandoned faith for his own ability to have a son? But wait, what's this? An altar, knife and fire, the precious Isaac, a victim – and, by a clear implication of what we heard him say to his servants, there is an expectation that God would reconstitute the burnt body and restore the boy to life. This is indeed faith!

We know, of course, that the Lord did not need this process of validation. He knew from the start. But he is represented as needing it; he is depicted as if he came to a final decision about Abraham's faith through observation of Abraham's works. And he graciously condescends to be represented to us like this, so that *we* can share his point of view. A true faith produces results, and in particular the result of costly and wholly trustful obedience to the word of God. It fell to James, alone in the New Testament, to bring out this total view of the faith of Abraham.

The primary works

What, then, would James look for as evidence of the reality and living quality of our faith? We have seen (p. 107, above) how, in the present passage, he clears the ground by ruling out the armchair philanthropist (14–17) and the demons (18–20) as examples of faith. That leaves Abraham and Rahab. The contrast is neat: Abraham, a major Bible figure; Rahab, a minor participant. Abraham the father of the faithful; Rahab a foreigner. Abraham the respected; Rahab the disreputable. Abraham a man; Rahab a woman. As so often, the contrast is intended to alert us to the fact that a fully comprehensive statement is being made – as it were, covering the situation all the way from Abraham to Rahab and back again. The primary works of faith, then, are the works of Abraham and Rahab and they apply to all without exception.

What was the work of Abraham? He held nothing back from God. God said, 'I want your son' and Abraham 'rose early in the morning' (Gn. 22:3) in prompt obedience. What was the work of Rahab? She reached out and took into her own care those who were needy and helpless, regardless of the cost to herself.

The life of faith, then, is the life which respects the glory of Jesus (Jas. 2:1), for in his obedience to God and his concern for needy sinners he 'emptied himself... humbled himself... unto death, even death on a cross' (Phil. 2:7–8). It is a life of obedience in particular to *the royal law* (8) – our obedience to the word of God seen in our concern for the needs of man. The life of faith is more than a private (long past) transaction of the heart with God. It is the life of active consecration seen in the obedience which holds nothing back from God, and the concern which holds nothing back from human need.

3:1–12
10. The master-key

*Let not many of you become teachers, my brethren, for you know that we who
teach shall be judged with greater strictness.* [2]*For we all make many mistakes,
and if any one makes no mistakes in what he says he is a perfect man, able to
bridle the whole body also.* [3]*If we put bits into the mouths of horses that they
may obey us, we guide their whole bodies.* [4]*Look at the ships also; though they
are so great and are driven by strong winds, they are guided by a very small
rudder wherever the will of the pilot directs.* [5]*So the tongue is a little member
and boasts of great things. How great a forest is set ablaze by a small fire!*

[6]*And the tongue is a fire. The tongue is an unrighteous world among our
members, staining the whole body, setting on fire the cycle of nature, and set on
fire by hell.* [7]*For every kind of beast and bird, of reptile and sea creature, can be
tamed and has been tamed by humankind,* [8]*but no human being can tame the
tongue — a restless evil, full of deadly poison.* [9]*With it we bless the Lord and
Father, and with it we curse men, who are made in the likeness of God.* [10]*From
the same mouth come blessing and cursing. My brethren, this ought not to be so.*
[11]*Does a spring pour forth from the same opening fresh water and brackish?*
[12]*Can a fig tree, my brethren, yield olives, or a grapevine figs? No more can
salt water yield fresh.*

Ask what James 3 is about and there is only one possible answer: the
tongue. By making this answer we have at once 'placed' this section in
the overall pattern of James' letter. In 1:26–27 three topics were
announced as the definitive marks of the person who (in the terms of
1:18) had been born through the word of truth. One of those marks, a
life of outgoing concern for the needy, has now been dealt with at
greater length (ch. 2). James, in his own headlong way, is about to
launch himself into another.[1] But he comes to this subject of the

[1]See pp. 74–78, above.

tongue by taking up and just as quickly putting down again another: the hesitation which should be exercised before undertaking any teaching task, because of the more searching judgment to which God will subject those who teach (3:1).

It is much the best to see this reference to teachers as James' way of catching his hearers'/readers' attention[2] – as if one should say to a group of young people at a vocation conference: Whatever you do, don't think of Christian service! Yet, while we must not make heavy weather over a passing allusion, what James says is important in its own right, and undoubtedly he intended it to score a bull's-eye when he said it. For even today it is not unknown for those who have only recently committed their lives to Christ to be pushed into making some sort of public declaration of their faith long before they have either the basic knowledge or the proper development of Christian character for it.

And it is certainly as true today as ever it was that we tend to over-value the more extrovert and public gifts and to over-admire those who possess and exercise them. If we had an 'imperishable jewel' to give as a prize to the possessor of the best gift, we would be unlikely to choose 'a gentle and quiet spirit'![3] The Lord Jesus saw around him a striving for the honours which accompany position and function, and commanded his disciples to refuse the title of teacher or rabbi.[4] How well the spirit of James matched that of his Lord! Jesus was concerned with the 'say and do not' style of contemporary church dignitaries, but James has a different side of the situation in mind. The tongue gives opportunities for many easy mistakes, and the mistakes of those who hold public position invite closer divine scrutiny and severer divine reaction than those of Christians in a private capacity. In this way, James brings us to his intended topic.

A serious business (3:1)

It comes as no surprise to us that James takes a serious view of the tongue. It arises from the particular way in which he stated the doctrine of salvation. Our heavenly Father made us his children by the powerful word he addressed to us, 'the word of truth' (1:18). His children should be marked out by their careful, controlled speech (1:26). But what James says in his way, the rest of the Bible says in its

---

[2]Laws, 'The first verse should... be seen as introducing the general topic by reference to a particular instance.'
[3]1 Pet. 3:4.   [4]Mt. 2 :1–8.

way, and there is hardly a sin more pervasively exposed and condemned than sins of speech. According to Genesis 3:12 the first actual sin following the fall was a sin of speech. Matching this, when Paul wants to exemplify the fact that the whole world, with no individual exception, is unrighteous, and without understanding or concern to do good, he crystallizes his general charges into this hard fact, that 'their throat is an open grave, they use their tongues to deceive. The venon of asps is under their lips. Their mouth is full of curses and bitterness' (Rom. 3:13–14, quoting Pss. 5:9; 140:3 and 10:7). Isaiah explained his alienation from the presence of the holy God, his inability to join the heavenly chorus of adoration, and his sense of personal doom, by admitting that 'I am a man of unclean lips' (6:5). To the contrary, Peter, recognizing that Christians long for a fulfilled experience, a good life, a rich blessing from God, commands any who 'would love life and see good days' to 'keep his tongue from evil and his lips from speaking guile' (1 Pet. 3:10, quoting Ps. 34:12–13). It would be impossible to pretend that ordinarily we see the tongue in this light. We rarely stand alongside Genesis or Paul in finding in our speech the primary evidence of our fallen state. We do not share Isaiah's sense that here is a sin which in a special way separates us from God and brings us to condemnation. Nor has anyone ever told us that a controlled tongue is the key to blessing, as Peter does, and as we are about to hear from James. Let us ask James, then, why the tongue is so important and humbly wait to hear his reply.

The key to holy living (3:2–5a)

As we shall see, James is going to answer our question along six lines. This is what he puts first (2–5a): the tongue holds a key place in holy living. Verse 2 explains verse 1. The more searching judgment to which teachers expose themselves arises this way: they belong to a talking profession, and while we all sin in many ways, it would take a truly perfect person to keep free of sins of speech. By *perfect* he means (as in 1:4) the completeness and maturity that will mark us when God has fully wrought in us all that he intends for us in Christ – in a word, the holiness of those who see him and are like him (1 Jn. 3:2).

But there is more to it than that. As Christians, *we all make many mistakes* (2). Sin remains our universal experience and it takes all sorts of forms. Among them, as every self-aware believer will admit, sins of speech are prominent – the hasty word, the untruthful statement, the sly suggestion, harmful gossip, innuendo, impurity. Indeed, not to

119

sin in speech would demand perfection, and we would be unrealistic not to see James' thoughts going back as he voices this thought to a thirty-year experience, within his own home, of one who 'committed no sin; no guile was found on his lips' (1 Pet. 2:22). Yet James' purpose in this section of his letter is not to warn us to be on our guard against the hasty or impure or lying tongue – or whatever our weakness may be – but to make the positive point that control of the tongue leads to a master-control of ourselves and our lives.

His two illustrations (vv. 3 and 4) show this. As to the horse (3), a comparatively tiny thing, a bit, controls and directs all its powerful and potentially unruly, even menacing, forces. As to the ship (4), the essential point is the same, that a comparatively small factor, a rudder, is the key to control and direction, but the forces now are not internal but external, the *strong winds* that would blow the ship off course and on to the rocks. James sees the tongue in the light of these illustrations, for he adds, *so* (*i.e.* in the same way) *the tongue is a little member* (as comparatively small in its setting as bit and rudder are in theirs) *and boasts of great things* (5a). The 'boasts' of the bit and rudder are not idle or hollow: they really do master the violence of the horse and of the storm. So too the tongue: 'It can make huge claims' (NEB) – and substantiate them, too! The tongue is the key-factor in *controlled* living. We ask ourselves how we are to control the powerful forces within us that drive us into sin, and James replies by talking about something we never considered – do we control our tongues? Are we the masters of the master-key? The tongue is the key-factor in consistent living. Circumstances vary. There are the pressures of adversity and the (often greater) pressures of prosperity; there are sudden and unexpected shocks – the blows which life administers to us. Can we hold our course? James' marine illustration is not at all wide of the mark as a description of life with its tides, currents and storms. Once again, there is a rudder to hold the ship on course, and the tongue is that rudder.

This teaching strikes us as so unexpected that we had better survey it a little longer to make sure we are grasping exactly what the Bible says. It is not that a person strong enough to control the tongue is therefore also strong enough for every other battle. It is much deeper and more important even than that: it is rather that winning this battle is in itself a winning of all battles. Think of a switchboard in a church or other large building. Each switch controls the lights in its own section of the church and the person who controls the switch controls those lights. But on the board there is also a master-switch. It does not need any special strength to operate it. There is no way in which anyone could say, 'If you are strong enough to operate that switch then you are strong enough to operate any of them.' The simple fact is that, if you control the master-switch, you control all the lights; you are lord of the switchboard. It is in this sense that the person who controls the tongue is *able to bridle the whole body also* (2). This is the great (and not unreal) boast the tongue can make (5a).

But should this surprise us quite so much? The tongue is so much more than what we actually say out loud. In fact actual speech is probably only a small percentage of the use of the tongue. We cannot think without formulating thoughts in words; we cannot plan without describing to ourselves step by step what we intend to do; we cannot imagine without painting a word-picture before our inward eyes; we cannot write a letter or a book without 'talking it through' our minds on to the paper; we cannot resent without fuelling the fires of resentment in words addressed to ourselves; we cannot feel sorry for ourselves without listening to the self-pitying voice which tells us how hard done by we are. But if our tongue were so well under control that it refused to formulate the words of self-pity, the images of lustfulness, the thoughts of anger and resentment, then these things are cut down before they have a chance to live: the master-switch has deprived them of any power to 'switch on' that side of our lives. It is in this way that *if any one makes no mistakes in what he says he is a perfect man* (2). The control of the tongue is more than an evidence of spiritual maturity; it is the means to it.

Fire! (3:5b–6)

Secondly, the tongue has enormous power for actual harm (5b–6). There is another little matter, as small in its sphere as bit and rudder in theirs. But whereas they are passive, waiting to be used, this is active, a force in its own right: *fire*. Tiny as the spark is, once it is fanned into flame and the flame takes hold, then it will keep on spreading till all is ablaze. So the tongue is an actual power for evil.

James covers four aspects of the fiery potency of the tongue (6), starting with its *character*. The tongue (lit.) 'appoints itself as the world of unrighteousness among our members'.[5] The *world* (*kosmos*) is

---

[5] The verb here is *kathistatai*, used in 4:4 where the friend of the world 'sets himself up' as God's enemy. The meaning of *kosmos* includes the idea of 'created world' (Mt. 13:35), but mainly refers to the system which refused Jesus (Jn. 1:10), where Satan is prince (Jn. 12:31), which is spiritually blind (Jn. 14:17); *etc.* Believers are 'not of the

121

this present state of affairs or scheme of things organized on the basis of man's sinfulness, hostile to God, rejecting Christ. 'The world of unrighteousness' means 'the unrighteousness world', the world characterized by all that falls short of being right with God, the world in all its unrighteousness. The tongue makes itself available as the focal point of all that unrighteousness, actually within us, 'the enemy agent within God's rightful kingdom, a ready tool at the disposal of God's enemy'.[6] Our *members*[7] are literally our 'limbs', but in its use the word regularly looks beyond the actual physical limb – such as the hand, foot or eye – to the capacities of our nature which are expressed through that limb. In this sense, then, the tongue is inflammatory of all our capacities, doing its utmost to make them the organs of a whole cosmos that is hostile to God.

James next speaks of the tongue's *influence*: *staining the whole body* (6). This is the other side of the positive mastery over the body which can be achieved by a controlled tongue, the power illustrated above as that of the master-switch. Left to itself, since the tongue is involved so fundamentally in all the thoughts, imaginings, longings and plans which lie behind the whole of our earthly life, it leaves the mark of its own defilement everywhere. *Body* is here used in the same sense as *members* just above. In the Bible it is equally valid to define a person (so to speak) from the inside by speaking of the soul and spirit, or from the outside by speaking of the body, for the person is the unity, the ensouled-body or the embodied-soul. Thus the *members* are identified with the capacities (for good or ill) which find expression through them, and *the body* is the total vehicle for expressing individual life. Everywhere the tongue makes its presence felt and leaves its stain.[8] There is some profit in supposing that James began by describing the Godward aspect of the tongue – its affiliation with 'the world' in opposition to and rejection of God – and that now he goes on to the self-ward aspect – the defilement which the tongue spreads through the person. But it would not do to press this, for the idea of sin as

world' (Jn. 15:19), *etc.* E. H. Plumptre suggests that 'the world of unrighteousness' means 'that which contains in itself all the elements of unrighteousness'. This would suit James' meaning, but such a use of *kosmos* is unexemplified in the New Testament. Sophie Laws, 'The tongue effects in a man the defilement that is inherent in the world.'

[6]Mayor, quoted by Mitton.

[7]Gk. *melos*, *e.g.* Rom. 6:13, 19.

[8]The verb is *spiloō*. Its only other appearance in the New Testament is Jude 23, which provides a good illustration of its meaning. See the noun *spilos* (spot, blot), Eph. 5:27; 2 Pet. 2:13.

leaving a mark which God can see is thoroughly biblical and, indeed, expresses the most serious side of the sinner's problem. I may regret that sin holds me back from a fully satisfying, fulfilled life, but this is as nothing compared with the fact that sin makes me offensive to the Holy One. Even so, the defiling mark is left on the person; the personality has been stained. It is not what it ought to be; life itself is diminished in the sinner and the tongue is the culprit.

For the third aspect of his analysis of the evil force of the tongue, James uses the unusual expression, *setting on fire the cycle of nature* (6).[9] C. L. Mitton sensibly offers the opinion that James is referring to 'the whole range of human life'. We are accustomed to the poetic 'time, like an ever-rolling stream' and 'through all the changing scenes of life'. 'Time rolls on' we say – and James takes this into account in relation to the tongue. 'Other vices are corrected by age or by process of time. They drop off from our lives' (Calvin), but from earliest to latest days the baneful influence of the tongue remains. This is its *continuance*.

In the fourth place, James notes the tongue's *affiliation: and set on fire by hell* (6). The first feature of the tongue was that it is anti-god (the world); the final feature is that it is pro-Satan. *Hell* (Gehenna)[10] is the place of fire and James sees the fires of Gehenna reaching up to that part of our sinful, fallen nature where they will most easily find their touch-paper. The tongue becomes the instrument of Satan himself. This is by no means to be thought of as something confined to what we would recognize as improper or questionable uses of the tongue. One day Peter took the Lord aside to give him the best advice he was capable of and to do so with the most loving and concerned intentions. But the Lord Jesus replied, 'Get behind me, Satan! You are a hindrance to me; for you are not on the side of God...'[11] James' warning, then, is timely.

The untameable tongue? (3:7–8a)

Recapitulating James' teaching about the tongue: he began (2–5a) by showing what good followed from a controlled tongue; he followed

[9] In 1:23 James speaks of a man seeing in a mirror 'the face of his nature', *i.e.* 'his natural face'. The parallel phrase here would then mean 'the natural wheel/cycle'. The phrase seems to have a background in philosophy where it referred to various cycles of reincarnation. Sophie Laws suggests that James represents a popularization of the expression in which it had left its unacceptable background well behind and 'passed into common use as a term for the course of human life'.

[10] Gk. *geenna, e.g.* Mt. 5:22; 23:33; Mk. 9:47–48.   [11] Mt. 16:22–23.

this up with the alarming harm brought about by an uncontrolled tongue (5b–6). He now turns to develop a third major point: the tongue is humanly uncontrollable (7–8a). We shall presently have to ask what we are to make of this truth, but there is no doubt that this is what James is saying in these verses.

In the beginning the Creator gave to the man and the woman their joint dominion over the whole creation (Gn. 1:28) and in pursuance of this the animal creation has been subdued and is being subdued. The God-given dominion over creation is still being exercised, for good and ill. But, by contrast, *no human being can tame the tongue – a restless evil* (8). [12] The word *restless* [13] has been well represented by J. B. Phillips as 'always liable to break out', as if it were an untamed, half-tamed or poorly tamed beast accepting for a time the imposed restrictions and then suddenly turning savage. Sadly we acknowledge – within the bounds of personal experience – how well James knows human nature and the tongue. Looking back into the past there are very many deeds we would like to go back and leave undone, but they are vastly outnumbered by the words we would now wish unsaid. This is not always the hasty, angry word either, but often the pondered word, the word meant kindly, but all of them, whether hostile or with loving intent, now seen as the unpredictable outbreaking of the restive tongue.

If we could say no more about these verses than this, then they would still have their place in a section designed to make us alert to the significance of the tongue. For we would learn from verses 7–8a the constant need for watchfulness in case this restive beast should suddenly rouse itself to our shame and hurt. But there is probably something more. In verse 7 the words *by humankind* are literally 'by human nature' or, possibly better, 'by a nature that is merely human'; [14] and in verse 8, *no human being* is 'no-one is able to tame – (that is to say) of men'. James does not simply say that the tongue is untameable, but that it cannot be subdued by any power resident in mere human nature or possessed by a mere human being. Beyond this he does not go, but he may feel that the hint is plain enough. On the day of Pentecost

[12] The verb 'to tame', *damazō*, is well illustrated by its only other New Testament appearance, in Mk. 5:4.

[13] *Restless* is *akatastatos*, only in James (1:8, 'unstable'); *cf. akatastasia*, 'disorder', 3:16. Laws translates *akatastatos* well as 'restive'; Adamson, 'irreducible to order'.

[14] Gk. *tē physei tē anthrōpinē*. The adjective *anthrōpinos*, 'human', quite often seems intended to stress the contrast between the human and the divine: *e.g.* Acts 17:25 requires the emphasis 'served by *human* hands'; likewise 1 Cor. 2:13, 'not taught by *human* wisdom', or 1 Cor. 4:3, 'any *human* court'; *cf.* 1 Cor. 10:13; 1 Pet. 2:13.

(Acts 2:2–4) a different fire from that which ascends from Gehenna descended from heaven to kindle new powers and give new speech to the human tongue. If we must say that the outworking of sin first appeared in the abuse of speech (Gn. 3:12; see p.119, above), we must also say that the first act in the new creation was the renewal of the power of speech, a tongue intelligibly declaring the wonderful works of God (Acts 2:11). Maybe this is what James wants us to learn from verses 7–8a. Would not this be a marvellous display of the glory of the Lord Jesus Christ in our lives, if our tongues were as his: 'No man ever spoke like this man!' (Jn. 7:46)?[15]

Inconsistency, that deadly sin (3:8b–10)[16]

The fourth element in James' searching analysis of the tongue is that it involves us so easily in the deadly sin of inconsistency, one of James' special themes as we see in 1:6–8 and 2:4. It is this sin which is the *deadly poison* of which he speaks.

The repeated words *with it . . . with it* underline the use of the same faculty for two opposite, irreconcileable purposes, to *bless* and to *curse*. Not only so, but our inconsistency is further compounded by the fact that we bless and curse the same thing, the image of God. We look upwards to *the Lord and Father*[17] and our awareness of his greatness, his glory – everything that is true and lovely about him. The thought, too, that Jesus is 'the image of the invisible God'[18] prompts us to *bless*

[15]In the Greek of John's Gospel these words have the same sort of order as that in v.8 of the present passage in James: the noun 'man' is held back right to the end of the sentence for emphasis: *oudepote elalēsen houtōs anthrōpos*, 'never did one speak thus – no man'. James could well have had Jesus in mind throughout. The Lord's wonderful speech often caught people's attention; *cf*. Lk. 4:22; Jn. 6:68.

[16]RSV reflects accurately the way James added two descriptions of the tongue to the end of the sentence in v.8. NIV creates a separate sentence: 'It is a restless evil, full of deadly poison.' This is permissible, but it obscures the fact that James is making two separate assertions – that the tongue is restive and that it is poisonous. The former belongs with the picture of the untamed beast (7–8a), while the latter prepares for vv.9–12. Two sentences would perhaps be preferable: first, 'It is a restive evil', concluding the beast-analogy; secondly, 'It is a deadly poison', introducing the reference to the sin of inconsistency (9–10) and the illustration of the bitter fountain (11–12).

[17]This phrase is unique in the New Testament. Doubtless James deliberately chooses it to underline the special and unique glory of the Father and therefore of the image in which we were created.

[18]Col. 1:15. James uses the word *homoiōma*, 'likeness'; Colossians uses *eikōn*, 'image'. The words *who are made* (9) translate a Greek perfect participle, *gegonotas*, *i.e.*

125

him.[19] We look around at our brothers and sisters, whether in the human family or in the family of God,[20] and think nothing of defaming, denigrating, criticizing, making the sly innuendo; yet they bear the image of God. We think of Jesus and count it a shame if his glory is despised or his name used dishonourably; we write to the papers to complain of blasphemy on radio or television. But the same glorious image of God in other people we hardly think of and rarely hesitate to speak ill of. James, however, was shocked and moved. *My brethren*, he appeals, *this ought not to be so* (10). Clearly, James was a warm-hearted man, delighting to belong within the family of the people of God. Time and again he presses home his point with *brethren, my brethren* and even *my beloved brethren*.[21] The words are as much rebuke as appeal. If Stephen could picture Moses as crying, with outrage, 'Men, you are brethren, why do you wrong each other?'[22] how very much more should James call out to us who have been brought into family unity by the precious blood of our Saviour! *This ought not to be so.* A word appearing nowhere else in the whole New Testament proclaims that this is 'intrinsically not right', not right, by reason of its own internal constitution, 'no way right'.[23]

James makes us face something we can and must do. As he examined the tongue, its place among our bodily faculties, the dangers it threatens, the fearful task of controlling such a restive beast, we may well have found it all too much, far beyond the capacity of our present state of sanctification. But we can make a start here. Here is something precise, limited, manageable. This is not beyond us; this is something we can tackle. It concerns the way we speak inwardly about a brother or sister, the way we speak to somebody else about a brother or sister, the way we speak to a brother or sister. If we are in earnest as we sit before the Word of God, then we admit what seems far in excess of our powers, but we can start here with a new respect for the image of God seen in the members of his family.

'who came into being in the image of God and bear that image still'. Sin has defiled but not destroyed the image of God in man.

[19]The idea of 'blessing' God should not be watered down to 'praising' God (as NIV). It is a distinct idea. When God 'blesses' us he reviews our needs and responds to them; when we bless God we review his glories and respond to them. 'Praise' can arise from a multitude of causes; 'blessing' arises from an awareness of God's glory.

[20]*Cf.* Gn. 1:26–27; Eph. 4:23–24.

[21]*Cf.* 1:2, 16, 19; 2:1, 14; 3:1; 4:11; 5:7, 9, 10, 12, 19.

[22]Acts 7:26.   [23]The word is *chrē*.

Brackish waters (3:11)

There is a fifth reason why we need to guard our tongues. It is this, that its pollution, not its sweetness, prevails (11). The question James asks expects the answer 'no', and for a very obvious reason. Suppose two separate sources of water flowed together into the same outlet, one sweet water, the other brackish and unpalatable, we would never know of the double source because the bitter flavour would prevail. That is what would prove to be the stronger element; that is what would leave its mark. So the tongue needs guarding lest it leave a bitter taste behind it wherever it makes itself felt.

An index of the heart (3:12)

The illustration in verse 12 is different from that in verse 11. In verse 11, so to speak, we stood beside the tap and registered the fact that, though a pure source flowed to the tap, yet it was joined there by another source, bitter and undrinkable. But in verse 12 we are invited to go back beyond the tap to the spring itself. A salt spring cannot yield fresh water. James leads up to this conclusion by a reference to plant life. Again the question is asked so as to suggest the answer 'no'. But why is this? Because the Creator has so organized plant life that each plant bears 'fruit . . . according to its kind' (Gn. 1:11–12). The nature of the plant determines the fruit; the fruit borne bears witness to the nature of the plant. Jesus said: 'Out of the abundance of the heart the mouth speaks' (Mt. 12:34). This is James' sixth reason for keeping a watchful eye on our speech. A fig must have a fig tree as its source, a grape can come only from a vine, an olive from an olive tree; salt water has a salt source; sweet water a sweet source; bitter words a bitter heart; critical words a critical spirit; defamatory, unloving speech issues from a heart where the love of Jesus is a stranger.

3:13–18
11. The two wisdoms

Who is wise and understanding among you? By his good life let him show his works in the meekness of wisdom. [14]*But if you have bitter jealousy and selfish ambition in your hearts, do not boast and be false to the truth.* [15]*This wisdom is not such as comes down from above, but is earthly, unspiritual, devilish.* [16]*For where jealousy and selfish ambition exist, there will be disorder and every vile practice.* [17]*But the wisdom from above is first pure, then peaceable, gentle, open to reason, full of mercy and good fruits, without uncertainty or insincerity.* [18]*And the harvest of righteousness is sown in peace by those who make peace.*

Without sounding any trumpets James introduces the third of his leading topics. He announces its arrival in 3:13 with the words *his good life*. Greek has two words which receive the English equivalent 'good'. One (*agathos, e.g.* Lk. 18:18) means 'that which is intrinsically good', 'possessing the quality of goodness'. The word James uses, however, is *kalos,* 'lovely',[1] and what he speaks of is the loveliness of goodness, the attractiveness of the good life, its wholesomeness and helpfulness, as seen in the Lord's people: a way of life whose goodness is plain to all who see. There is a phrase in 4:4 which – with all the bluntness of James – assures us that we have launched into the third main topic: 'a friend of the world . . . an enemy of God'. When James sketched out his three topics (1:26–27), the third was 'to keep oneself unstained

---

[1]The New Testament does not use *kalos* at all in its simple, basic sense of 'lovely', but always in a derivative sense: 'good fruit' (Mt. 3:10), a 'good tree' (Mt. 7:17), 'good ground' (Mt. 13:8), 'good' fish (Mt. 13:48), the goodness of entering eternal life (Mt. 18:8), the 'good shepherd' (Jn. 10:11), 'good servant' (1 Tim. 4:6), 'good works' (Tit. 2:14). Possibly Mt. 13:45 comes nearest the meaning of 'lovely', yet even there a great deal more is involved: in fact it illustrates pretty well for us the way the word *kalos* is used to combine beauty and worth.

from the world'. But when he laid the foundation for the major teaching sections of his letter in 1:18, the third segment was that the Father brought us forth to be 'a kind of first fruits of his creatures' – something that is specially his and notably holy. It is this requirement that James introduces when he calls for a life which displays the beauty and benefits of goodness.

This unheralded introduction of the topic of the holy life is due not only to James' general way of going about things, but also because the new subject grows so naturally out of what has preceded. At the end of his analysis of the place and power of the tongue (3:12) James went right to the heart. If only the source is pure the outflow will be pure. The question is therefore automatic: how do we deal with the source? To which James replies by showing that there are two wisdoms, the one productive of all the divisiveness and worthlessness of sin (15–16), the other bringing in a harvest of righteousness (17–18).

Wisdom

Wisdom means a lot to James. It is both the key to steering a straight course through life's varied experiences (1:5) and the key to that basic rectification of the heart from which the new life will flow. In this, he is simply leaning back on the understanding and place of wisdom which he found in what he would have called simply 'the Scriptures', but which we (sadly and to our loss) have become accustomed to call 'the Old Testament'. It is plain from his letter that his mind was saturated with scriptural information. It is understandable that his practical nature would find satisfaction in the insistence of the Scriptures that God's law is for living, and his truth is for thoughtful application to the varied circumstances of the day. In this, the purpose of Wisdom is, as Derek Kidner delightfully implies, to make 'the good people nice'.[2]

Wisdom begins with knowing God. When Proverbs speaks of 'the fear of the LORD' (1:7) we need to be clear that it is going far beyond a prudential recommendation to watch our steps because big brother is watching us. Proverbs 2:5 and 9:10, for example, bring fear, knowledge, understanding (discernment) and wisdom together in a way which makes them inseparable. Our fear, then, is a proper reverence for one who has made himself known and whom we therefore know for

---

[2]Derek Kidner, *Proverbs, An Introduction and Commentary* (Tyndale Old Testament Commentaries, IVP, 1964), p.13; *cf.* pp.31–35.

ourselves. But the Bible nowhere places much value on knowledge that remains merely cerebral or credal. Nothing is known until it also reshapes the life. For this reason, the way of wisdom is the way of obedience (*e.g.* Dt. 4:5–6). 'Knowledge', at its deepest, is living out a deep personal relationship. The Bible does not say that 'Adam knew Eve' (Gn. 4:1) through any reticence to speak plainly about sex. The verb 'to know' is not a polite periphrasis; it is a definition. Marriage exemplifies true knowledge; it also shows that knowledge is pretty dramatically life-changing! Wisdom is the God-given ability to see how 'in all our ways' (*i.e.* throughout the whole course and style of life) we may 'acknowledge (lit. 'know') him' (Pr. 3:6).

In a very brief way, this sketches the background to James' introduction here of the idea of wisdom. He has a two-pronged thrust to his teaching, exactly catching the Old Testament emphases which we have noted. First (3:13–18), there is a God-given wisdom and it is our personal responsibility to seek it, to put it at the centre of our beings and to live by it. Secondly (4:1–10), this God-given wisdom cannot be had if our lives are not constantly being kept in a right relationship with God himself, in which we are daily nourished with grace and more grace (4:6–10).

Relationships (3:13–14)

In this way, then, the new section on the 'good life' arises by way of answer to the question implicit in the section on the tongue: how are we to purify the source? But there is another relationship between 3:13ff. and 3:1–12 which is worth exploring. James began his section on tongue and speech with an introductory and cautionary allusion to those who might be tempted to rush into a teaching position in the church (1). Did it now seem to him that in putting a brake on the exercise of gifts of wisdom and knowledge in this way he might have introduced a sense of frustration for some? In any case, his opening words in verse 13 come to us as both a corrective and an encouragement.

What is a Christian to do who (in all humility) can be reckoned as *wise and understanding*? The description *wise* must be understood in the light of our discussion of Old Testament Wisdom. There are those who live closely to God, see more clearly into things than others do, and just know how to manage life's varied circumstances. They are godly in character, sharp in discernment and helpful in their advice and counsel. Equally they are *understanding*. The word does not appear

elsewhere in the New Testament, but it points to 'professional knowledge' (Tasker), 'like our "expert"' (Ropes). Provided we do not push
the ideas of 'professional' and 'expert' too far, this is exact. At the very
least the word describes the well-informed person (Alford).[3] Here,
then, is the one who has a veritable mass of stored-up, useful, helpful
knowledge. What place has such a person in the church? Well, of
course, some will be called out and recognized as teachers of the flock
of God (cf. Eph. 4:11; 1 Tim. 5:17). James does not say that none are
to become teachers! Yet even in their case he would recommend
caution. For not only is that wordy task full of hazard (2), but also it is
not the priority use of the gifts of wisdom and understanding (13–18).
The great priority is to put whatever gift the Lord has given to the task
of living the *good life*. Again, how true to its Old Testament background: a wisdom of deeds; an understanding and knowledge that
reshapes life.

James does not yet tell us anything that we must actually do, any
course of conduct to follow. He offers us an ethic not of verbs (do this),
nor of nouns (naming this or that item of good conduct), but of
adverbs (about the sort of people we are to be whatever we do).
Everything (his good life . . . his works) is to be done in *the meekness of
wisdom*, or, to unwrap the phrase slightly, 'in a wisdom which always
bears the mark of meekness'. *Meekness* is a word which we have already
met at 1:21 (see pp.68–69, above) when we noted that it means
self-subduing gentleness, both Godward and manward. What a
remarkable priority target for the great gifts of wisdom and understanding! Plainly the Word of God and the ways of man move along
different paths and in opposite directions! Sophie Laws notes that 'the
dominant morality of the day associated (meekness) with meanness
and grovelling. It is linked with adjectives like ignoble, abject,
servile . . . Epictetus names it first in a list of moral faults.' Perhaps
today this would be unspoken rather than written down for all to see,
but, spoken or not, the lives of many who would like to be thought of
as wise and expert tell what they think of meekness. But for James,
self-subduing gentleness has to be the first mark of wisdom. Did not
the Lord Jesus say, 'I am meek' (Mt. 11:29)?

Meekness is a word which requires the context of relationships for its
full meaning to emerge. Alone, Robinson Crusoe might have had to

[3] *Wise=sophos, wisdom=sophia*; cf. Mt. 23:34; 1 Cor. 3:10; 6:5; Eph. 5:15; *under-
standing=epistēmōn*. The words ocur in LXX, Dt. 1:13, 15; 4:6, translating the
Hebrew *ḥākām* and *nāḇon* or (1:15) *yᵉduʿim*, the latter two words meaning respectively
'discerning' and 'knowledgeable'.

shun pride; once Man Friday came along the scene was set for the practice of meekness. This, too, is the emphasis we find in James. The wisdom he advocates will put an end to jealousy, selfish ambition and disorder (16) and will be seen in peace, gentleness, reasonableness and mercy (17). It is an antidote to the personal whims and fancies that are productive of wars and fightings (4:1ff.). Again, this is all very different from our view and experience of the wise and expert! Yet not unexpected in James! His chosen metaphor of Christian experience is the family-metaphor of birth (1:18); the family lives under the rule of the Father (1:17), and it is a family of brethren (1:2; *etc.*[4]); its first duty is caring love (2:1ff.), and its second, guarded speech (3:1ff.). There is nothing unusual, then, when James teaches that its third duty is to cultivate a wisdom which promotes good relationships and peace, and to live a lovely life of holy meekness.

To James anything other than this life of self-submission and peace is a denial of the truth (14). In verse 14 James makes a very clear connection with the conclusion of his passage on the tongue: he refers to the *heart* which needs to be purged of *jealousy and selfish ambition*, and uses the same adjective which is here translated *bitter* and appeared in verse 11 as *brackish*. It is clear, therefore, that he is dealing with this matter of the source from which our lives issue out (*cf.* Pr. 4:23). What should dwell in our hearts is *the truth*, but the evidence of jealousy and selfish ambition — in a word, bad relationships and a divisive attitude towards others — shows that the truth and our hearts are strangers to each other.[5]

The word translated *jealousy*[6] really means no more than 'strong feeling'. It does not of itself contain the thought of a hostile envy of other people's gifts or affections, which our word jealousy implies. Plainly, when allied to the adjective *bitter*, it must have a bad meaning. There are those who are 'quick on the draw', more than ready to fight for their rights and easily prepared to feel that they are in some way threatened by others. It is more this sharpness of spirit in personal relationships, this over-concern for one's own position, dignity, rights or whatever, that James has in mind. There is a sharpness of self-

---

[4]See p. 126, above and n. 21.

[5]*False to the truth* could simply mean 'false to what is the real truth about yourselves. In this case the force of the words would be to drive us more determinedly to seek the *wisdom from above* (17) to put things right in our hearts.

[6]The word (*zēlos*) is used in Heb. 10:27 of the blazing heat of fire. This sets its basic sense. It is used of commendable, strong feeling (*e.g.* Jn. 2:17; Rom. 10:2); also of animus against (*e.g.* Acts 5:17; Phil. 3:6); *etc.*

interest, that easily leads into the formation of parties and cliques, which is the inner force of the word translated as *selfish ambition*[7]: 'an inclination', says J. H. Ropes, 'to use unworthy and divisive means for promoting one's own interests.' If we stress the word 'divisive' then we see the meaning exactly.

Church history would have a very different tale to tell – as would, indeed, the bit of church history that is being written in our own day – if Christian people had paid attention to the fact that James contrasts division and truth. Over and over again the formation of a party, the growth of a clique, the promotion of a split have been justified as standing for the truth. It is said that, unless we divide, the truth cannot be safeguarded; the body from which we are dividing has rejected all truth, or this truth or that. But when Paul withstood Peter to the face over the really cardinal issue of the truth of the gospel (Gal. 2:14), he did not separate, form a party, send word to the churches he had founded that they were now a new denomination. The sad thing is that we who are born into a divided, wretchedly denominational situation are inured from birth to separation, and we have lost James' realization that in Christian division, as in time of war, truth is the first casualty.

Make your choice (3:15–17)

We come now to the central issue James has in mind. We have seen through his eyes our need of a pure source (12). He has outlined his basic position (13–14) that there is a wisdom, working through self-subduing gentleness, productive of a life of lovely goodness; but, alternatively, there is sharp, defensive self-concern leading to division and party-spirit, exposing the absence of the truth from the heart. Now he is ready to put the vital choice to us: is the wisdom of earth (15–16) or of heaven (17–18) to rule our lives? No compromise is allowed, for they are true alternatives, standing in contrast to each other in origin, characteristics and results (as set out in the diagram on the next page).

[7]Gk. *eritheia* appears mostly in lists of vices (*e.g.* 2 Cor. 12:20; Gal. 5:20); Rom. 2:8 links (as does James) divisiveness and disobedience; Phil. 1:17 shows *eritheia* resulting in parties and factions.

	Verses 15–16	Verses 17–18
Origin	not from above earthly unspiritual devilish	from above
Characteristics	jealousy selfish ambition	pure peaceable gentle open to reason full of mercy, *etc.* without uncertainty without insincerity
Results	disorder every vile practice	the harvest of righteousness

The key section is the middle one, for by it we can identify which of the wisdoms is prompting our life. A wisdom which is *earthly* is not necessarily easily identifiable. The word[8] means 'belonging to this (earthly) order of things' – but such a wisdom can recommend much that is true. A wisdom that is *unspiritual*[9] is not necessarily identifiable. The natural man, unaided by special regenerating grace (for such is the meaning of *unspiritual*), is nevertheless not wholly bereft of that which the Spirit approves. The constituents of the fruit of the Spirit (Gal. 5:22–23) are often seen – and in remarkable depth – in those who would be the first to deny any special touch from on high. The same applies to a *devilish* wisdom.[10] Peter showed such wisdom when in a spirit of concern he counselled the Lord not to go the way of the cross (Mk. 8:32–33). If in other respects Satan can masquerade as an angel of light (2 Cor. 11:14), why not in this also?

But there is no mistaking the characteristics as they manifest themselves, or the fruit they bear. James requires us to affirm that whatever displays a sharp, antagonistic spirit of self-concern (*jealousy*), whatever leads to or favours party spirit or the creation of parties or the

[8]Gk. *epigeios*; *cf.* Jn. 3:12; 1 Cor. 15:40; 2 Cor. 5:1; Phil. 3:19.

[9]Gk. *psychikos*. Jude 19 defines the word: 'worldly (*psychikos*)..., devoid of the Spirit'; *cf.* 1 Cor. 2:14; 15:44, 46.

[10]Gk. *daimoniōdēs*, only here in the New Testament. *Cf.* Wesley (quoted by Ropes), 'Such as Satan breathes into the soul'. In 1 Cor. 2:8 Paul links human wisdom with the demonic powers ruling this age.

dividing of fellowships (*selfish ambition*), whatever issues in *disorder*[11] (restlessness, instability, disturbance in the fellowship) and in meanness in thought, word and deed (*every vile practice*[12]) – this is the wisdom which in no way comes down from above.[13] We need to ask ourselves very seriously whether we believe this or not. We look about us and see fellowships being sundered – sometimes in the name of the Holy Spirit, the Spirit of fellowship himself! It does not look as if we really believe James when he says that the spirit which promotes, tolerates and brings about divisions is of the earth (not of heaven), of the natural man (not of the Spirit of God) and of the devil (not of the Lord). We look about us and find Christians being catty and petty, as anxious to keep their end up, and to defend their rights, and so on, as the next man. It does not look as if we believe James when he says that all that is mean lacks heavenly validation. We need to ask ourselves very seriously whether we believe James or not.

The James of Acts 15:13ff. and 21:18ff. was pre-eminently the peacemaker. There was much that tended towards division and disharmony. James laboured to keep the opposed causes together in Christ. It is that same spirit which breathes through this passage, with its hatred of all that sunders and its evident delight in all that unites. Unity is the main thrust of the wisdom from on high (17–18). The heavenly wisdom is depicted before us in seven adjectives (17). It has, first of all, that which is of special value to God: moral purity and holiness,[14] the likeness of Jesus who is pure (1 Jn. 3:3). In its significance in James' lists, *pure* balances *jealousy* (16). There, the spirit of harsh, abrasive self-concern easily gave rise to inability to tolerate and get on with others (*selfish ambition*), but here, purity from all such defilement, a purity like that of Jesus, naturally reaches out to others in *peaceable* ways, peace-loving and peace-making.[15] But if peace is to

[11]Gk. *akatastasia*; *cf.* on 'unstable' (*akatastatos*) 1:8, p.41, above.

[12]*Vile* translates *phaulos*, *e.g.* Jn. 3:20; Tit. 2:8; *etc.* Trench (p.318): '... worthlessness is the central notion of *phaulos* ... light ... mediocre, of no account, worthless, bad.' In a word, 'mean'.

[13]The Greek of the opening phrase of v. 15 places the emphasis on 'is not' and 'comes down from above'.

[14]Gk. *hagnos* in general has the idea of spotlessness, though if we were to ask what blemishes it is free from or in what sense it implies purity, the answer is that it depends on the context in which the word appears (*e.g.* 2 Cor. 11:2 with 1 Tim. 5:2; Tit. 2:5; 2 Cor. 7:11; 1 Tim. 5:22). In the present passage it could mean 'free from the blemishes arising from the false wisdom', as if James had written that the wisdom from on high is 'free from all this'. But it is probably best to take it is an absolute sense: *pure* (as God is pure).

[15]Gk. *eirēnikos*. Elsewhere only in Heb. 12:11.

135

be achieved and kept, then there is need to be *gentle*,[16] tolerantly though not weakly accepptive of the other person, graciously amenable, yielding wherever yielding is possible rather than standing up for one's rights. And, matching this, *open to reason*,[17] not necessarily easily persuaded but certainly readily persuaded and possibly also winning, able to gain the consent of others. And just as the mercy of God is moved by our plight so that his love finds free rein to pour grace on unworthy, wretched sinners (Eph. 2:4ff.), so the wisdom from on high inculcates a spirit of *mercy* to the full. We live with each other in a full consciousness of the other person's neediness and helplessness. We are therefore ready to forgive as he has forgiven us (Eph. 4:32), ready to welcome as he has welcomed us (Rom. 14:1, 3), ready to be to them in all things what he has proved himself to us. Furthermore, all this must come from the heart: this is not a face we wear for the occasion, but a nature which we display in our deeds. *Without uncertainty*[18] means that we are not in two minds about it all. James reaches back in this word to the waverer of 1:6–8, the person who has not finally settled the issue of where his loyalty lies. *Without . . . insincerity*[19] means that we are not trying to be two different people, with an outward life maintained for appearance' sake but an inward heart kept secret and very different. The former word demands a firm commitment of mind and heart; the latter, an equally firm commitment to a matching life.

The harvest of righteousness (3:18)

The third chapter of James has proved to be a most concentrated and challenging piece of teaching. Every verse has had its point to make and each one of deep importance for our Chritian lives. Yet none surpasses in significance the final verse, to which we now turn. As we saw in the analysis (see p. 134), each of the two wisdoms brings about its own results and in the case of the wisdom from above it is this: *The harvest of righteousness is sown in peace by those who make peace.*

[16]The lovely word *epieikēs*. The verb *eikō* (Gal. 2:5) means 'to yield'. The noun *epieikeia* is used of the Lord Jesus (2 Cor. 10:1). For the adjective, *cf.* Phil. 4:5; 1 Tim. 3:3; Tit. 3:2; 1 Pet. 2:18.

[17]Gk. *eupeithēs*, persuadable or persuasive. E. H. Plumptre speaks of 'that subtle yet gentle power to persuade and win', but most think rather of openness to what the other thinks, says, wants. The word occurs only here.

[18]Gk. *adiakritos*; *cf.* on the verb *diakrinomai*, p.40, above.

[19]Gk. *anypokritos*, 'without hypocrisy'.

There are two ways in which the words *the harvest* (lit. 'fruit') *of righteousness* may be understood. They can mean 'the fruit which grows out of righteousness', *i.e.* righteousness is the seed which bears the fruit.[20] The 'fruit of the Spirit' is the fruit which the Holy Spirit produces; the fruit of repentance is the evidence in our lives that we have truly repented. In the same way, the fruit of righteousness is the fruit righteousness bears. There is no strong case against understanding James' words in this way. As in 2:23, *righteousness* is the fundamental reality of being right with God. In the immediately preceding verses (13, 17) James has been detailing the life which is directed by the heavenly wisdom. It is perhaps surprising that he should now describe it in a different way as the life right with God, but there is no reason why he should not. In 1:18, 26-27 he spoke of the life which proceeds out of the new birth, but in 2:1 he changed his terminology to speak rather of the life which grows out of believing in the Lord Jesus Christ. Maybe this is his way of integrating his teaching. The life of wisdom is not a new thing or something different; it is just another way of talking about being right with God and of the life which, by good works, shows what a lovely thing being right with God is. If this is the correct way of understanding *the harvest of righteousness*, then *harvest* refers back to all the good things mentioned in verse 17, characterizing the heavenly wisdom. They are all the proper and natural outgrowth of being right with God.

On the other hand, *the harvest of righteousness* could equally mean 'the fruit which consists of righteousness'.[21] In this case *righteousness* is a summary description of the life approved by God – the same sort of use of the word as in 1:20 (see p.65, above). But, once more, in the present context, if we were to ask what sort of fruit this might be, we could only look back to verse 17 for the answer or, with Sophie Laws, say broadly that the fruit of righteousness is wisdom.[22]

Along each of these roads of interpretation we have been led, then, to the same broad conclusion. Either *harvest* is a summary of the covetable characteristics named in verse 17, with righteousness as the seed from which they grow, or else *righteousness* describes the life in which they come to harvest. Now a seed needs its own proper conditions

[20]Plumptre takes this view. Ropes ('the reward which righteous conduct brings') appears to, but his whole note on the point is not easy to follow. Tasker prefers another view but counts this one 'possible', calling attention to Is. 32:17.

[21]Most seem to take this view: Tasker, Davids, Alford, Adamson.

[22]Sophie Laws alludes to Pr. 3:18; 11:30. 'The promise of *the fruit of righteousness* . . . is implicitly a promise of the true wisdom from above.'

for germination, growth and fruitage. However good the seed, it cannot thrive out of its environment. Even if it does not die, it will not properly grow; even if it grows, it will not properly bear. The conditions must be right. So it is also in this case. The crop demands the context for its true growth.

James takes his gardening metaphor seriously. *Peace* is the soil and *those who make peace* are the green-fingered gardeners. The only way in which this clear picture needs any further explanation is to say that our usage narrows unduly the meaning of *those who make peace*, for we call peacemakers those who have a ministry or gift of helping others to compose their differences. H. Alford is correct in seeing here those who 'work peace', or 'peace-workers'. They are those whose whole life, ministry, influence and relationships are peace-creating. They are those who are out for peace in the fellowship, as Acts 15 and 21 reveal James himself to have been.

Once more we need to ask ourselves if we really believe this. Is it not too surprising? Do we find it recommended as a way of Christian growth in our churches? Certainly, the idea of Christian growth is not neglected by any manner of means: there is a suggestion here, an experience there, a crisis to pass through, a new touch from God to receive, a special blessing into which to enter. But how often do we hear of a harvest of righteousness sown in peace by those who prize and promote peace? How very important Christian fellowship is! A harmonious fellowship of believers is the soil out of which grows the whole life that is pleasing to God.

4:1–10
12. The beginning of wisdom

What causes wars, and what causes fightings among you? Is it not your passions that are at war in your members? [2] *You desire and do not have; so you kill. And you covet and cannot obtain; so you fight and wage war. You do not have, because you do not ask.* [3] *You ask and do not receive, because you ask wrongly, to spend it on your passions.* [4] *Unfaithful creatures! Do you not know that friendship with the world is enmity with God? Therefore whoever wishes to be a friend of the world makes himself an enemy of God.* [5] *Or do you suppose it is in vain that the scripture says, 'He yearns jealously over the spirit which he has made to dwell in us'?* [6] *But he gives more grace; therefore it says, 'God opposes the proud, but gives grace to the humble.'* [7] *Submit yourselves therefore to God. Resist the devil and he will flee from you.* [8] *Draw near to God and he will draw near to you. Cleanse your hands, you sinners, and purify your hearts, you men of double mind.* [9] *Be wretched and mourn and weep. Let your laughter be turned to mourning and your joy to dejection.* [10] *Humble yourselves before the Lord and he will exalt you.*

To put the matter bluntly, it is all very well to tell us that there are two wisdoms and to describe them in terms which makes us long to reject the one and to embrace the other. But long ago Job asked the key question: 'Where shall wisdom be found?' (28:12). If Job could ask such a question, we may be sure that James would ask it too – and have an answer!

This is, in fact, the relationship between the end of James 3 and the first ten verses of James 4. James is dealing with the same situation. In 3:14, 16 he wrote of *jealousy* (a strong emotion of self-interest) and *selfish ambition* (the positive promotion of self-interest), *disorder* (unrest) and *every vile practice* (every sort of mean, unworthy deed). He said in 3:14, *If you have,* but the Greek would be better served by 'Since you have'.[1] Now in chapter 4 he speaks of *wars, fightings, passions* (1), *desire, covet* (2), unfaithfulness and *friendship with the world* (4). The opening question (4:1), *What causes . . . ?* declares his purpose to trace unrest, bad feeling, hostile relationships and the rest, to their root, and then to tell us what to do about it all. As to the latter, we shall find that James' remedy is the same as the answer Job found (Jb. 28:28), 'Behold, the fear of the Lord, that is wisdom; and to depart from evil is understanding.' But James puts it in his own way.

Symptoms and diagnosis (4:1–5)

These five verses look in two directions: verse 1 speaks of *fighting among you* and verse 4 speaks of *enmity with God*. Up to the middle of verse 2 James is speaking about the ill relationships that exist between Christians. Then he turns from that with the words *You do not have, because you do not ask*. Something makes even prayer ineffectual. The channels of communication with God and of supply from God have become blocked. In each section the same word pinpoints the trouble. Verse 1 points out that the cause of the *wars and . . . fightings* is *your passions*; verse 3 says that requests remain unanswered because whatever God gave in response would be spent *on your passions*. There is, then, the outward symptom of really bad relationships among believers. This has its inner side in a flawed relationship with God, and the root of all the trouble is *passions*. Having reached this point by the end of verse 4, James rounds his teaching off by an appeal to Scripture (5).

Christians at war (4:1–2a)

We begin, then, with what James sees in the relationships of Christians *with each other* (1–2a). The words he uses are frighteningly strong: *wars, fightings, at war, kill, fight, wage war*. We know, of course, that James does not mean actual killings. He is using the language of war metaphorically, as do other New Testament writers.[2] But at the same time we must not allow metaphor to take away from the force of his

[1] A simple conditional clause expressed with the indicative. Blass and Debrunner, *A Greek Grammar of the New Testament*, para. 371: '. . . denotes . . . emphasis on the reality of the assumption . . . the condition is considered "a real case".'

[2] Neither the noun *war* (*polemos*) nor its verb (*polemeō*) are used outside James in this metaphorical sense, though both are used extensively in Revelation of the war of the Lord and his angels with Satan (*e.g.* Rev. 12:7) and of the war of Jesus against those who corrupt his church (2:16). *Fightings* (*machē*) and its verb (*machomai*) are used, *e.g.* 2 Tim. 2:23; Tit. 3:9; Jn. 6:52; 2 Tim. 2:24.

words and the horror they are intended to strike. Sadly, the world around us has hardened our senses even in respect of war. The prospect of a 'real' war between the so-called superpowers has diminished our awareness of the small but heart-breaking conflicts which constitute the unfinished story of many parts of the world. The devastation and loss of life on the horrendous scale of nuclear war make us less than realistic about the thousands of deaths caused equally indiscriminately by what we comfortingly describe to ourselves as conventional weapons. The daily tale and toll of death by terrorism and battle makes it not worth the while of the media to report run-of-the-mill killings in drunken brawls and the like. We are, in fact, of all generations, least capable of feeling a sense of personal and moral outrage at the vocabulary of war. But very likely we each have some threshold of awareness which we can try to cross. You yourself lie dead, 'picked off' by the accidental or deliberate bullet of the enemy; the news is brought to your family — that is what war is like. Or you return on leave from the front to find a bomb crater where your home was, your dear possessions and dearer family simply there no longer — that is what war is like. Or, miraculously, you are among the unlucky survivors when the bomb is at last dropped and from a rising ground you see the return of the formless void from which the Creator's hand once made a fair and habitable earth; nothing is left. Or you have heard of — or, for some of us, grew up amongst — those who bravely kept the home fires burning for the boys who never came home. That is war.

James chooses the vocabulary of war to express controversies and quarrels, animosities and bad feeling among Christians, not because there is no other way of saying it, but because there is no other way of expressing the horror of it. He is seeing the relationships of the church through the eye of God. He speaks of a fact (1a), a condition (1b) and a practice (2a).

It is a depressing commentary on church life that James can write to a scattered people (1:1) and make the same general comment on all alike. He does not, of course, mean to imply that they are perpetually at loggerheads among themselves, but he does seem to take for granted that the peace of the churches is by no means unbroken. The words *wars* and *fightings* may simply be used for the sake of variety, but if we are to draw a distinction between them C. L. Mitton gives us as good a lead as we can get. '"War" represents a continuing state of hostility' and *fightings* 'a specific outburst of active antagonism', enduring feuds with recurring quarrels flaring up. This is the fact to which James addresses himself. Behind it lies, as its cause, a condition existing in each individual.

We have met the word *members* already (see 3:6, and p.122, above). Its basic and physical meaning of 'limb' leads into its extended meaning of whatever capacity of our nature is expressed through that limb. In saying *your members* James points to each one of us, and what he says of us is not flattering. We are, he says, inwardly like an armed camp ready for the bugle call that will send us into battle. The phrase *passions . . . at war in your members* might suggest a condition of internal conflict – as, for example, when we choose what is right, but are overpowered by forces within ourselves determined upon evil, which forbid us to implement our choice (*cf.* Rom. 7:15–20). James, however, is not examining our inner conflicts, but the wars we wage against each other. All our desires and passions are like an armed camp within us, ready at a moment's notice to declare war against anyone who stands in the way of some personal gratification on which we have set our hearts.

Our condition (1b) is one of self-willed determination, summed up as *passions*. This word, like the words *desire* and *covet* in verse 2a,[3] is in itself morally neutral. It means 'pleasures'. All would be well except that in us 'pleasures', 'desires' and strong longings are allied to, and at the service of, a sinful nature. Consequently the sinful self, setting its heart on this satisfaction or that, will not allow anything to stand in its way: *so you kill*[4] *. . . so you fight and wage war* (2a). The condition becomes a practice.[5]

James' language sounds so extravagant, so exaggerated in our ears, that we feel we must positively refuse to see our small-time disagreements and occasional squabbles as meriting such a description. But if

---

[3] *Passions* is *hēdonē*, as in Lk. 8:14; 2 Pet. 2:13, *etc.*; *desire* = *epithymeō*, *cf.* used with its cognate noun *epithymia*, Lk. 22:15; *covet* is a poor translation of *zēloō*, which we met as the noun *zēlos* at 3:14 (see p.132, above). The verb is used in LXX of the Lord's jealousy and has, therefore, no essentially bad meaning. It covers any 'strong feeling' but it easily moves on to express emulation or rivalry (*e.g.* Acts 7:9; 17:5) or sinful envy.

[4] Sophie Laws urges that if James intended a metaphorical meaning for 'kill' he would need to have made this clear. Oddly, however, she does not make the same remark about 'wars' and 'fightings' in v.1. James is simply being faithful to the terms of the total metaphor which, to him, is the only way to bring out the exceeding sinfulness of Christian quarrels.

[5] The punctuation of v.2a is by no means certain, as a glance at the English Versions will show. RSV offers the most neatly balanced rendering. The alternative, *cf.* NIV, has a separate sentence 'You kill and covet . . .'. The essential meaning remains unchanged, except that the NIV-type renderings do bring out the inability of the passionate self to achieve satisfaction – even killing for gain still leaves the self coveting.

we take this line we only show how imperfectly our thoughts have been brought into captivity to the obedience of Christ. When the Lord Jesus undertook to explore the length and depth of the sixth commandment, he spoke of anger, derogatory, dismissive remarks, name-calling. He illustrated his serious intent by the story of the sudden realization, during worship, that a brother has 'something' against us (Mt. 5:21ff.).[6] He spoke not of great, prolonged or unjustified anger, or anything of the sort. He did not specify 'something big', or 'something important', which a brother might be holding against us – or even some charge with which we agreed – just 'something'. Was the Lord Jesus exaggerating when he brought it all under the heading of murder? Or was John extravagant when he said that anyone who failed to love his brother was like Cain (1 Jn. 3:11–12)? It is we who diminish the importance of right relation ships, not the Scriptures which exaggerate the importance of quarrels. We smile with the wrong sort of tolerance over a touchy and difficult brother or sister; we shrug our shoulders over two who have fallen out. But we should not be tolerant of war, or shrug our shoulders over fightings.

Unanswered prayer (4:2b–3)

James now moves the area of his enquiry from our relationship with other believers to our relationship with God. Here, all is far from well. First, prayer would be a solution (2b), but in practice (3a) prayer goes unanswered because of the hindrance interposed by our *passions* (3b). The symptom is different but the diagnosis is the same. We find that the unfettered flow of prayer upwards, and of response downwards, is no longer operating; we are somehow out of sorts with God. The *passions* are at work again. We want it all for self.

Is James speaking here of some particular prayer, or of all prayer? If he has a particular prayer in mind it will be the request for wisdom mentioned in 1:5. A Christian faced with unsatisfactory or broken relationships – or the threat of such – remembers that anyone who lacks wisdom can ask for it. But as there, so here, God (as Calvin remarks on Jn. 15:7) does not permit us undisciplined asking. James wanted to know, in 1:5–8, if our hearts are solidly loyal to the Lord from whom we seek wisdom; here he simply charges that the one thing our hearts are solidly loyal to is our personal satisfactions. Therefore

[6]See John Stott's comment on this passage in *The Message of the Sermon on the Mount*, pp.82ff.

the prayer for peace-making wisdom seems to fall on deaf ears. Interestingly, however, James does not say that God does not hear, but that we *do not receive* (3). He always hears; there is no such thing as unheard prayer or, for that matter, unanswered prayer. But time and again the answer has to be 'no' or 'not yet', because we are incapable of receiving the heavenly gift. Most commentators, however, make the reference to prayer general rather than specific. Prayer itself, not just prayer for wisdom, is defiled by the insistently self-centred heart, so that 'we must either cleanse our hearts or stop our prayers'.[7]

It is to this very need for cleansing of the heart that James is leading us (6–10); this is the beginning of wisdom which he wants to share with us. But before he does he must face us (and frighten us) with what *passions* (self-centred feelings given their head) really do to our relationship with God (4), and what Scripture has to say about it (5).

We ought to notice that James does not set out lists of forbidden passions, or enter into a discussion of allowable and illicit desires. Maybe we could persuade ourselves to feel more comfortable if he did – our darling indulgence might, perhaps, not get mentioned! But none of us can side-step the accusation of self-pleasing. It is as likely to turn our highest endeavours into sins as it is to make our base passions more defiled. In the life of a full-time Christian minister, some may devote themselves to the activist pursuits of endless caring for the sick and house-to-house ministry to the unsaved, and skimp sermon preparation. It may be called 'getting our priorities right', but it may simply be an exercise in self-pleasing. Others lock the study door behind them. When they descend the pulpit steps on one Sunday they are already mentally climbing the same steps next Sunday. They may say that the pulpit is the best place to exercise pastoral care, and that they are putting first things first – but they may in fact just be indulging a passion. While it is useful to face the fact that there are 'polite' passions like those just illustrated, it is in the cruder passions of men and women that we see most plainly the outcome of the self-regarding life. John Blanchard rightly says that 'it is one of the most astonishing evidences of the sovereignty of God that in spite of the fact that man has . . . turned his back on his Maker . . . the fact of the matter is that we cannot cast off restraint, run riot, please ourselves and be completely hedonistic without a price having to be paid'.[8] The human

[7] J.G.S.S. Thomson, addressing the South of Ireland Convention on this passage in 1968.

[8] Blanchard, Vol. 3, p. 17.

price is the destruction of relationships; the spiritual price is a breach with God.

Plotting our course

Coming to James 4:4, we have reached a watershed in his treatment of the last of his three chosen topics, the unspotted life. We will find it worth while therefore to take a moment to look back and to have a preliminary glance forward.

In 3:13–18 James made two basic points. First, the *good life* (3:13) is the product of the true or heavenly wisdom (3:17). The alternative wisdom gives rise to *every vile practice* (3:16). But, secondly, this heavenly wisdom is like a seed demanding its own characteristic environment for growth, and it will not reach its harvest in righteousness outside the *peace* of a fellowship intent upon peace (3:18).

Here, precisely, is our problem! James draws it out in two stages: first, the churches he writes to are marked and marred by *wars* and *fightings* (4:1). By this (as we noted above) he neither means actual murders, nor does he mean specially outrageous examples of Christians falling out with each other. He uses words indicative of extreme violence to expose the actual enormity of every dislocation of fellowship within the people of God: it is a declaration of war, an act of murder. But, secondly, he is pitilessly insistent in exposing the cause of the problem, which is a collection of very ordinary things within the individual heart. Pleasures, desires and needs! Seeking and demanding for self! We need, in fact, to read the verses again (4:1–3) and, as it were, to insist on the ordinariness of what they say. It is not only the notorious, most outrageous and insistent demands, to have our own way and feed our own needs, that make for wars and fightings. It is at root no more than the existence in each of us of a self-centred heart, a controlling spirit of self-interest.

This is the militant cause of all disturbance. But what a problem is raised in this way! Think again of the diagnostic path along which James has led us. The good life arises from the true wisdom, but the true wisdom requires a genuine peace. Our hearts are such that they refuse peace – our members are armed and mobilized for war (4:1). Our central affiliation is with that wisdom which is earthly, unspiritual and demonic and, through that wisdom, is productive of every manifestation of jealousy and selfish ambition (3:15–16; 4:2–3).

The whole movement of James' thought, therefore, from 3:13 to 4:3, is to reveal that public problems (a disrupted fellowship) have

145

private causes (the self-pleasing heart), and that if the highest (the good life) is to be achieved in the harvest of righteousness there is need of a deep, penetrative work of transformation to be wrought upon the individual heart.

As we seek now, with James, to move forward from this point, we find that his first thought is to put the entire problem into a different context. For with his cry *Unfaithful creatures!* his concern is not that we have played false with each other, but that we have played false with God, and that in befriending our own interests we have become friends of the world and the Lord's enemies (4:4). Our problem is, in fact, a spiritual one: how to get right with God and how to stay right with him.

The basic dislocation (4:4)

Verse 4 brings us two distinct pictures of our relationship with God: one is marital and, for a moment, we will call the other one political. *Unfaithful creatures!* is, literally, 'Adulteresses', that is to say, wives who have betrayed their marriage vows.[9] Here James takes up a theme very dear to the whole Bible. When the Lord chose a people for himself, he was like an ardent young man pursuing and claiming his bride.[10] On the Lord's side, the Bible does not shun taking the metaphor seriously with its implications of loving choice and passionate intimacy. In our ears it may sound somewhat dispassionate to call this 'the grace of election' but, biblically speaking, it is not so, for God's election or choice of his people to be his very own is his deepest love in action (Dt. 7:7–8; Eph. 1:4–5). It brings to effect his determination that we should be 'in Christ', that is to say, 'in' the fullest, richest and most intimate union and communion with himself.

With his second, or 'political' picture, James turns to the grace of reconciliation. Two states have 'made peace' after a period of tension and war, but one has reneged on its treaty obligations, going back to its old alliances and affiliations and becoming once again the enemy to its new-found friend. We need to exercise some care in handling this picture. *Enmity* is such a strong word, with overtones of the sundering of relationships, the undoing of treaties, returning to a former state of affairs. In the most fundamental sense, this simply cannot be. Peace with God has been achieved by the blood of Christ's cross (Col. 1:20);

[9]Not as AV, 'adulterers and adulteresses', but as RV, 'adulteresses'.
[10]*E.g.* Is. 54:5; Je. 2:1–3; Ezk. 16:8ff.; Ho 2:14–20; Rom. 7: 1–6; 2 Cor. 11:2; Eph. 5:22–33; Rev. 19:7ff.

we were once enemies but we have been reconciled (Rom. 5:10). The reconciliation was achieved while we were still in our enmity, and it was accomplished not on condition that we would become friends, but on the ground of the will and determination of God in Christ that it would be so. Peace was declared, and will never be 'undeclared'. However fluctuating may be my desire and determination to live in peace with him (Rom. 5:1), the new-formed relationship itself cannot be put into reverse:

> My name is graven on his hands;
> My name is written on his heart;
> I know that while in heaven he stands
> No voice can bid me thence depart.

Nevertheless, though this is gloriously true, we who are AD children can live BC lives. It is for this reason that James amplifies the marital picture with the political, lest we deceive ourselves by clouding over the practical, daily-life realities of our situation. A marriage may to all appearances be intact, and even to some extent in the experience of the partners remain what it always was, and yet — as the world says, 'on the side' — one partner may be playing false. James challenges us, therefore, with the sharp contrast of the words *friendship* and *enmity,* and drives them home by the *therefore*-clause with which he ends verse 4. There is the reality of the two irreconcilables, *friendship . . . enmity.* There is the choice we make: *whoever wishes to be a friend of the world makes himself an enemy of God.* We must not, in other words, deceive ourselves into thinking that we can live in intimate fellowship with him when the set of our hearts (*whoever wishes*) is towards *the world.* From such unimpressive and unsuspected sources great rivers of consequence flow! He does not say 'whoever wills', as though some mammoth and critical decision had to be made each time. It is just this same circle of pleasures, desires, wants, wishes — the priority of the daily bread and butter of the self-pleasing life — that is what takes us into the world, the arena in which Christ's Lordship is not recognized and where his writ does not run.

The testimony of Scripture (4:5)

James 4:5 is a minefield of unsolved problems for the expositor, and yet there is a wide sense in which both the place of the verse in James' argument and the thrust of what he is teaching are plain.

147

It is clear, for example, that he aims at driving his point home by an appeal to Scripture, but as soon as we seek to go beyond this we flounder in uncertainty. The problem is that the words *the scripture says* create an expectation that some passage is about to be quoted,[11] or at the least alluded to,[12] but this expectation is not fulfilled. RSV ambitiously places quotation marks around the second half of the verse, but the words cannot be identified with any other scriptural passage – and, of course, our problem is compounded by the fact that final certainty even about translation (contrast, for example, RV, RSV and NIV) cannot be reached. Most commentators hold that James is using the formula *the scripture says* to refer to what is in fact not a direct quotation but a concise summary of the mind of Scripture on this point, though, of course, the list of passages brought within the summary varies according to a commentator's estimate of what the following words may mean.[13]

And what, indeed, do they mean?[14] Without making any pretence to settling problems which continue to exercise and vex commentators, the following points must be allowed a major influence in understanding verse 5b. First, the emphasis rests on the adverbial phrase *jealously*, or 'with jealousy'. Whatever the half-verse may mean, this is what it is about. Since this word 'jealousy' (*phthonos*), in the New Testament and in the Greek of the Apocrypha, 'is always used of a base human or devilish emotion' (Laws), it fits most easily into the present passage as a summary word for the *jealousy* (*zēlos*) *and selfish ambition* of 3:14 and the pleasures, desires and wishes of 4:1–3 which disrupt the fellowship. It looks at first sight therefore as if James is intending to drive some lesson home about sinful human self-seeking. Secondly – and arising directly from this – the word 'jealousy', because of its insistently sinful connotation, would be a most unsuitable way of expressing the divine jealousy – in the way in which, for example, RSV takes it. This

[11]See, *e.g.*, Jn. 19:37; Rom. 4:3; 9:17; 10:11. *Cf.* Mk. 12:10; 15:28; Lk. 4:21; Acts 1:16.

[12]*Cf.* Jn. 7:38, 42; Eph. 5:14.

[13]Most commentators make *the scripture says* look forward. John Blanchard has the interesting suggestion that James is rather looking back to and driving home the teaching about enmity in v.4b. There is no reason why this should not be the case. He sees James as making a summary allusion to the fact that Scripture takes the Lord's hostility to sin seriously (*e.g.* Is. 1:24; 63:10).

[14]See Mitton for a fine summary of possible translations and the commentators in general for argument and counter-argument. A full review would take the present exposition far into the realms of technical commenting and we must be content as above to offer some ground rules for understanding the verse.

is not to dispute the truth of a 'jealous God'[15] or even to find difficulty with such an idea. Jealousy, properly considered, is a necessary ingredient of all true love. It is, on the one hand, a ceaseless longing for the loved one's welfare and, on the other, a desire for a responsive love as intense and as loyal as the love bestowed. In this sense the Bible insists on the jealous love of God over and for his people. But none of the Hebrew vocabulary of jealousy is ever translated into Greek by *phthonos,* which does not, as a matter of fact, occur at all in LXX. Sophie Laws rightly says that 'a writer of James' familiarity with the LXX is highly unlikely to write of God's jealousy in a way that neglects the usual terms and adopts (unprecedented) language.'[16]

Thirdly, the reference to *the spirit which he has made to dwell in us* is much more likely to be a reference to the gift of the indwelling Holy Spirit than a (mere) reference to the human spirit resident in man. If this spirit is simply the spirit of man, what is the point of the descriptive clause *which he has made to dwell in us*? Why should James call attention to the fact that our spirit, involved as it is in sinful longings, was nevertheless placed in us by the Lord? It would, of course, underline our sinful corruption of a good design of God, but the context does not seem to need such a point to be made. On the other hand, if the reference is to the Spirit, made to indwell us by the act and purpose of God, then the unique verb 'to make to indwell' (*katoikizō*), used nowhere else in the New Testament, is justified and the 'greater grace' of verse 6 has added force in the light of this considerable grace noted in verse 5.[17]

Arising from this discussion, there are two ways in which we can now present verse 5b. The first is this: 'Or do you consider that Scripture speaks in this meaningless way: "The Spirit he made dwell in us yearns with sinful jealousy"?'[18] The second is this: 'Or do you think scripture speaks meaninglessly, Does the Spirit he made to indwell us yearn with sinful jealousy?'

These two renderings have a single common point: God's people are indwelt by God's Spirit and there is no way in which the living

[15]*Cf.* Ex. 20:5; 34:14; Dt. 4:24; 5:9; 6:15; Ezk. 39:25; Zc. 1:14; 8:2; *etc.*

[16]H. Alford, for example, offers '"Or do you think that the Scripture saith in vain, The Spirit that He (God) placed in us jealously desireth (us for his own)?"' The thought is acceptable but the word 'jealous' cannot express a divine emotion.

[17]See NIV for the 'spirit of man' understanding of the words. This is obviously a possible rendering.

[18]This rendering avoids the problem of what passage of Scripture James is quoting. It sees him as exposing the error of his readers by asking them to imagine Scripture saying something which it manifestly could never say.

presence of that Spirit is compatible with those sinful yearnings and promptings to self-interest which are destructive of the peace of the church. This would then be a third aspect of divine grace: the grace of election (4a), the grace of reconciliation (4b) and now the grace of indwelling (5b) – and all alike contradicted by the self-concern of the believer and the wars and fightings which arise from it.

The way of greater grace (4:6–10)

But he gives more grace; therefore it says, 'God opposes the proud, but gives grace to the humble.' [7]*Submit yourselves therefore to God. Resist the devil and he will flee from you.* [8]*Draw near to God and he will draw near to you. Cleanse your hands, you sinners, and purify your hearts, you men of double mind.* [9]*Be wretched and mourn and weep. Let your laughter be turned to mourning and your joy to dejection.* [10]*Humble yourselves before the Lord and he will exalt you.*

Since so much difficulty and uncertainty surrounds the meaning of verse 5b, it would be unsafe to draw out extensive conclusions from it. Yet in the light of the foregoing discussion, especially the fact that a reference to God's yearnings must surely be excluded, James must be understood as underlining either how sinful our human spirits are, notwithstanding that the Lord gave them to us (so, NIV), or that these sinful impulses remain and may even predominate, notwithstanding that the Holy Spirit now indwells us. Either way, we must look to God for fresh and greater aid. This is the promised 'greater grace' of verse 6.

What comfort there is in this verse! It tells us that God is tirelessly on our side. He never falters in respect of our needs, he always has *more grace* at hand for us. He is never less than sufficient, he always has more and yet more to give. Whatever we may forfeit when we put self first, we cannot forfeit our salvation, for there is always *more grace*. No matter what we do to him, he is never beaten. We may play false to the grace of election, contradict the grace of reconciliation, overlook the grace of indwelling – but *he gives more grace*. Even if we were to turn to him and say, 'What I have received so far is much less than enough,' he would reply, 'Well, you may have more.' His resources are never at an end, his patience is never exhausted, his initiative never stops, his generosity knows no limit: *he gives more grace*.

But grace, in God, has a correlative in man. James, having pointed to *God's sufficiency*, points on to *our responsibility*. In verses 7–10 there are no less than ten commands to obey. James does not see the indwelling Spirit (5b) as a means of instant and effortless sanctification – rather, the Holy One may dwell within even while we pursue the pathway of sinful self-seeking. In the same way he does not see the inexhaustible supply of grace as sweeping us along to an effortless holiness. He knows of no such easy victory. The benefits of grace and more grace are ours along the road of obedience and more obedience. The God who says 'Here is my grace to receive' says in the same breath, 'Here are my commands to obey.'

James forges the link between the experience of grace and the life of obedience by means of two 'therefores' (6b, 7a). First, because *more grace* is available by God's gift (6a), *therefore* (6b) Scripture makes clear by whom this grace may be enjoyed: God gives his grace to *the humble*. But this still leaves unanswered the vital question how we may take our place within this favoured category. *Therefore* (7) we are given a series of commands to obey which spell out the terms of a humble walk with God, commands whose effect is summarized in verse 10 as humbling ourselves before God, with the promised result that he will lift us up. In other words, the Bible, as so often, not only tells us what is true but also how to respond to what is true. The truth is a superabundant supply of grace (6); the response is an obedient walk with God, itemized in verses 7–9.

James begins his description of the humble walk with God by commanding *active allegiance* (7). Christians must have no doubt in their minds whose side they are on; and by their lives they must leave no doubt in the minds of others that they are God's enlisted subordinates and the devil's unyielding opponents. The English translation *submit* does not do full justice to the Greek it translates, chiefly because some ways in which we use the idea of submission point to the end of struggling and the onset of passivity. In this way, we 'submit' to superior forces: further resistance is useless. For the duration of the war we will stand idly by as prisoners of the enemy. But the word James uses is much more an 'enlistment' word, the taking up of allegiance to a great Superior in order to engage in the fight under his banner. The Lord Jesus 'was obedient' (Lk. 2:51) to his parents; Christian citizens are to 'be subject to' the authorities (Rom. 13:1) – the verb (*hypotassō*) speaks of a subordinate's readiness to await commands and to do the will of the superior. Francis Schaeffer aptly uses the phrase 'active passivity'[19] to cover this important idea.

If the translation *submit* is too passive, the translation *resist* is, if

19 F. A. Schaeffer. *True Spirituality* (STL, 1979), pp.57–59, 86–87.

anything, too active! It is not a word for one who is carrying the attack over into the enemy camp, but for one who is manning the defences, knowing that enemy pressure is ceaseless and that he is constantly under fire. We do well to notice that it is those who have subordinated themselves to God who are commanded to stand firm against the devil. James knows of no act of consecration to God which takes us out of the conflict. On the contrary, it is the very act of decisive enlistment as his underlings which brings us into the firing-line and calls the devil's attention to us as objects of attack.

James continues his description of the humble walk with God by commanding a *deliberately cultivated fellowship* (8a). The command is *Draw near to God,* and we find ourselves encouraged to obey it by the promise which goes along with it, *and he will draw near to you.* We shall, of course, find a tendency in ourselves to want to reverse this order. How easy it would be to keep a daily time with God if only we had, to begin with, a more vivid sense of his presence – in other words, we want the promise to come before the command! But we learnt at the outset (6–7) that *more grace* is given to those who set their feet on the path of obedience. God enriches with the grace of his presence those who obey his command to seek his presence. Indeed, if we are true to James, we will see this command to *draw near* as the first obedience required of those who have subordinated themselves to God and propose to resist the devil. For James is not snatching haphazard commands out of the air. He is setting out for us an ordered programme of obedience. The first element in the conflict is this central battle to live near God, the battle for regularity and discipline in Bible reading, prayer, private and public worship, feasting at the Lord's Table, devoting ourselves to Christian fellowship, cultivating every appointed avenue whereby we can draw near to him. Fellowship with God – and its consequent blessing of his fellowship with us – does not 'just happen'; we cannot drift into it any more than we drift into holiness. It is our first obedience.

Thirdly, we are commanded to put in hand *a thoroughgoing purification* of our lives (8b), to clean up the outer life of the *hands* and the inner life of our *hearts.* It touches our specific acts of wrong-doing, for the designation *sinners* points to individual sins; it touches too the inner disloyalty of the *double mind.* Here James uses the same word as at 1:8: the sin of being two-faced with God, of wavering inconsistency. In this thoroughgoing purification, notice who is to be the agent: *cleanse your hands, you sinners.* This is not the work of the Holy Spirit; it is the work of the energized believer. Just as James said to us in 1:21

that we are to go to it like a gardener, and hoe out the weeds from our lives, so here we are commanded to clean up our conduct and our hearts. But again, we must keep this command at its proper place in the sequence. Logic might suggest that we must clean up our lives and then draw near to God. James' logic is otherwise, for it is when we know the reality of his presence and come under its holy influence that we are at last in a position to face the demands of holiness, and find ourselves motivated by the desire to be like our God.

In this way, fourthly and finally, we are prepared for the command *to lament our sin and to repent of it* (9). Such an awareness of our wretchedness is, of course, beyond us. But then, equally so is every command in the sequence! It is in fact grace alone which makes it possible for us to obey any of God's commands. Our position is one of perpetual supplication for grace to obey in order that we may experience the *more grace* which God gives to the obedient. Nevertheless, the purpose of God is to lead us *down* into the lowest place of self-awareness and lamentation (9). This is the goal of the programme: the decisive taking of sides (7) leads into the practice of the presence of God (8a). This in turn prompts the longing (8b) to be like him in holiness. As always, the more we pursue his likeness, the more deeply and sorrowfully our sinfulness and shortcomings are exposed (9). But the Lord sets the downward path before us because there is no other way up (10).

4:11 – 5:6

13. Areas of high risk

Do not speak evil against one another, brethren. He that speaks evil against a brother or judges his brother, speaks evil against the law and judges the law. But if you judge the law, you are not a doer of the law but a judge. ¹²There is one lawgiver and judge, he who is able to save and to destroy. But who are you that you judge your neighbour?

¹³Come now, you who say, 'Today or tomorrow we will go into such and such a town and spend a year there and trade and get gain'; ¹⁴whereas you do not know about tomorrow. What is your life? For you are a mist that appears for a little time and then vanishes. ¹⁵Instead you ought to say, 'If the Lord wills, we shall live and we shall do this or that.' ¹⁶As it is, you boast in your arrogance. All such boasting is evil. ¹⁷Whoever knows what is right to do and fails to do it, for him it is sin.

¹Come now, you rich, weep and howl for the miseries that are coming upon you. ²Your riches have rotted and your garments are moth-eaten. ³Your gold and silver have rusted, and their rust will be evidence against you and will eat your flesh like fire. You have laid up treasure for the last days. ⁴Behold, the wages of the labourers who mowed your fields, which you kept back by fraud, cry out; and the cries of the harvesters have reached the ears of the Lord of hosts. ⁵You have lived on the earth in luxury and in pleasure; you have fattened your hearts in a day of slaughter. ⁶You have condemned, you have killed the righteous man; he does not resist you.

Time and again in James our problem is not how to understand what he is saying, but to explain why he is saying it at this particular point. He published his letter without headings and, ever since, commentators have either opted for the counsel of despair, that the letter of James is a series of unconnected topics, or else they have tried to read between the lines and fathom out a coherent line of development.

Beginning at 4:11 there are three obviously separate paragraphs. Verses 11–12 forbid defamatory talk about a fellow-Christian on the ground that we are individually called to render obedience to God's law, and that the task of giving the law, and of judging how far we have obeyed the law, must be left to the Lord himself. With the challenging call *Come now,* the paragraph 4:13–17 takes up a different topic. It is easy for Christians to act with presumption when they plan their future moves, but the future and its outcome is in the Lord's hands and not ours, and we should be humble enough to acknowledge this. Indeed, the more clearly we know this, the deeper our sin if we fail to order our lives accordingly. Thirdly, the paragraph 5:1–6 is a fierce denunciation of the misuse of wealth, whether by selfish hoarding (1–3) or dishonest fraud (4–6). And the Lord will be the judge of such things, for they have not escaped his notice.

Though the topics are so different, yet there are indications that James saw them as interwoven. Thus, for example, he links verses 11–12 and 13–17 by asking similar questions: *Who are you...?* (12)... *What is your life?* (14). In other words, honest and humble self-awareness would guard us from the sins of which he is warning; both are sins against humility. Again, the sections 4:13–17 and 5:1–6 are linked by the identical opening summons, *Come now* (4:13; 5:1), by the topic of wealth (4:13; 5:2, *etc.*), and by pictures of the frailty of life (4:14; 5:3).

We can take our review a stage further. The three topics are presented in such a way as to bring out two themes running through them. One of them is the theme of human weakness and insecurity. First, there is the weakness of unworthiness (4:12). A dreadful lack of self-knowledge lies behind every judgment passed on a fellow-Christian. Who am I, indeed! Secondly there is the weakness of sheer frailty in the face of the changes and chances of this life (4:14). I presume to decide about the future – I, who cannot foresee one day ahead; I, who am as perishable as a mere vapour! And finally, there is the weakness inherent in all forms of earthly security (5:2–3). All valuables fluctuate with altering circumstances. All alike suffer devaluation when things turn against them. Riches are uncertain.

The second theme is that of divine greatness and strength. *There is one lawgiver and judge, he who is able to save and to destroy* (4:12)... *Instead you ought to say, 'If the Lord wills...'* (4:15)... *the ears of the Lord of hosts* (5:4). It is for the Lord to decide what constitutes the good life (lawgiver) and to judge to what extent each has fulfilled the ideal (judge). None can appeal against or resist his judgment (able to save,

155

etc.). He is the arbiter of the experiences in the daily life of each individual (the Lord wills) and of the extent of individual life itself. No earthly circumstance or misdemeanour escapes his attention (ears) who is the absolutely sovereign One (Lord of hosts).

The three topics which sprang so suddenly upon us at 4:11 are not in fact out of place at all, but continue the theme which James was exploring in 3:13 – 4:10. If we are to live according to the wisdom from above, and to avoid the ill-fruits of earthly wisdom (3:13–18), then we need to cure the selfish and chronic covetousness of our hearts by humbling ourselves individually before God (4:1–10). In 4:6–10 James itemized for us a programme for the humble walk with God, our individual humility before him in the context of our personal fellowship with him. But there are other areas also where, if we are not alert, the self will raise its proud head and where we must learn to cultivate a truly lowly estimate of ourselves and a fully worthy estimate of our God. This is particularly in relation to other people and what we say about them (4:11–12), in relation to the ordering of our lives and the laying of plans (4:13–17), and in relation to the husbanding and use of this world's resources and goods (5:1–6).

The root cause

One further question remains: why these three topics? It is clear that they are all aspects of the basic thrust of this whole section, the need for humility before God. But is there any reason why James isolated these three areas as demanding special mention? The answer seems to be that these were the typical areas in which James saw the spirit of self-interest displaying itself. In 4:1–3, when he opened up for the first time the ways in which selfish pleasures, desires and wants make their presence felt in the church, he showed us *wars* and *fightings, i.e.* not just ill-relationships, but a determination on the part of each to come out on top. Next he saw a determination to possess, albeit constantly foiled of its objective (*you desire and do not have*), but yet insistently returning to the attack (*you fight and wage war*) because of the dominance of the profit motive. Thirdly, the aim was to possess (not in order to share, but) solely for self-gratification (*to spend it on your passions,* lit. 'pleasures').

When we were dealing with these verses we took them first as descriptive of those to whom James was writing. But then we noted the contrast between the ferocity of the vocabulary of war and the 'ordinariness' of the vocabulary of pleasure and desire, and realized that he was pressing beyond description to diagnosis. A really serious, fundamental ailment was being brought to light. Its symptoms were such as not to arouse suspicion or anxiety – just people being themselves, showing signs of average self-concern – but its root cause was in the sinful human spirit, the spirit of sinful and savage 'jealousy' (*phthonos*, 5) itself. If this is the case, then there are three ways in which the self-concerned heart displays itself as the root of the fallen nature, the antithesis of the wisdom from above, the epitome of the earthly, sensual, devilish wisdom. These are a determination to dominate others, an insistent profit motive (what's in it for me?) and a possessive attitude towards things. These three are now found to be the themes respectively for 4:11–12; 4:13–17 and 5:1–6. They concern the arrogance that would denigrate others, the presumptuousness that would be master of its own life in order to *get gain* (13), and the grasping covetousness that hoards wealth and defrauds others of what is due to them.

Against defamation (4:11–12)

Do not speak evil against one another, brethren. He that speaks evil against a brother or judges his brother, speaks evil against the law and judges the law. But if you judge the law, you are not a doer of the law but a judge. [12]*There is one lawgiver and judge, he who is able to save and to destroy. But who are you that you judge your neighbour?*

The command *Do not speak evil against* (11) is, more specifically, 'do not defame' or 'do not denigrate'. A defamatory word may be perfectly true: we do not have to tell lies in order to defame. But the fact that it is true gives us no right to say it. True or false, it makes us superior to the other person so that, as even the very form of James' verb suggests,[1] we 'talk down' to them, ourselves adopting a superior position. Defamation is forbidden not as a breach of truth, nor even as a breach of love, but as a breach of humility. If we are really low before God (6–10), we have no 'altitude' left from which to 'talk down' to anyone!

James elaborates his prohibition of defamatory talk along four lines. First, he tells us *how we should regard each other.* We are brothers (11)

---

[1]The verb is *katalaleō*, found elsewhere only in 1 Pet. 2:12; 3:16 of the dismissive condemnations of the world directed against Christians. The noun *katalalia* is found in 2 Cor. 12:20; 1 Pet. 2:1 and the adjective *katalalos* in Rom. 1:30. James Adamson notes that 'the OT denounces evil speaking, both against God (*e.g.* Num. 21:5) and man (*e.g.* Ps. 49:20) oftener than any other offence'.

and neighbours (12). Brotherliness is emphasized by repetition, *brethren . . . brother . . . brother*;[2] neighbourliness is emphasized by being put last, the word that hangs in the air at the end of James' final question. *Brethren* belong together within the love which marks family membership. Behind it lies the saving grace of God reaching out to us in Christ, the Father's self-imposed determination (1:18) to have us as his children. The relationship of brethren puts us all on the same level, so that it is improper for one to claim or exercise any superiority over the other. We are, none of us, the first-born (Rom. 8:29); we are simply the co-equal family members. It is probably right to bring in here also the description of God the Lawgiver as the one *who is able to save and to destroy*. These words have a plain meaning (as in Mt. 10:28) that God as Judge has power to settle the final and eternal issues of life or death. Yet this seems an unnecessarily heavy way in which to dispose of the sin of one Christian in criticizing another. The meaning is more likely a reminder that the God who could justly have condemned and destroyed chose rather to save. It is on this ground of undeserved mercy that both critic and criticized stand together as *brethren* of the same Father. Neither has the 'superiority' which makes 'talking down' possible; each is bound to the other in family love.

Neighbours belong together in the love which manifests itself in mutual care and concern, the love that sees need and reaches out to meet it. Our Lord's definition of neighbourliness in the Good Samaritan (Lk. 10:25ff.) leaves no room for 'talking down', but only for coming down to where the needy is, identifying with the need and abandoning self-interest so as to meet it. My fellow-Christian is my neighbour *par excellence*. Suppose I do know something to his discredit – and be it never so true – my task is not to publicize it, nor even privately to berate him with it, but to go where he is and lift him up. I must be the Samaritan to him. He is my neighbour.

Defamation begins and lives on in the mind. It is something we say to ourselves long before we pass it on. But if our minds were drilled in biblical attitudes, then love for our brothers would begin to root out censoriousness. Consideration for our neighbours would begin to replace the hurtful and arrogant word by helpful and caring pastoral concern.

Secondly, James tells us *how we should regard the law*. God has given us his 'royal law' (2:8) that we should love our neighbours. What

---

[2]It is extremely unfortunate that NIV has thought fit to cancel out James' emphasis by replacing the noun 'brother' by the pronoun 'him' after the verb 'judges'. This is an unwarranted watering down of the rigour of James' Greek.

happens, then, when we desert the path of love for that of criticism and denigration? Outwardly we speak against a brother and neighbour, actually we speak *evil against the law* (11). First, we break the law as a precept which we were meant to obey. It commands love; we respond with defamatory talk. Secondly, we set ourselves up as knowing better than the law, we *judge the law*. In effect we say that the law is mistaken in commanding love. It ought rather to have commanded criticism — and if we were lawgivers it would do so. The law no longer expresses the highest values as far as we are concerned. We know values — those of 'talking down' to our brothers — which are higher still. And, thirdly, we take up a new position, *not a doer of the law but a judge*. We seek to usurp the authority of God himself.

This leads us straight to James' third main point: *how we are to regard God*. He says, *There is one lawgiver and judge* (12). When we disobey the law, what are we doing in respect of the lawgiver? We are disputing his authority and that, of course, would be error and offence enough. But there is more. As we saw in the parallel discussion of 2:10–11, God's law is not an arbitrary collection of precepts which happens to contain this selection of all possible commands. His law is the expression of who and what he is; he gave us his commands in order that, by obeying them, we might fashion our lives in his image. Elements which exist as principles of the divine nature have been expressed as precepts for believers, so that the life of God may be seen in our mortal bodies. Very well then: to disobey his law is to contradict him. To value our opinions above the law is to value ourselves above him. To take up the position of judge is to elbow him off his throne. Where now is the humility and lowliness before God which is the essence and key to the heavenly wisdom?

It is to this point that James brings his whole discussion: *how we are to regard ourselves. But who are you . . . ?* (12). Do we sense an element of warmth in James' question? We would be right to do so! In the light of his teaching in this context how would we answer the question? 'I am a person seeking to walk in the lowliest humility with God, for I know that this is the way of blessing. I have learnt that the way down is the way up. I seek for myself the lowest place.' But if we exalt ourselves over a brother, is not the reality of our life with God called in question?

Against presumptuousness (4:13–17)

Come now, you who say, 'Today or tomorrow we will go into such and such a town and spend a year there and trade and get gain'; ¹⁴*whereas you do not know about tomorrow. What is your life? For you are a mist that appears for a little time and then vanishes.* ¹⁵*Instead you ought to say, 'If the Lord wills, we shall live and we shall do this or that.'* ¹⁶*As it is, you boast in your arrogance. All such boasting is evil.* ¹⁷*Whoever knows what is right to do and fails to do it, for him it is sin.*

James turns to a second area of high risk. He has shown us that by a wrong understanding of other people, and of their significance as brothers and neighbours, we can jeopardize our humility before God, which is the key to the whole situation. But there is also the sin of presumptuousness, which comes from a wrong understanding of ourselves in relation to our own lives and ambitions. It is interesting – and typical of James – that this sin too is put before us as a sin of speech. We are not now, however, defaming a brother; we are talking with a like arrogance to ourselves. We assure ourselves that time is on our side and at our disposal (*today or tomorrow*). We make our plans as if personal ability (*and trade*) and the profit motive (*and get gain*) were the only issues to take into account. We overlook frailty (*a mist*), and ignore the fact that even the small print of life is in the hands of a sovereign God (*if the Lord wills*). Yet we know better all the time (*knows what is right*), but self-confidence makes us *boast*, and *all such boasting is evil* and a sin against knowledge.

What is this presumptuousness of which James speaks? It first touches life: *today . . . tomorrow . . . a year* (13). It is the presumption that we can continue alive at will. Secondly, it touches choice: *today or tomorrow we will go . . . spend a year . . . trade*. It is the presumption that we are masters of our own life, so that we need to do no more than decide and, lo and behold, it will happen like that. Thirdly, it touches ability: *and trade and get gain*. Of course we shall succeed if we want! We can do it!

Once more it is all so ordinary, indeed so natural. That is exactly the point. When James exposes the blemish of presumptuousness, he exposes something which is the unrecognized claim of our hearts. We speak to ourselves as if life were our right, as if our choice were the only deciding factor, as if we had in ourselves all that was needed to make a success of things, as if getting on, making money, doing well were life's sole objective.

Now how do we guard against presumptuousness? The three verbs in verses 14–15 will put us on our guard against presumptuousness. First, there is our ignorance, *you do not know*. James indulges here in a little irony. He is talking about a person who was busy laying out his programme for next year (13) and he quietly notes that *you do not know about tomorrow* (14). This fact alone is enough to keep us low before the God who created, controls and apportions time. Then there is our frailty — *you are a mist that appears for a little time and then vanishes*. We are insubstantial (*mist*), transient (*a little time*) and gone without trace (*vanishes*). Finally there is our dependence, *you ought to say, 'If the Lord wills . . .'*. We come here to the heart of the matter.

James is not trying to banish planning from our lives, but only that sort of self-sufficient, self-important planning that keeps God for Sunday but looks on Monday to Saturday as mine. Certainly the words 'God willing' or their equivalents are not to become a fetish, or used as a protective talisman. John Calvin aptly notes that 'we read everywhere in the Scriptures that the holy servants of God spoke unconditionally of future things, when yet they had it as a fixed principle in their minds that they could do nothing without the permission of God'. C. L. Mitton goes to the central point when he contrasts 'evil doers' who make the transience of life 'an excuse for snatching all the pleasure out of it while there is time', while 'others use it as an excuse for doing nothing', but 'James refers to it as a reason why men should be *humble before God*'.[3] Once more it is this key factor of the lowly walk with God that is threatened. Our initial determination is to commit ourselves decisively to God's side (7), to live in close fellowship with him (8a), to purge our lives and our hearts (8b), to come to the place of wholesale repentance (9) and so to humble ourselves before God. All this can be lost, however, if, once outside the doors of our private room, we take the reins of life into our own hands, we forget our ignorance, frailty and dependence and plan our day, our week and next year as if we were lords of earth and time, and there was no God in heaven. To be sure the words 'If the Lord wills' can be a protective superstition; but they can also be the sweetest and most comfortable reassurance to a humble and trustful spirit.

The words are also intended for practical application to the hard details of real life. James addresses himself here to the Christian businessman, planning the expansion of his company into a new area, engaged in forward budgeting for a year's trading. Too often Christians leave God in the church or at home with their wives when they take

[3] Italics mine. *Cf.* Acts 18:21; 1 Cor. 4:19; 16:7; Phil. 2:19, 24; Heb. 6:3.

161

the train to their offices. James sees that either God is honoured as Lord in the place of business, or else the crucial factor of the humble spirit has been sacrificed on the altar of presumptuousness. In verse 14 it was the contents of tomorrow which were unknown, but in verse 15 it is the very existence of tomorrow and our own existence which is in question. We may take tomorrow for granted, thinking of it as a mark on the rim of time's wheel, coming on inevitably as the circling years proceed. But in the Bible the years do not circle. They go in a straight line from eternity to eternity, and on that line we receive another day neither by natural necessity, nor by mechanical law, nor by right, nor by courtesy of nature, but only by the covenanted mercies of God.[4] The very existence of tomorrow is as much part of our dependence on him as is our life itself[5] and our ability.[6]

The sin of presumption

Finally we must ask, with James, how serious the sin of presumptuousness is, even though in essence we have already faced the issue. It is, as we have seen, a most direct challenge to the life of lowliness before God, for it involves taking into our own hands the reins of planning and command. It involves seeing life itself as a continuing right rather than as a daily mercy. All this, however, is by implication from verses 13–15, and it would seem that James sees here something too serious to be left to implication. He uses verses 16–17 to drive his point home.

The verb 'to boast' (*kauchaomai*) is often used in the New Testament in a good sense for exultant, abounding joy in something, as when, for example, we are encouraged to boast in our hope of the glory of God (Rom. 5:2). But what an unholy, unacceptable thing this exulting becomes when it arises from *your arrogance*! Here is a word (*alazoneia*) used elsewhere only in 1 John 2:16, and translated the 'pride' of life. In other words, when even in little, secret, almost unrecognized ways we forget how frail we are, and stop short of conscious dependence on our God, it is an element of the proud, boastful, vaunting human spirit, flaunting its supposed independence and self-sufficiency. As such it is *evil* (16) – and James offers no qualification of the word: he merely says *evil*, the word which other scriptures use of the devil, the 'evil one'.

Verse 17 finds James at his abrupt best! He moves without preparatory warning from the particular of verse 16 to the general of verse 17,

[4]*Cf.* Gn. 8:22; Je. 33:25.   [5]*Cf.* Ps. 104:29–30; Dn. 5:23b.
[6]*Cf.* Dt. 8:18; Pr. 10:22; Je. 10:23–24; Ho. 2:8–9.

from the evil of the sin of arrogance to a searching statement of the principle of the sin of omission. In fact, the whole idea of sinning by default has never been given more pointed expression. It is a principle which exposes the insufficiency of even our best accomplishments, and makes us realize that we are never more than unprofitable servants. 'We may be able', says C. L. Mitton, 'to avoid committing forbidden evil; but who can ever seize positively every opportunity of doing good?'

Verses 16 and 17 are not, however, as unconnected as RSV might suggest. In the Greek the connective 'therefore' (*oun*) appears at the opening of verse 17. It must not be overlooked: 'All such boasting is evil. Whoever, therefore, knows . . . .' To James the sin of presumptuousness is so important, so basic, that it is as if the category of sins of omission had been deliberately devised in connection with it: that is the force of the 'therefore' of verse 17. We might consider it a small thing, a passing feature of life, if we forget how dependent we are and act in mere self-will. He sees it as the hard core of vaunting pride which is the mark and curse of fallen man. Here, above all places, we cannot afford to fall into the sin of omission.

Against covetousness (5:1–6)

Come now, you rich, weep and howl for the miseries that are coming upon you. *[2] Your riches have rotted and your garments are moth-eaten. [3] Your gold and silver have rusted, and their rust will be evidence against you and will eat your flesh like fire. You have laid up treasure for the last days. [4] Behold, the wages of the labourers who mowed your fields, which you kept back by fraud, cry out; and the cries of the harvesters have reached the ears of the Lord of hosts. [5] You have lived on the earth in luxury and in pleasure; you have fattened your hearts in a day of slaughter. [6] You have condemned, you have killed the righteous man; he does not resist you.*

With the beginning of chapter 5 we come to the third area of high risk to our humble walk with God. It is clear what James' topic is and what are the main lines of his teaching, even though much else remains unclear. He addresses himself to the wealthy and has pretty straight things to say about the use and abuse of wealth: this much is clear. But who are these rich people? Are they Christians who have been so drawn off course by the power wealth bestows that they have turned to oppress their fellow-believers? It may sadly be so, for there has surely been no period in church history when James' strictures against the rich would not apply to some church members. In support of the view that James is addressing rich Christians, we may note that this is suggested by the opening words of verse 1, where *Come now, you rich* is parallel with *Come now, you who say* in 4:13, and since the latter are Christian business folk, why should not the former be wealthy Christians? If they are Christians, then we may treat the command to *weep and howl* as the same implicit summons to repentance that was similarly expressed in 4:9. And, of course, if James is addressing believers, we do not need to ask any further questions as to why the passage occurs here. It is a feature of church life among those whom he is addressing, and gives him an opportunity to alert believers to an area in which their all-important humility could so easily be lost.

Commentators who argue against interpreting the rich as members of the church urge, for example, that there is no call to repentance (Laws, Adamson), nor any holding out of an expectation of salvation but only of judgment to come (Knowling). But they do not tell us why the call to weeping (1) cannot be a call to repentance, nor do they explain why the references to judgment day have to be simply the threat of doom to unbelievers, and not a sharp reminder to believers to mend their ways while there is still opportunity to do so. Sadly, the only compelling argument against understanding verses 1–6 as a challenging call to believers would be this – if we could say that believers could not possibly behave in this way. A. Barnes is unfortunately correct, and our experience of the church has been blissfully restricted if we have never met earnest, believing Christians who have allowed financial power to turn their heads, who remain blind to the fact that Christ is not Lord of their exchequer and whose worldly wealth has hardened their hearts against brothers and sisters less amply provided for.

The strongest argument that the rich are outside the church arises by implication from the conclusion James draws in verse 7, but it is far from decisive. In fact we hardly dare to do more than ask questions. Does the address to *brethren* (7) imply that those previously under James' lash in verses 1–6 are, by contrast, not 'brethren'? Does the fact that he encourages the *brethren* to hold on patiently until the coming Lord release them from such duress imply that for the rich of verses 1–6 the coming day (3, 5) can bring only condemnation? Maybe so, but in this case what is the point of verses 1–6 in a letter to the church? We could understand it if James alluded to financial oppression and described the form it was taking as a preliminary to speaking the word of comfort. But he actually addresses the *rich* as if they would be there in the church to hear his letter read out. Surely this would be a great exercise in pointlessness!

Many commentators rightly note how alike James is in verses 1–6 to the Old Testament prophets. Time and again they addressed stern denunciations to absent audiences – particularly, for example, oppressive or potentially oppressive foreign nations.[7] In doing this they fulfilled three distinct purposes. First, the word of God is an effective, potent thing in its own right. It accomplishes 'that which I purpose' and prospers 'in the thing for which I sent it' (Is. 55:11). The word goes out like a plenipotentiary to bring the will of God to pass. The prophets were in fact dealing the most powerful of all possible blows against the enemies of their people. Secondly, the people of God were present to hear the word being pronounced, and to draw comfort from it and power to persevere. The Lord would, in his own good time, deal with the threat; their position was to watch and wait and remain faithful. The *therefore* of verse 7, and its call to wait with confident hope and firm endurance, shows that James, with the prophetic mantle upon him, was living within the area of these two purposes.

The prophets also had a third purpose in mind. By making the mind of God plain in relation to whatever topic, sin or situation they were facing, they were teaching the people of God and calling them to the life that is pleasing to God. It is along this line that James' words to the rich have their greatest continuing significance. We might say: If we are not sure they are Christians, how can we take the denunciations as saying anything to us? Or we might say: They were obviously extremely wealthy and we are not; let those whom the cap fits wear it. But all this is beside the real point.

By facing a clear-cut case of those who have wealth at their disposal, James teaches all of us in respect of whatever resources, however small, God has entrusted to us. By exposing such glaring abuses, he teaches us how we ought to use our wealth as an adjunct to a humble walk with God. He shows us the pits, so that we may not fall into them.

Hoarding (5:2–3)

As James looks at the rich, he starts by condemning the hoarding of wealth. Garments are stored away and become the prey of the moth (2). Gold and silver bear on them the marks of disuse (3a). The rich have *laid up treasure* (3b) or, as NIV aptly says, 'have hoarded wealth'.

James sees all this as senseless – what is the point of feeding moths?

[7] E.g. Je. 46 – 51; Am. 1:3 – 2:3; Na. 1:1.

– from the earthly point of view, but he has his eye on eternity. Hoarding is condemnatory and spiritually foolish. The use of the idea of *rust* in relation to non-rusting metals like gold and silver makes an important point. Sophie Laws puts it this way: 'Gold and silver might well be base metals for all the worth they really are for their possessors.' In fact, when all comes to all, they would have been better without them, for they are yet another condemnatory voice bearing witness before God. Gold and silver, bearing on it all the marks of disuse, will reveal where the real faith of the wealthy lay: their trust was in their resources. It will speak too of their disregard of spiritual realities, specially the reality of having to give an account to God, for (again with NIV) 'you have hoarded wealth in the last days'. They lived without watching God's clock. They stored earthly goods as if there was nothing to expect but this life and its needs; they planned to live for ever – on earth!

We see, behind what James is teaching, the truths spoken by the Lord Jesus. It was he who showed how condemnatory hoarded wealth is in the day of divine scrutiny (*e.g.* Mt. 25:24–30), and how 'foolish' is the man who says he has more than enough stored away for many years, and who overlooks that he will promptly be called to account before God (Lk. 12:15–21).

Hoarding is a denial of proper use (*cf.* Lk. 12:33), of true trust (*cf.* 1 Tim. 6:17) and of godly expectancy (*cf.* 1 Tim. 6:18–19).

Fraudulence (5:4)

The wealthy against whom James is inveighing were landowners employing farm-workers. They were proving to be dishonest and dishonourable in paying the wages of their staff. As in the accusation of sinful hoarding, so here, James takes us straight from the earthly facts to their heavenly significance. He might well have dwelt on the insensitivity involved in withholding payment: families left unfed and so on. But one thing alone is important to say. The Lord is aware of what has happened, the fraud has not escaped his attention. The pain of his people has *reached the ears of the Lord of hosts*.

The phrase *the ears of the Lord of hosts* comes straight from the LXX of Isaiah 5:9,[8] and doubtless James expected his Christian readers to pick

---

[8]*Cf.* the comments of Laws and Davids. In LXX only the translators of Isaiah customarily use *kyrios sabaoth* ('Lord of hosts') in preference to the interpretative *kyrios pantokratōr* ('Lord Omnipotent') or its equivalent. In Is. 5 *kyrios sabaoth* comes in vv. 7, 9, 16, 24.

up the allusion. There too the rich were using their 'muscle' to gain every piece of available land for their own aggrandizement and comfort; there too (though the withholding of wages is not mentioned) the poor were suffering loss of land and income. When the Lord came to his vineyard (Is. 5:1ff.) he looked for righteousness, but heard only a cry of outrage and pain (Is. 5:7). His ears are still sensitive to the sufferings of the oppressed. It may be that the unexpected description of God as *the Lord of hosts* is intended to do no more than achieve this cross-reference to Isaiah 5 and thereby to bring an even deeper reassurance and comfort to the Lord's beleaguered people. He has always been on their side. The message through Isaiah all those years ago proved to be a word from the Lord. He did step in to judge the oppressor – and he will still do so today. But in its own right the title is worth pondering. In its Old Testament use it points to the Lord who has within himself and at his sovereign command every possible potency and resource: he is 'hosts'.[9] No power, however great or solid to the earthly eye, is beyond his capacity; no need, however pressing, is beyond his means, or outside his attention. What can the powerless labourer do against the all-powerful employer? Nothing for himself, but he can be sure that his very situation has already registered an appeal in the highest court of all. Here the all-powerful Lord sits as judge of the oppressor and the all-sufficient God attends to the needs of his people.

Indulgence (5:5)

In two words James now exposes the fact of wealth used for self-indulgence (*luxury . . . pleasure*) and in two more the folly of it (*on the earth . . . in a day of slaughter*).

You have lived in luxury translates a verb (*tryphaō*) not found elsewhere in the New Testament but of well-established meaning. It points to extravagant comfort, stressing the softness of luxury; it does not suggest dissolute living. On the other hand, *you have lived in pleasure* (*spatalaō*, *cf.* 1 Tim. 5:6) does suggest the breaking down of divine restraints, going beyond pleasure to vice. Together the words offer a picture of a life without self-denial, not necessarily corrupt in every way, but certainly offering no resistance to sin where there is promise of comfort and enjoyment.

In the parable of the rich man and Lazarus (Lk. 16:19–31) the Lord

[9] *Cf.* G. A. F. Knight, *A Biblical Approach to the Doctrine of the Trinity* (Cambridge University Press, 1953).

167

Jesus tells of a man who 'feasted sumptuously every day' but who, in a lost eternity, could only be reminded that 'in your lifetime' you enjoyed everything you counted good. How well this offers a backcloth for James' portrayal of people living *on the earth* as if this life were all that is, without thought of a heaven to be gained or a hell to be avoided. It is this latter thought that comes to the fore with the accusation that they *fattened* their *hearts in a day of slaughter*. The picture is fearfully vivid. They are like so many unthinking beasts, luxuriating in their rich pasture day after day, growing fat by the hour and careless of the fact that each day, each hour, brings the butcher and the abattoir nearer. Only the thin beast is safe in that day; the well-fed has made itself ready for the knife. In such a way James saw the wealthy, blind alike to heaven and hell, living for this life, forgetting the day of slaughter.

Betrayal (5:6)

As James balances out his teaching on wealth, there are two sections exposing the use of wealth for self-care (2–3 and 5), and each is followed (4 and 6) by a condemnation of the way wealth is used to hurt others. The final charge (6), now before us, is blunt: the murder of an unresisting victim. It is also obscure in its meaning! Taking the words as they come, *you have condemned* (*katadikazō*) does not necessarily imply condemnation by a court of law but (*e.g.* Mt. 12:37) can have that meaning. It would suit the Old Testament background of James' prophetic style of denunciation of the rich if we were to think of them as using the processes of law to get their own way, and to feather their own nests at the expense of the poor. This first verb is followed, without a connecting 'and', by another: *you have killed*. Is this James' implied comment on the way the courts have been used? The verdict was dressed up with every appearance of legality, but its actual effect was to violate the law; it was nothing short of murder. The victim is called *the righteous man*, which could either point to some notable, well-known individual or else it could be a collective description of a whole class against whom the rich set themselves. But in either case no resistance was offered; the victim accepted uncomplainingly whatever came his way.

The weight of opinion among the commentators is that we must understand *the righteous man* collectively – as Sophie Law says, 'not a known individual but a representative figure.' This would have the advantage of making the present passage in James match what he referred to in 2:6b: Christians found themselves the target of the hostility of the rich. But in the present passage, James adds the words *he does not resist you*, and this makes a collective reference to the persecution, even murder, of Christians in general more implausible. If he had said 'he cannot resist you', or 'he ought not to resist you', he would be saying what is true of all weak Christians under persecution. But there again, the target of persecution is not the weak who cannot (and who if they are believers ought not to) resist, but the 'righteous'. There have always been at least some well-provided Christians who could certainly offer some rejoinder at law or otherwise to the hostility of the wealthy. It is by no means the case that 'the righteous' is always ready and willing to be the passive recipient of injustice, opposition and death. But there was one who was notably such, our Lord Jesus Christ, and if James Adamson has ground for saying that a reference to him here would be 'hopelessly cryptic', it is proper to reply that a reference to non-resistance by the righteous in general would be hopelessly inaccurate.

It is in fact surely impossible to read the words *killed the righteous man; he does not resist* without the lone and wonderful figure of the Lord Jesus coming before the eyes of the mind. He is pre-eminently the Righteous One[10] – his response of non-resistance is at one and the same time the most demanding example and the sweetest consolation in time of oppression. However unexpected the reference, no sooner is it made than we exclaim over its suitability. Judas sold his Lord for money and the wholly Righteous One bowed to the act. Thus James exposes the sinfulness of those whose lives acknowledge only the lordship of money, and plots the pathway ahead for those who suffer as a result.

Drawing conclusions

A. Barnes is right when he says that 'there is no sin in merely being rich; where sin exists among the rich, it arises from the manner in which wealth is acquired, the spirit which it tends to engender in the heart, and the way in which it is used'. How very perceptive of him to include the second of his three qualifications! James would have thoroughly agreed – the way it is gained, the way it is used and 'the spirit which it tends to engender in the heart'. Maybe James would have gone just a shade further? The spirit which it almost inevitably

[10]*Cf.* Acts 3:14; 7:52; 22:14; 1 Pet. 3:18; 1 Jn. 2:1. See also Mt. 27:24; Lk. 23:47; 1 Jn. 1:9; 2:29; 3:7.

engenders? Compared with the loving tone which made him address us as *brethren* (4:11), when he warned us against arrogant criticism and the reasoned way in which he made his case against presumptuous planning (4:14), is there not something almost intemperate in the way he flies at the rich? It is all denunciation without qualification or relief. Strong language indeed!

We must not shirk the implication of James' harshness and directness. More than any of the areas of high risk, wealth threatens its possessors with coming misery (1). Its earthly cushioning dulls the sense of spiritual urgency (2–3) and of the reality of divine judgment (5). Affluence opens the door to commercial carelessness and insensitivity to what is both due and needful to others (4). It leads finally to setting aside the honour and dignity of the Lord Jesus Christ (6). He says nothing of the great good that those who possess wealth can do – maybe because the actual doing of good still leaves those who are rich within the high risks he has outlined. Good may be done with all the implicit arrogance, and sense of self-importance, that is more plainly seen when riches are wreaking their more obvious ill-effects on the human spirit.

Through James, as from a veritable prophet of the Lord, we have listened to the unsparing denunciation of the rich. But if, like the prophets of old, James has allowed us to hear such words in order to make principles and issues plain to us, what is he teaching us about our attitude towards and use of such possessions as we enjoy? Following the teaching in verses 2 and 3, we must strike the right balance between prudent saving and sinful hoarding. We know that we live 'in the last days' (3, not as RSV), and that the Lord may return at any time. When he does, the wealth we have amassed will be meaningless. But we also know that, though we live in the last days, his coming may not be yet. We do not know the day or hour of this, and the Scriptures put no premium on improvidence or imprudence. James' fire seems to be reserved for possessions left to rot in idleness, and this is a practical pointer for us. We should always put a priority on the use of possessions – following our Lord's own teaching about so using our resources as to heap up treasure in heaven (Lk. 12:32–34). And, as regards what may legitimately be put aside to shelter us in the earthly rainy day, we must ask the question where our trust is being placed. Are we keeping our reserve of earthly riches at such a level as indicates that they are our security, or does the level of earthly security represented by stored wealth prove that our trust is in the living God (1 Tim. 6:17–19)?

The teaching of verse 4 leaves no room for speculation. All our financial dealings must be honest. Every honourable debt must be paid; there is no room for anything else. The ears of the Lord of hosts are still open to the cry of any whom we might defraud of their due, and we must 'aim at what is honourable not only in the Lord's sight but also in the sight of men' (2 Cor. 8:21). There are few Christians who would steal another's money, but not a few fail to return borrowed books. There are few who would shop-lift in the local supermarket, but dare we have the same confidence about Inland Revenue returns, and our behaviour at customs barriers?

Moving to verse 5, we must keep the tightest hold on all luxury spending. The more we surround ourselves with possessions which only minister to creature comfort, the less we are likely to cultivate the spiritual trimness of physique which keeps us fit in the battle for holiness. Furthermore, when we allow such wealth as we possess to focus attention on ourselves and our satisfactions, we are ministering to that spirit of pleasure, desire and wanting for self which is the root of all unholiness and unfaithfulness to God (4:1–4).

Finally, we must have it constantly before our minds that it was love of money that betrayed the Lord Jesus. In Matthew's Gospel the word 'then' occurs again and again, like the pegs which hold his story to the line. He writes a very significant 'then' at 26:14. In a most beautiful and moving gesture a woman whom Matthew leaves unnamed (but *cf*. Jn. 12:1–8) pours a precious anointing oil on Jesus' head. To her it was an act of loving devotion. To Jesus it was a delight, something worthy to accompany the preaching of the gospel all round the world; to the disciples it was waste compared with what might be done to relieve world poverty; and, to Judas Iscariot, it was the last straw. 'Then' he left to barter away his Lord for thirty pieces of silver. We are not told why the incident acted like a trigger in this way. There was just something about a devotion which put Jesus so incomparably above this world's goods which he could not accommodate but must rather contradict. Would we be surprised if only we could remember how often the Lord Jesus Christ has taken second place to possessions, and has been much less than Lord of our financial arrangements?

Worldly wealth is an area of high risk in the battle to walk humbly with God. It is hard to be rich and lowly at the same time. The use of money and the life of self-pleasing are never far apart.

171

5:7–12
14. Enduring to the end

Be patient, therefore, brethren, until the coming of the Lord. Behold, the farmer waits for the precious fruit of the earth, being patient over it until it receives the early and the late rain. ⁸You also be patient. Establish your hearts, for the coming of the Lord is at hand. ⁹Do not grumble, brethren, against one another, that you may not be judged; behold, the Judge is standing at the doors. ¹⁰As an example of suffering and patience, brethren, take the prophets who spoke in the name of the Lord. ¹¹Behold, we call those happy who were steadfast. You have heard of the steadfastness of Job, and you have seen the purpose of the Lord, how the Lord is compassionate and merciful.

¹²But above all, my brethren, do not swear, either by heaven or by earth or with any other oath, but let your yes be yes and your no be no, that you may not fall under condemnation.

With the reappearance of the key idea of patience (7–8, 10) or steadfastness (11) James makes his letter return at the end to the point from which he started. As regards the two words which he uses, R. J. Knowling expresses their respective meanings very exactly when he says that patience[1] is the self-restraint which does not hastily retaliate against a wrong, and steadfastness[2] is the temper which does not easily succumb under suffering. Examination of the biblical use of the two words bears this distinction out. James began his letter with a call to *steadfastness* under trial (1:2–4), and we saw that holding up through the God-sent afflictions and difficulties of life is actually the pathway

[1] The verb *makrothymeō*, to be patient, long-suffering, appears in vv. 7–8 and the noun *makrothymia* in v. 10.

[2] The verb *hypomenō* and the noun *hypomonē* are both in v. 10. In Lk. 2:43; Acts 17:14 the verb means 'to stay on in the same place', illustrating well the idea of remaining steady, not giving up, under trial.

of sanctification, the progressive road to becoming *perfect and complete, lacking in nothing* (1:4). His conclusion (5:7–20) opens with the same theme set in the same context. He encourages us to the life of steadfastness by holding before us the bright prospects of the last Day. In 1:12 there is the bestowal of the crown and in 5:7–8 the personal coming of the Lord. In 1:4 and 12 respectively, he speaks of the goals of completion and life and, in 5:7 and 11, *precious fruit* and a promised experience of the compassion and mercy of the Lord.

If for a moment we stand back from 5:7–20 we see how completely it rounds off the letter. At the beginning, the pathway of steadfastness was linked with the pathway of prayer (1:5) as we sought from the Lord the wisdom needed to plot our course amid life's trials. Prayer at that point was related mainly to our own welfare: how we can individually keep on course for the crown. In his conclusion, when James has dealt with steadfastness (7–12), he turns again to the topic of prayer (13–18), but this time it is prayer at the service of others, our prayers as the means of dealing with their needs. For between 1:4ff. and 5:7–20 James has shown us that a caring ministry (2:1–26) is the first mark of the child of God. Of course, then, this will invade the realm of prayer, and we shall be much in the presence of the Lord for the good of needy brothers and sisters. Another of James' central characteristics of the child of God is the controlled tongue (3:1–12), and this topic, too, is woven into his conclusion, for he insists (as we shall see) that an unguarded tongue is the chief threat to a life of patience and steadfastness for God (see 5:9, 12). In the same way, his third element in the rounded Christian life, a holy freedom from the world's blemishes, finds its place in his conclusion. The expectation of the coming Lord (7–8) attracts us to the thought of patiently living to please him; the fact that the coming Lord is also the imminent Judge (9, 12) challenges and motivates us to the same end. Furthermore, verses 19–20 leave us in no doubt that sin is a thing of the utmost seriousness and that our greatest care for each other is to reach out in true pastoral concern to keep our brother's feet in the way of righteousness.

Within the total complex of this conclusion to his letter, James takes up two major topics as the setting in which he allows his major themes to receive their final expression. In verses 7–12 the foremost subject is patience or steadfastness, but it is shown as under constant threat – not (as in 1:2–4) from external circumstances, but from a factor within ourselves, the impatient and hasty tongue (9, 12). In verses 13–20 the foremost subject is prayer, but the prayer which in 1:5 sought the meeting of our own needs now pleads on behalf of brothers and sisters (14, 16). It is this note of outreaching care for our fellow-members in the Lord's family that finally closes the letter (19–20).

The pattern of 5:7–12

Standing back from verses 7–12 we see, as a first observation, that two subjects alternate with each other:

7–8 Patience	9 The tongue (mutual recriminations)
10–11 Patience/ steadfastness	12 The tongue (using oaths)

We can open up this pattern in further detail:

7–8 *The coming Lord* The farmer's patience is related to God's programme of the seasons and issues in precious fruit. Patience will bear precious fruit for the coming Lord.	. . . 9 *The coming Judge* Sins of speech will bring us under condemnation. The Lord who is near (8) is also the Judge who is at the doors (9).
10–11 *The coming end* The 'end' (RSV *purpose*, 11) towards which the Lord is working is to bestow compassion and mercy on those who have endured.	. . . 12 *The coming judgment* Sins of speech, the use of oaths, make us liable to fall under condemnation

In this way we see that not only do sections on patience and speech alternate, but that sections dealing with joyful hope (7–8 and 10–11) lead into sections dealing with fearful expectation (9, 12). The whole unit (7–12) is, in fact, wonderfully symmetrical and balanced.

It remains true, of course, that James – as usual – omits connecting phrases. He does not stop to tell us why he sees it as logical to write about the patience that waits for the coming Lord (7–8), and to move on immediately to a warning against mutual recrimination (9). Nor does he say why he then returns (10–11) to further exhortations to endure, only, once again (12), to revert to warnings against a particular sin of speech (the use of oaths). But when all is said and done, is it so very hard to trace out his logic? Looking again at the detailed outline above, the word that springs to mind to replace the dots between the sections is 'forfeiture'. We can forfeit the blessing of joyful hope, and replace it by fearful expectation of a coming Judge – and it is the tongue through which this grim forfeiture takes place. There is more to this than James' celebrated emphasis on the seriousness of sins of speech. The very circumstances which call for patience (7–8) beget impatience. Think of such times of stress and hardship as verses 1–6 describe. (Note how James makes this connection by the 'therefore' in v.7.) Pressed from outside by opponents, waiting for a Lord who is coming yet seems not to come, how easily tempers can fray and the fellowship begin to fall apart! How easy to begin to take it out on each other, to find cause for complaint within the family! Yet, as James taught in 3:18, *the harvest of righteousness – the precious fruit* of 5:7 – can grow only in the soil of a peaceful fellowship. The tongue which destroys peace blights the harvest for which the coming Lord is looking.

Since this is the case, the call for endurance (10–11) must be pressed home. James does it now by a strong appeal to the examples of the prophets and Job, and by a lovely reminder that the Lord's purposes are worth waiting for. But again, the tongue could rob us of our prize. Under stress of what he saw as personal danger, Peter began to call down curses on himself and to swear (Mt. 26:74). The tight corner and the loose tongue went together. It was all very far from what Peter intended. He had started out with a very different vow (Mk. 14:29) but the stress exposed the weakness, and this weakness found the tongue. This steadfastness is exactly what James has in mind: the tongue needs to be made the object of special guardian care.

There, then, is the passage in its unity, its pattern and its main teaching. We must now turn to its details.

Coming Lord, coming Judge

As we have noted, each of the four sections in this passage concludes with a forward look. In verses 7–8 we expect a coming Lord; in verse 9 there is a Judge already *at the doors*; in verses 10–11 James speaks of *the purpose,* lit. the 'end' or 'objective' (*telos*) *of the Lord.* The immediate relationship of this expression to the illustration of *Job* shows that the

Lord may in fact bring his 'end' to pass in this life (Jb. 42:12), yet the word 'end' cannot, in this present context, be without its fuller significance. There is a supreme outpouring of the compassion and mercy of the Lord which can come only when Jesus comes. Finally, in verse 12, the warning note is again sounded: the misused tongue may bring us *under condemnation*. If this were translated 'under judgment' then verse 12 would display its close link with the parallel verse 9. But taking the verses as a whole, the Lord comes (7–8) bringing divine compassion and mercy (11); the Judge comes (9) bringing judgment (12).

Very often in the Bible when a word has a special, almost technical, sense it is also used in what we might call an 'ordinary' way. In verse 7–8 James uses a special and lovely word for the *coming* of the Lord, and we can begin to enjoy its flavour by noting that it is also used in a very ordinary sense. Paul speaks of 'the coming of Stephanas'[3] and uses the same word for his own personal 'presence'[4] with this or that church. In relation to the coming of the Lord, we can bring these two meanings together in the word 'arrival'. That is to say, the coming is an expected event, but when it happens it will be the Lord's personal arrival and presence with his people. Our main source of information regarding this *parousia*, or *coming*, is the Lord Jesus himself. We have, therefore, a sure foundation for our expectant faith. He taught that his coming would be preceded by signs[5] and would, when it happened, be as vivid, visible and unmistakable as lightning which illuminates the whole sky.[6] It will happen on a day which cannot be known in advance,[7] and will bring about a separation or taking away of the people of God.[8] Those who are Christ's[9] will be gathered for ever into his presence,[10] caught up to meet him in the air,[11] transformed into an unblemished holiness[12] as they are at last made fully alive in Christ.[13] To unbelievers the expectation of the Lord's return is a matter for cynical doubt and dismissal,[14] but to believers this sure hope constitutes a strong call to endure[15] and to prepare by holiness of life.[16] For the Lord himself[17] will come in power,[18] his foes will perish,[19] and the

[3] 1 Cor. 16:17. The word is *parousia*. Note here how well the translation 'arrival' fits. See also 2 Cor. 7:6–7; Phil. 1:26.

[4] 2 Cor. 10:10; Phil. 2:12.

[5] Mt. 24:3.   [6] Mt. 24:27.   [7] Mt. 24:36ff.

[8] Mt. 24: 8ff.   [9] 1 Cor. 15:23.   [10] 1 Thes. 2:19; 2 Thes. 2:1.

[11] 1 Thes. 4:17.   [12] 1 Thes. 3:13; 5:23.   [13] 1 Cor. 15:22.

[14] 2 Pet. 3:3–4.   [15] Jas. 5:8.   [16] 1 Jn. 2:28.

[17] 1 Thes. 4:16.   [18] 2 Pet. 1:16.

[19] 2 Thes. 2:8; *cf.* 2 Thes. 1:7–10.

heavens and the earth will be replaced by new heavens and a new earth in which righteousness will dwell.[20]

It is striking that all James needs to say to his readers is that the Lord is coming. He does not enter into long explanations and descriptions. He can assume that they know all about it, for it was a familiar truth to the New Testament church. If we wish to be New Testament believers, and to think in terms of New Testament priorities, then the fact of this great Advent, the sure expectation of it and the desire not to be ashamed before him at his coming should be in the forefront of our thoughts. John Blanchard says that 'it is certainly probable that there are about 300 references in the New Testament, one for every 13 verses from Matthew to Revelation'.

In the first instance James intended the expectation of the coming Lord to bring comfort and joyful expectation to those to whom he wrote. They were undergoing stresses and strains (5:1-6), *therefore* (7) they needed to be called to patience, but they needed too the reminder of that *coming* which would put an end to all opposition and make suffering a thing of the past. When Jesus comes, then indeed the Lord's great and eternal 'end' (11) will have been reached, and it will be compassion and mercy all the way (11). We could better translate *compassionate* as 'tender-hearted' or, even more accurately, 'abundantly tender-hearted'.[21] *Merciful* requires a much more emotional rendering, for we see from its background that it sums up that moving of the heart of God towards us from which all his blessings and saving mercies flow.[22] Behind all that God has ever done for us lies his heart of love – behind his choice of us, his gift of his Son, the temporal and eternal blessings of his great salvation, his daily and nightly care for us, his provisions for body, mind and soul, his presence day by day, and the hope of glory. The wonder of the day of Christ's coming is that then the full content of that heart of love will come home in experience to the people of this great and tender-hearted God.

---

[20]2 Pet. 3:12-13.

[21]James seems to coin a word, unused elsewhere, *polysplagchnos*. The *splagchna* are, literally, the intestines and then came to express those deep and surging emotions which move us physically as well as mentally and spiritually. The prefix *poly* means 'much'. God is, thus, 'much' in tender feeling.

[22]James says he is 'pitiful' (*oiktirmōn*). The related noun (*oiktirmos*) occurs in Rom. 12:1 as 'mercies', a summary-word for all that God has ever or will ever do for us in Christ. The verb (*oikteirō*), in Rom. 9:15, translates the Hebrew (Ex. 33:19) *riḥamti*. We can feel the force of this Hebrew verb by noting that its noun (*raḥamim*) is translated 'heart' in 1 Ki. 3:26, a verse full of the yearning, passionate love which the verb expresses.

But there is another side to the expected coming, for *the Judge is standing at the doors* (9). James is here speaking to Christians, those whom he can address as *brethren*. He is stating a truth which we find it easy, even convenient, to forget, but which is central to the New Testament revelation of the returning Lord. Again, James does not have to prove or elaborate his point. He can assume that his readers know about this aspect of the Lord's return. We must, therefore, go outside the letter of James to remind ourselves of the fact and nature of this inescapable judgment.

Before the Judge

The teaching of the Lord Jesus is again our starting-point. Similar parables are found in Matthew 25:14–30 and Luke 19:11–27. Each concerns itself with servants entrusted with their lord's good during his absence, and each includes the lord's enquiry, on his return, into the way the servants have discharged their stewardship. In each parable there is the exposure of one who claimed to be a servant but was not. This matches that strand of teaching regarding the return of Christ, that there will be a separation, one taken and one left (*e.g.* Mt. 24:40–41). But in each parable the real focus of attention is on the servants who were servants indeed, and what they can present of the fruits of their service before the judgment seat.

First, then, when Jesus comes again we will appear before his judgment seat (2 Cor. 5:10). What is in question is not our salvation but our reward. Paul insists that even the Christian who makes (if we may so put it) the poorest showing before the Judge, and whose works simply will not bear scrutiny, but are revealed as insubstantial, will nevertheless himself or herself be saved. The fire of judgment will expose and destroy the 'works' but cannot touch the person (1 Cor. 3:12–15). In his parables, the Lord Jesus speaks (in Lk. 19:13) of servants who each receive the same sum of money to trade with. At the end they are invited to bring the fruits of their work for their lord's inspection. This speaks to us of those things which each Christian alike possesses: salvation, the indwelling Spirit, the Scriptures, the gospel message, and so on. What have we done with these since they came into our possession? What gains have we made? Have we become more like Christ through entering into the riches of the full salvation that is ours? Have we grown in holiness and maturity through the indwelling Spirit? Do we know the Scriptures in an ever extending and deepening way? How many others have we told about Christ? In

Matthew 25:15, however, the thought is different. Individual Christians have differing abilities or, as we say, 'talents'. These are God-given. The thrust of the Lord's teaching here touches on our consecration: have we devoted every talent we possess to him and his service? Are we really all for him?

But, secondly, we ought to note how positive the judgment is. The returning lord in the parables is looking for what he can praise, and when he finds it his praise is immediate and warm (Mt. 25:21, 23; Lk. 19:17–19). We must never forget the searching nature of the enquiry: it is such that Paul can use the metaphor of fire (1 Cor. 3:13) and in prospect of the judgment can say that he is moved by the fear of the Lord (2 Cor. 5:11). Yet the Judge is our own loving, caring Saviour, and our constant thought should be how we can delight him at his coming by having something of eternal, lasting value to lay at his feet.

There is one thing that James stresses regarding the coming Lord and coming Judge: the coming *is at hand* (8), the Judge is *at the doors* (9). Nearly two thousand years have passed since James wrote those words, and still the Lord has not come; the Judge has not stepped over the threshold. There is a real problem here, and one which many find it easy to solve by supposing that James (and the rest of the New Testament) entertained a wrong expectation. Yet, what are we to make of James' words? Even if the Lord Jesus were to come tomorrow it would still be a lapse of many centuries since James insisted that his coming was (lit.) 'near'. This is certainly not what we would call nearness!

Lovers of Narnia will remember with what perception C. S. Lewis recognized the fact that different spheres might operate with different time-scales. The children slip through the magic wardrobe and engage in what really are months and years of Narnian adventures, yet they return to find that earth-time has not perceptibly moved on. How could we understand, then, the relationship between earth-years and the eternal, 'timeless' sphere of the life of God? It was in these terms that Peter saw the problem of the Lord's imminent return, and offered the Bible's authoritative solution. First, God is not dilatory in keeping his promise that Jesus will come soon (2 Pet. 3:9); secondly, his time-scale and ours are not concurrent (2 Pet. 3:8); and, thirdly, what we call 'delay' is in fact the outward evidence of God's merciful longing that none should be unready when Jesus comes (2 Pet. 3:9). Scoffers may scoff (2 Pet. 3:3–4), but the day will come (2 Pet. 3:10). Jesus insisted that the date of his return is unknown and unknowable (Mk. 13:32; Acts 1:7). He also countered false expectations with clear hints of a protracted period before he would return (*e.g.* Mt. 25:19; Lk. 19:11). Yet he summoned us to a constant state of readiness (Lk. 12:35–46). The remainder of the New Testament underlines the need for an expectant spirit, and James 5:7–9 is as good an example as we could wish. He was not mistaken in calling for sustained readiness for a soon-returning Lord and Judge. Such readiness, such longing and expectation, is rather the mark of a truly apostolic faith – and James is typical in this also, that in relation to the second coming of the Lord Jesus our first responsibility is not to devise a calendar of the future, and to predict as near as may be when he will come, nor even to try to interpret world events in order to discern signs of his coming. Rather, it is to look to our hearts and lives to see whether we are ready to stand before him without shame and to his praise, glory and pleasure.

The fruitfulness of patience (5:7–9)

Be patient, therefore, brethren, until the coming of the Lord. Behold, the farmer waits for the precious fruit of the earth, being patient over it until it receives the early and the late rain. [8] *You also be patient. Establish your hearts, for the coming of the Lord is at hand.* [9] *Do not grumble, brethren, against one another, that you may not be judged; behold, the Judge is standing at the doors.*

If we are studying the words of James the Lord's brother, then we could be tempted to think that when his elder brother followed James' father, Joseph, as a carpenter, and maybe other brothers were drawn into fishing on Galilee, James himself worked on the land. He loves the imagery of gardening and farming (*e.g.* 1:10–11, 18, 21; 3:18). In the present verses he presses home his call to patience by noting how necessary and how fruitful a virtue patience is for a farmer. The farmer sets out to obey the laws of God as they are built into the way things work. He plants his seed at the appointed time, in the appointed conditions, and having done so he waits, for there is no other way to harvest-time.

In the climate of Palestine *the early and the late rain* (7) were a unique feature. The early rain came in October, preparing the soil for the seed and helping the seed, once planted, to begin the process of germination. The late rain, in March and April, swelled the grain and guaranteed a good crop. The illustration fits well not only at this point in the letter but also into James' characteristic way of thinking. It was at this very point that he opened his letter. Faith meets life's tests and, through patience (and not without it), grows into full maturity of settled character (1:2–4). James' doctrine of the Christian life is a doctrine of process or growth, and patience is its central requirement. We neither drift into holiness nor are we wafted there by some heavenly visitation; we grow to holiness and, like every harvest, it is a process.

Nothing can hurry on the early and late rains and nothing can speed up the imminent coming of the Lord. James thus speaks to assure us that all will be well. Along the line of the processes he has appointed, God the Creator germinates the seed, promotes growth, swells the grain until, when harvest-time comes, the harvest is ready. It is his annual miracle in the sphere of the created world. Surely James wishes us to see the same mighty hand at work in our lives. The Father will have us ready too, so that nothing will mar the excellence of the day he brings his Son back in glory.

But we have our part to play. In one of the Lord's parables (Mk. 4:26–29), the farmer, who cannot explain or understand the processes of growth, nevertheless superintends and watches over the developing crop with persistent care. In verses 8–9 James summons us to this task. First, we need to watch *our own hearts* (8). The words *establish your hearts* do indeed repeat and enforce the call to *be patient,* but they do so by focusing attention on a central need: the fixed heart. The same verb (*stērizō*) appears in Luke 9:51, where Jesus 'set his face' to go to Jerusalem and to all that awaited him there. In this one example we feel the whole force of the word: determination, steely resolution, persistence. All this is to be directed towards our *hearts*. In other words, James is faithfully warning us against the old enemy of inconsistency (*e.g.* 1:6–8; 2:4; 3:11–12; 4:4, 8). He looks for a heart fixed on the harvest, fixed on the returning Lord, a heart which leaves no room for the double-mind. R. A. Ward neatly contrasts the fattened hearts of 5:5 with the fixed hearts of 5:8. Whatever our life-style, the heart lies at the centre. It is either the focus of indulgence or the focus of determination. We can forfeit the harvest by a failure in true, sustained commitment.

Secondly, we need to watch *our fellowship* (9). The call for patience needs to be made only in situations where there is a temptation to impatience. Under the stresses of living for God we may so easily round on our fellow Christians, our *brethren,* in all sorts of grumbles and recriminations. Our hearts may let us down (8) through failure in commitment and resolution. Our tongues may let us down and rob us of the harvest through failure to cherish the family (*brethren*) and fellowship of the people of God among whom he has set us. James has already taught us that the harvest requires the soil of fellowship (3:18). When our tongues disrupt the fellowship they rob us of the harvest. Of course it is true that the Judge, when at last he steps over the threshold, will bring every aspect of our lives and service under review, but the one aspect that led James to recall the imminent Judge and the inescapable judgment was the tongue which brings divisions into the fellowship.

The blessing of steadfastness (5:10–12)

As an example of suffering and patience, brethren, take the prophets who spoke in the name of the Lord. [11]*Behold, we call those happy who were steadfast. You have heard of the steadfastness of Job, and you have seen the purpose of the Lord, how the Lord is compassionate and merciful.*

[12]*But above all, my brethren, do not swear, either by heaven or by earth or with any other oath, but let your yes be yes and your no be no, that you may not fall under condemnation.*

As we noted above, verse 10 flows naturally out of verse 9. If such serious consequences can follow upon impatience of speech, so that we are called into question by the Judge on the day of his coming, then indeed it is important to give ourselves to the task of bearing up under stress. James brings out three points in sequence. First, we have reason to expect in our experience the sort of *suffering* which requires *patience* (10). We see it exemplified in the prophets, who were highly privileged but not protected against the strains of life. They had a special place in God's plans as they *spoke in the name of the Lord.* But, as C. L. Mitton notes, 'faithfulness to God's commands so far from giving them immunity from suffering actually involved them in it'. Their privilege and their trials went hand in hand. Jeremiah (11:21) was hunted by the men of his home town specifically because they wanted to stop him from speaking in the name of the Lord. Ezekiel suffered painful bereavement as the setting in which he delivered his message (24:15ff.). If Daniel had not suffered deportation we would never have heard of him (1:3–6) or benefited from his ministry. Hosea's marriage breakdown was in itself the Lord's word to and through him (1:2–3). Privilege and suffering, suffering and ministry just belonged together in the lives of the prophets.

Secondly, James points out that *we call those happy who were steadfast* (11), that is, we look at them and instinctively recognize that the blessing of God has rested on them. We would rightly call Jeremiah,

Ezekiel, Hosea and the other people on whom God's blessing rested. Indeed we often react in the same way to contemporaries in whom we see the virtue of endurance. We covet it for ourselves. We would like to think that in similar circumstances of oppression or of illness we would be as resolute, even if we have grave doubts that we could manage it. But is there solid ground for feeling like this? Is there a blessing in having exercised steadfastness? The example of Job makes James' third point. The Lord subjects his servants to those trials which call for steadfastness, because it is along this line that he wills to achieve his own *purpose* for them in some signal outpouring of his compassion and mercy.

The story of Job is an example of faithful steadfastness, but even more of divine purpose. The blessedness which came to him eventually was not a 'fairy-tale ending' in which all lived happily ever after. It was the objective of God from the start: above all it was the enrichment of knowing God more fully. This is where Job puts his finger, and James also. Doubtless neither would discount or despise the earthly prosperity which the Lord gave to Job, for this too is part of his compassion and mercy (Jb. 42:10ff.). But Job's own word is this: 'I had heard of thee by the hearing of the ear, but now my eye sees thee' (42:5). His new knowledge of the Lord was as vivid as the replacement of hearsay by encounter. James too brings out, not the blessings the Lord bestows, but the knowledge of the Lord himself, *how the Lord is compassionate and merciful,* for, as the Lord Jesus said, 'eternal life' is to 'know thee the only true God, and Jesus Christ whom thou hast sent' (Jn. 17:3).

Steadfastness has great blessings to bring to us but, once more, the blessings must be safeguarded and, once more, the danger arises from the tongue (12). The blessing can be jeopardized if, through impatience, we seek to enforce our words by oaths. As we have seen (pp. 174–175), the general connection between verses 10–11 and 12 is easy enough to establish: experiences calling for endurance can quickly provoke looseness or rashness of speech. But it is more difficult to pin James down to specific meanings. Possibly we should start by saying that it is unlikely that James would find any difficulty in taking an *oath* when required to do so by a court of law. He does not seem to have this situation in mind, but rather how Christians behave in ordinary conversations, and what they say in a purely private capacity. The formal oath, taken in court, is part of the way in which we safeguard the control of speech, on which James is so insistent. It is a solemn and considered use of the tongue which could not possibly come under condemnation. It would be absurd to expect that law-officers would intuitively recognize in us the quality of character which could not tell a lie, and therefore the request for a spoken guarantee of truth simply reflects our involvement in a society of sinners. As those who love the truth, we should be glad to make a serious affirmation of our truthfulness.

Maybe the similarities between James 5:12 and the teaching of Jesus in Matthew 5:33–37 and 23:16–22 can guide us to James' intention. The Lord Jesus was tackling a situation in which oaths were used in order to give the appearance of making a binding statement or agreement, but the actual wording of the oath contained an escape-hatch whereby the speaker could not be held to what he had said. The oath was, in fact, an assertion of truth used as a means of falsehood. Many commentators tell us that this was a widespread feature of contemporary life, and R. J. Knowling, among them, is able to quote one pagan source as noting the prevalence among Jews of the time of 'heedless and false swearing'.[23] It would be splendid if only we could say that this would never happen among Christians, that we never would use and never have used duplicity and misleading affirmations, promises and undertakings to get our own way, or to get ourselves out of a tight corner. It would be splendid if only we could say that we have never suffered from the white lies and intentionally misleading words and pledges of believers. It would be even more splendid if we had never been guilty ourselves. Rather, Isaiah spoke for us all when he confessed to being a man of unclean lips, living among a people of unclean lips (6:5).

We are extremely lacking in self-knowledge if we even begin to think that James' words in this verse have no application or bearing for us. We should cultivate an unadorned manner of speech, free, of course, from bad language, certainly free from any light use of the name of God, but free too from unnecessary (even if harmless) expletives. The merest whiff of exasperation makes us exclaim 'for heaven's sake', but, apart from the fact that 'heaven' here is a circumlocution for 'God' and therefore a concealed misuse of his name, the light expletive opens the door a crack and prepares the way for the greater. James Adamson is correct when he notes that even the sincere but needless invocation of God's name in common speech can only lead in the end to irreverence.

There is another aspect of oath-taking which is worth mentioning.

---

[23]Knowling refers to Martial, *Epig.*xi. 94.

As we look back in our lives, we see that God graciously brought us into seasons of difficulty in order to bring us nearer to himself. Indeed the older we get the more we can look back with heartfelt thanks for the benefits reaped through experiences which at the time were full of grief and pain. Yet sometimes our backward look is touched with sadness, and even remorse, because the spiritual ground gained during the trial has not been held when once again the sun shone and our circumstances became more manageable. It is very likely for this reason that in Old Testament times people made vows to God while their trouble lasted, promising to fulfil the vow when the cloud of trial lifted again. But within the Old Testament it is also recognized that it is easier to vow than to fulfil and the warning is given that 'when you vow a vow to God, do not delay paying it; for he has no pleasure in fools. Pay what you vow' (Ec. 5:4). This is so close to what James is teaching that it may well have been in his mind also. Our stresses could give rise to an unreal pledge to God, made in the most solemn terms. But in James' practical book it is essential to be real rather than dramatic, and to mean what we say, for in this matter also it is not unusual for a believer to carry about an unfulfilled promise to God.

Yet, while we may feel after this meaning or that which may have been in James' mind, his central concern is all too plain. To say 'yes' and mean it, to say 'no' and equally mean it, is a matter of integrity of character rather than a form of words. In this way James returns (as with his reference to the heart in v.8) to his favourite topic, that we should be people without internal division, free of the double-mind, whole-hearted with God and with man. We practise a devotion to the truth with our lips because the truth dwells in us.

15. The last word: prayer and care

Is any one among you suffering? Let him pray. Is any cheerful? Let him sing praise. [14]*Is any among you sick? Let him call for the elders of the church, and let them pray over him, anointing him with oil in the name of the Lord;* [15]*and the prayer of faith will save the sick man, and the Lord will raise him up; and if he has committed sins, he will be forgiven.* [16]*Therefore confess your sins to one another, and pray for one another, that you may be healed. The prayer of a righteous man has great power in its effects.* [17]*Elijah was a man of like nature with ourselves and he prayed fervently that it might not rain, and for three years and six months it did not rain on the earth.* [18]*Then he prayed again and the heaven gave rain, and the earth brought forth its fruit.*

[19]*My brethren, if any one among you wanders from the truth and some one brings him back,* [20]*let him know that whoever brings back a sinner from the error of his way will save his soul from death and will cover a multitude of sins.*

James is much too practical to leave us with only the wearying ideas of patience and steadfastness as guides for life till Jesus comes again. He is also much too consistent to offer us any programme other than that which he has already presented. When he insisted in 1:2–4 that life's trials are not unnatural barriers to our walk with God, but are the appointed way forward to spiritual maturity, he at once called us to prayer. This is so that in answer to believing, undoubting prayer we might receive from God the wisdom which would guide us on our way to the crown (1:5ff., 12). The sequence 'patience . . . prayer' was thus established (1:3–4 . . . 5). It is the same here at the end of his letter. The seven references to patience, waiting and steadfastness in verses 7–12 are matched by seven references to prayer in verses 13–18. The positive way forward in situations demanding endurance is the way of prayer.

The passage before us (13–20) is bound together by the words *any one among you* which open the first and last sections (13, 19), but within its unity there are two unequal parts. In the first of these (13–18) prayer is mentioned in each verse, as James introduces us to the praying individual Christian (13), the praying elders (14–15), the praying friends (16a) and the praying prophet (16b–18).

The individual at prayer: a basic principle (5:13)

James makes the neatest possible transition from the previous section of his letter to this one. In the course of his varied exhortations to the life of patience and steadfastness, he referred *as an example of suffering* to *the prophets* (10). The word which he used in verse 10 as a noun, *suffering*, he uses as a verb in verse 13, *suffering*. It is as if he said, 'We mentioned suffering. Well, suffering will come your way too and you had better know what to do about it.' The word (*kakopatheia, kakopatheō*) is wider than the sufferings of sickness.[1] Jeremiah suffered opposition, Ezekiel bereavement, Hosea marital breakdown. It is any ill circumstance which may come upon us, any trial, anything of which we or an onlooking friend might say 'That's bad'. Alternatively, life has other experiences in store for us as well. James asks, *Is any cheerful?* The word means, broadly, 'to be in good heart'. It does not necessarily mean to be trouble free but to be buoyant, whatever the circumstances, to be happy in spirit.[2] Here, then, in two words, are all life's experiences, and each of them in turn can so easily be the occasion of spiritual upset. Trouble can give rise to an attitude of surly rebellion against God and the abandonment of spiritual practices. Equally, times of ease and affluence beget complacency, laziness and the assumption that we are able of ourselves to cope with life, and God is forgotten. James is fully aware of all this, for the persistence, throughout his letter, of the themes of trial, alongside warnings against allowing the heart to stray after riches, indicate his acquaintance with the full run of life, and his concern to armour us against its varied assaults.

His insistence, nevertheless, is that none of these things should

[1] The noun occurs only here. The verb is found also in 2 Tim. 2:9; 4:5 and a compound form of the verb, *synkakopatheō*, in 2 Tim. 1:8; 2:3. These references bear out the very general meaning of the words, covering all 'bad experiences'.

[2] The verb is *euthymeō*, found also in Acts 27:22, 25; the adjective, *euthymos*, appears in Acts 27:36 as 'encouraged'. These references show that the meaning concentrates not on outward circumstances (which there could hardly have been worse), but on the state of the heart.

THE LAST WORD: PRAYER AND CARE

move us. Neither suffering nor ease should find us without a suitable Christian response in prayer and song. We may say that James is asserting, in verse 13, principles which cover life in all its widely differing forms. Our religion should cover all experience, finding expression in prayer or praise as the occasion may demand. Calvin puts it well when he comments that James 'means that there is no time in which God does not invite us to himself'. It is not so much that our religion should cover all experience, as that we have a God for all seasons. Both in periods of suffering and trouble, and in times of joy, prayer and praise alike acknowledge that he is sufficient. To pray to him is to acknowledge his sovereign power to meet our needs, and to praise is to acknowledge his sovereign power in appointing our circumstances. Whether as the source of supply in need, or the source of the gladness of our joy, God is our sufficiency.

James, however, would not be content with the bare proposition that God is our sufficiency. He would want to be certain that we are finding him to be sufficient, that we are, in practical terms, making use of him as our resource. Therefore, he writes to us by way of command to pray and to sing. The Christian life is to be an exercise in practised consecration, to 'hallow every pleasure, sanctify each pain'. Our whole life, we might say, should be so angled towards God that whatever strikes upon us, whether sorrow or joy, should be deflected upwards at once into his presence. In particular, this is an exercise in glad acceptance of the will of God. This is the common denominator of prayer and praise. In praise, we say to him, 'Your will is good, perfect and acceptable; this is what you have done for me and I rejoice.' And as for prayer in time of trouble, it attempts – however poorly we may succeed – to copy the Gethsemane prayer of Jesus in saying, 'Not my will but yours.' R. V. G. Tasker notes helpfully that when Jesus was in agony, 'wrestling with the forces of evil at the moment of their strongest attack, "he prayed more earnestly" (Lk. 22:44). Prayer may not remove the affliction but it most certainly can transform it.'

This, then, is the individual at prayer. He is reflecting all his life upward, acknowledging the sufficiency and sovereignty of God, practising the grace of acceptance and rejecting the disgrace of stubbornness. In this the voice of prayer and the voice of praise are at one, for alike they say that the will of God is good.

The elders at prayer: a call answered (5:14–15)

Is any one among you sick? Let him call for the elders of the church, and let them pray over him, anointing him with oil in the name of the Lord; [15]*and the prayer of faith will save the sick man, and the Lord will raise him up; and if he has committed sins, he will be forgiven.*

We come now to one of the most fascinating passages in the whole letter of James, and one which has excited a great deal of difference of opinion and not a little controversy. James moves on from the general experience (13) of passing through life's ill-experiences to one particular adversity of life to which Christians are as prone as anyone else – sickness. He envisages the sick person summoning the elders, the local leaders of the church to which the sick person belongs. They engage in a twofold ministry: prayer and anointing in the name of the Lord (14). Two promises are attached. First, *the prayer of faith will save the sick man, and the Lord will raise him up* and, secondly, if sin should be involved in any way, *he will be forgiven* (15).

Setting the scene

Three comments of a general nature will help to set the scene.

First, we notice that James associates the healing ministry of prayer and anointing with the local church leaders. From the very earliest apostolic times it was customary to appoint elders in every church.[3] Their alternative title, 'overseers',[4] is more functional: it signifies 'caring for', 'watching out for the welfare of'. We not only meet such a group in Acts 20:17–35, but we find their work described there as guarding and feeding God's flock (28) and following the apostolic example of 'admonishing' (31). Elsewhere emphasis rests on their work as teachers (1 Tim. 3:2; Tit. 1:9), labouring in preaching and teaching (1 Tim. 5:17). Since it is not as much as hinted in the New Testament that the church would ever need – or indeed should ever want or tolerate – any other local leadership than that of the eldership group, we may say that James vests this ministry of prayer, anointing and healing in the ongoing life of the church.

A. Barnes turns this passage to good account with a piece of pastoral

---

[3]On the whole question of ministry in the New Testament church, see J. A. Motyer, *The Message of Philippians* (IVP, 1984), pp. 33ff. *Cf.* Acts 14:23; *etc.*

[4]Gk. *episkopoi*, e.g. Phil. 1:1, see RSV margin. The verb, *episkopeō*, means to watch over, care for.

guidance, that 'it should always be presumed of a minister of the gospel that he is ready to visit the sick'. This is very true, but we must observe how Barnes expresses the teaching of James, in the light of later practice. He speaks of 'a minister of the gospel', whereas James knows nothing of such a 'one man ministry'. For him it is 'the elders' who hold themselves in readiness to answer the call of the sick. Nevertheless the substantial point is well observed. This ministry to the sick belongs not to any specially gifted person – such a one as claims to have received the 'gift of healing' mentioned in 1 Corinthians 12:30. Nor does it belong to any unique and bygone order of ministry such as apostles.

It is, of course, true that miracles clustered round the apostles as a God-given sign to authenticate their unique ministry (*e.g.* 2 Cor. 12:12; Heb. 2:3–4) and this accords with the general pattern of the Bible. Miraculous happenings, whether cures or otherwise, are not evenly spread through Scripture. Indeed there is a sense in which we must say that as a general rule the Bible is more concerned with the providential than with the exceptional acts of God. It reserves miracles for the great turning-points of its story: Moses and the time of the redemption from Egypt, Elijah and Elisha and the inception of the work of the 'great' prophets, the life of the Lord Jesus, and the period of apostolic church-founding. Of all these periods, and not just of the time of the apostles, we might use the words of Acts 14:3, that 'the Lord . . . bore witness to the word of his grace, granting signs and wonders to be done by their hands'. But we cannot sidestep our present passage in James by urging that the apostles are dead and gone and, by the will of God, there are no longer living apostles in the church, either universal or local.[5] Nor can we limit the presence and availability of this ministry to the sick by making it depend on the fact that a person with the gift of healing happens to be present. It is a ministry exercised by those whom James envisaged as always being at the helm of the local church, *the elders*. Whatever, therefore, is the meaning, in doctrine and practice, of the verses before us, they continue to belong in every local church.

The second general comment we must make is one which can only

[5]In his article on 'Extreme Unction' in *The Protestant Dictionary* (1933), having noted the opinion that there is nothing to hinder a revival of a true, scriptural practice of anointing the sick, F. Meyrick expostulates, '"Nothing to hinder" – except that not being Apostles, we have not the miraculous gifts they had.' This states exactly the view we counter. James centres the ministry of prayer and anointing in the ever-present ministry of elders, not in the passing and now past ministry of living apostles.

be hurtful to every Christian spirit, for it involves an element of controversy — or, even if one resolutely refuses to engage in controversy, a denial of what some who profess the name of Christ would hold to be true. By the third century AD it had become the custom for oil used in anointing the sick to be 'consecrated' by the bishop of the area in which it was to be used. By the tenth century, it was increasingly the practice to insist that the anointing be carried out by a 'priest'. By the twelfth century, the terms 'extreme unction' and 'sacrament of the dying' are found and the anointing is restricted to those whose imminent death seems certain. In the thirteenth century, the ceremony of anointing was declared to be one of the 'seven sacraments' instituted by Christ himself, so that the Council of Trent (1545 onwards) can pronounce an anathema on anyone who denies that extreme unction is 'properly a sacrament, instituted by Christ... promulgated by the blessed apostle James', or who denies that the 'sacred unction' confers grace and remits sin, or who thinks that the ceremony is 'repugnant to the sentiment of the blessed apostle James', or that the elders to whom James refers 'are not priests who have been ordained by a bishop'.[6] The Jerusalem Bible may be exercising a diplomatic caution when it goes no further than to say (on the present passage) that 'the tradition that these prayers and this anointing... are the origin of the Church's "Sacrament of the Sick" (or Holy Unction) was endorsed by the council of Trent'. The second Vatican Council, however, continues to treat 'Extreme Unction' as one of the 'other sacraments' and, while urging that it is not 'for those only who are at the point of death', says that 'as soon as any one of the faithful begins to be in danger of death from sickness or old age, the appropriate time for him to receive this sacrament has certainly already arrived'.[7]

With all the love in the world, what can we say but that this has nothing to do with James 5:14–15? In the first place, there is no suggestion that the oil used has been previously 'consecrated', whether by the elders themselves or by anyone else. Indeed, it is difficult to see what such a ceremony might be supposed to mean or what difference it could possibly make. It cannot be anything but an unwarranted ecclesiastical superstition.[8] In the second place, the emphasis which

[6]*The Canons and Decrees of the Council of Trent*, translated by J. Waterworth (1848), pp. 110f.   [7]*The Documents of Vatican II*, (1965), p. 161.

[8]The practice of having oils 'consecrated' by the bishop is widespread in the Church of England, where very often clergy are encouraged to bring whatever oil they wish to set apart for anointing the sick to their cathedral church on Maundy Thursday. This misleading practice can only foster superstition.

has come to be placed on the anointing as carrying with it a spiritual efficacy, conferring grace and remitting sins, is not only wildly astray from the scriptural understanding of sin and its forgiveness, but also reverses the priorities which James sets out. For his primary emphasis is on healing the sickness, and he refers to sin only as something which may sometimes be involved – and even so there is no justification for thinking that the anointing as such confers forgiveness. But, in the third place, and most obviously, 'extreme unction' (even with the qualifications of Vatican II above) is a supposed preparation for death, whereas the ministry of the elders in prayer and anointing is designed for healing and restoration to earthly life.

It is a sad, even if inevitable, task to have to engage in denials like this, but it does bring to the fore a really key matter which will have to engage us a little later. This is the assumption that healing and restoration will follow the prayer of faith and the anointing in the name of the Lord. Before we come to this, however, there is a third general comment which must be made. We must not approach the special things which God does in such a way as to think little or to think less of his general and providential blessings. It is not only the special and the remarkable, the unique and the miraculous which are the works of God: *every good endowment and every perfect gift is from above* (1:17). Isaiah says that we have the Lord to thank for agricultural science (Is. 28:23–29, esp. vv. 26, 29). We learn from Exodus 31:1–11 that the Spirit of God is the moving force in artistic craftsmanship (*cf.* 1 Ki. 7:14).

There might be those who say or imply that the provisions of James 5:14–15 were intended for their own day, but that in our day the Lord has raised up medical and surgical practice, and that we should therefore call the G.P. to our aid rather than the elders of the church. They have at least this on their side – that the advance of medical knowledge, the discovery of medicines and the perfecting of surgical techniques are without doubt examples of the providential goodness of God. We must be careful lest we over-value the marvellous and the miraculous at the expense of the mundane and the providential. As to medical matters, there is enough in the New Testament to direct us to prize, to accept as a divine gift, and to call for, the specialist help of our medical doctors, and to thank God for the provisions of our health services. The Samaritan applied oil and wine (Lk. 10:34), using the medical knowledge of his day – the oil to soothe and the wine to cleanse – and for this as well as for his other care for his needy neighbour he received the praise of the Lord Jesus. Paul called Luke 'the beloved physician' (Col. 4:14), and we can understand the reference to Luke's profession only if Paul himself and others had enjoyed the benefit of it. Timothy was urged, in respect of his 'frequent ailments' (1 Tim. 5:23), to add a little wine to his diet. Trophimus, notwithstanding the healing powers of Paul, was left behind at Miletus (2 Tim. 4:20) because he was ill – presumably to rest until the medicines of the day, or the recuperative powers of the body, did their work. In our day the abundance, availability and effectiveness of medical care is a marvellous illustration of the goodness of God. Whether it is the humble sticking-plaster or the most advanced surgical therapy, we should never cease in our thanks to the God who gives us all these things so richly for our benefit. Yet there is more to be said. When he set out his basic attitude to the trials and joys of life in verse 13, James insisted that we should deliberately refer all life's experiences to the God from whom they come, for praise in a time of well-being, and prayer in a time of difficulty, are alike acknowledgments that one sovereign hand is over all. Even when we go to the doctor, then, our eyes are to the Lord. He alone can heal. There is no such thing as (so to speak) 'non-spiritual' healing. When the aspirin works, it is the Lord who has made it work; when the surgeon sets the broken limb and the bone knits, it is the Lord who has made it knit. *Every* good gift is from above! It is this aspect of things which James isolates when he tells the sick to summon the elders. He does not tell us whether he is offering a 'supplement' to the doctor, or an alternative, and we must not assume that he disapproves of what he simply does not mention. There is always a spiritual dimension in healing, and here it is in all its glory. On no occasion should a Christian approach the doctor without also approaching God, but there are those times when a notable and special approach to God will seem right and it is for this that James here makes a lovely provision.

The picture in detail

Turning now to the details of the passage, we will consider them under three headings: the sick person and his request, the elders and their ministry and the prayer of faith and its outcome.

a. The sick person and his request. There are indications in the passage that a fair degree of illness is present. We must be careful not to press hints beyond what is proper, but there is enough evidence to suggest that a minor or transient malady does not offer ground for summoning the elders in the terms James has in mind. First, there is the fact that the elders are called to the sick man rather than that he should go to them. Secondly, it is the elders who do all the praying, notwithstanding that verse 13 urges the one who is in trouble to pray for himself. If we sense here a good deal of weakness on the part of the invalid, then, thirdly, this is confirmed by the fact that he is called 'the weary/worn out one' (15; RSV *the sick man*),[9] pointing to a sickness either prolonged or serious enough to entail weakness. Fourthly, this same hint of failing health may be seen in the fact that the sick person is not called upon to exercise faith to be healed. The only faith mentioned is that of the praying elders (15). And, fifthly, the elders are said, in a unique expression, to pray 'over' him.[10] This does not necessarily mean more than that they stand while he sits or kneels, but it could possibly imply that the illness confined him to his bed. By itself it might not mean much, but in connection with the other indications of the degree of his illness it must be allowed to add its weight.

Ill though he may be, he is well enough to take the initiative in summoning the elders. It is proper to remark in passing that in this passage James is not thinking about public 'healing services'. In such services the elders summon the sick person, whereas here it is the sick person who calls the elders to his home for private ministry. In the same way, James is not prescribing a rite which could be used for a semi-conscious or unconscious patient. There must be that degree of alertness which makes a credible summons to the elders from the invalid possible. And there is another feature of the passage which points to a sick person 'with his wits about him'. It says (15) that *if he has committed sins, he will be forgiven.* There are three possibilities here.

One possibility is that, on his sick bed, he becomes aware that his sickness is a divine visitation resulting from some personal sin. The Bible does not teach that every sickness is the result of some foregoing sin, but it does teach that some sickness comes by way of punishment or warning. The Lord Jesus warned a man whom he healed to 'sin no more, that nothing worse befall you' (Jn. 5:14). Since the directive met with no demur on the part of the man concerned, we must assume that he knew what the Lord had in mind. When the Pharaoh of the day took Sarai, Abram's wife, into his harem, the Lord protected Sarai by

[9]The verb is *kamnō*; *cf.* its only other use, Heb. 12:3 ('grow weary').

[10]The verb 'to pray' (*proseuchō*) is here followed by the preposition *epi* with the accusative case, *i.e.* 'upon/over'. It could also mean 'towards' – that the prayers are very deliberately directed to the sick man and his needs – or 'over' in the sense of having power 'over' the sickness. *Epi* is nowhere else used in connection with either *proseuchō* or its noun *proseuchē*. The customary prepositions are *peri* or *hyper*.

afflicting Pharaoh and his house with great plagues (Gn. 12:17; *cf.* Gn. 20:17–18). We do not know what the 'plagues' were, or how the link with Sarai was discovered, but the onset of illness gave rise to a sense that all was not well. And so it could be for any of us in any illness. There may be a plain and obvious moral cause or there may be something which the Lord wishes to bring to our minds, a sin in the past which needs to be faced.

The second possibility – which in no way excludes the first – is that the period of lying-by should be used for quiet self-examination. In this way forgotten sins will come to light. They may have no bearing on the illness, but the illness is the occasion for recalling and repenting.

The third possibility is more general than the other two, but important in itself. As a person lies ill, he ought to realize that healing involves the whole personality. To be 'whole' includes being wholly right with God. There may, therefore, be no awareness of a specific sin such as might have provoked the illness, nor any memory of sins unconfessed. But there may be a deep desire to be fully reconciled with God, to lay the whole life open to his searching so that all that God knows about him may be reviewed and put right. Therefore he sends for the leaders of his local church for their ministry of prayer and anointing in the name of the Lord.

b. The elders and their ministry. When the elders arrive, what is their ministry? Two things only are specified, prayer over the sick and anointing with oil in the name of the Lord (14). Since we must ponder their prayer fully in verse 15, we shall reserve that aspect of their ministry for a moment and think here only about the anointing. In New Testament times, oil was used medicinally. The Good Samaritan poured on oil (Lk. 10:34) as a soothing ointment and Isaiah 1:6 takes the practice even further back. The practice of anointing the sick with oil is found in Mark 6:13. We are not actually told that the Lord Jesus, when he sent the twelve out, commanded the practice, but we may assume at least that the apostles would not have used it against his will. James is very likely relying on this apostolic example and tacit dominical approval. Both these aspects of the use of oil, the medicinal and the spiritual, would be in the minds of the elders and of their sick brother. As to its medicinal significance, it is rather like the way the Lord himself sometimes used his own saliva in healing miracles. The commentators say that in contemporary popular thought the saliva of an important or powerful person was considered to have curative properties in its own right. It is unlikely that the Lord Jesus subscribed

195

to this superstition, and we ought to note that he used his saliva only in ministry to the deaf (Mk. 7:31–37) and the blind (Mk. 8:22–26; Jn. 9:6–7). That is to say, where ordinary communication was not possible he used this tangible way of assuring the afflicted one that he intended to cure him, and of effecting a direct link between himself and the cure. In the same way the elders used oil. In itself it would speak of soothing and healing, and by linking it with *the name of the Lord* it would become a visible expression and token of the descent of the healing authority and efficacy of the Name. We can recall that Peter could say of the lame man healed at the temple gate that it was the name of Jesus that had effected the cure (Acts 3:6, 16). As the elders pronounced the name of the Lord over the sick, it was in the faith that power resided in the name of Jesus to heal.

Did the elders do anything else but pray and anoint? We have no ground for saying that they did. There is no reference to any 'laying on of hands' and no present-day elders who seek to minister to the sick according to James 5:14–15 should include the laying on of hands in their ministry. Nor is there any necessity to think of the sick person openly confessing his sins in the presence of the elders. As we have seen, sin is mentioned only incidentally, and its forgiveness is almost as it were a bonus for the sick man. It would be perfectly proper for elders seeking to minister to the sick to enquire if there was any sin needing to be confessed and forgiven. They would likewise wish to assure themselves that the sick person had indeed brought any such sin or sins personally and privately to the Lord, but it is not necessary that they should know what the sin is. It would be highly improper for them to press the sick to tell them any such intimate matter unless there was no other way of bringing relief to the conscience except confiding in them, and seeking to come to God with their help for an assurance of forgiveness. But there is a dividing-line which everyone who wishes to minister biblically will be careful not to cross, for a fundamental spiritual principle is involved. In the late sixteenth century Richard Hooker put it this way as he drew a distinction between the aims respectively of the Church of England and the Roman Catholic Church, a distinction which remains vital today between biblical and 'catholic' theology and pastoral care. Hooker said, 'We labour to instruct men in such sort, that every soul which is wounded with sin may learn the way how to cure itself; they, clean contrary, would make all sores seem incurable, unless the priest have a hand in them.'[11]

[11]Richard Hooker, *Laws of Ecclesiastical Polity* (1888), Book 6, vi. 2.

c. The prayer of faith and its outcome. Our third theme offers a fascinating topic. At first sight nothing could be clearer than what James says: *the prayer of faith will save the sick man, and the Lord will raise him up.* We are taught that the whole efficacy of the ministry resides in the prayer (not in the anointing) and that the Lord promises his own healing, restoring power in response to *the prayer of faith.* But, of course, we see at once that this is far from being a problem-free statement. What are we to make of the very many cases where the ministry of the elders has been faithfully carried out, believingly applied, and no healing has followed? Are we to say that there must have been a failure of faith? If so, then we need to understand that it can only have been deficient faith on the part of the elders, for the faith of the sick person is not mentioned at any point in the verses. It is they who *pray* (14) and it is *the prayer of faith* that is effective (15). Somehow such an explanation savours of a get-out. It is by far too simplistic and superficial. We need to try to approach the question at greater depth, taking into account the key-expression *the prayer of faith,* the other significant words which are used — *save, raise up* — and the setting of this passage on healing within a context of wide-ranging teaching on prayer.

It cannot be accidental that in speaking of *the prayer of faith* James both uses an expression not found elsewhere in Scripture and also departs from the usual Greek word for 'prayer' in favour of a word rarely used with this meaning.[12] A writer as sure-footed in his Greek as James, and as sensitive to the task of getting the right word in the right place, must have intended to signal to his readers that he was bringing something special before them. The words are, of course, in line with what James has already taught about prayer in 1:5, yet the emphasis is not quite the same. In 1:5–8 James was stressing that the faith which expresses itself in effective prayer is the product of a clear and absolute commitment to the Lord in total loyalty to him. As we saw, he contrasts faith with 'wavering', and defines wavering as being 'double-minded', *i.e.* keeping one foot in the world, allowing an element of disloyalty to remain, not being absolutely honest with God. This was, again, the vitiating factor in the prayer of 4:2b–4. What was asked for was intended for self-gratification; there was not

---

[12]Gk. *euchē* is used in Acts 18:18; 21:23 in its ordinary sense of 'a vow' and only here in the New Testament meaning 'prayer'. In LXX it usually means 'vow', but appears as 'prayer' in Pr. 15:8, 29. Likewise the verb *euchomai* must mean 'to pray' in v. 16, and we might compare 2 Cor. 13:9; 3 Jn. 2; but its basic meaning is 'to wish', Acts 26:29; 27:29; 2 Cor. 13:7.

an uncompromising commitment to the Lord himself, and to the life that goes his way. Now, in the light of 5:13, this truth certainly cannot be absent from verses 14–15. This whole passage (13–18) is about prayer, and the central truth about prayer is a deliberate but peaceful acceptance of the will of God. To this we shall return in a moment. But when he writes of *the prayer of faith* James seems intentionally to direct our gaze not into the hearts of the praying elders, but to the result that such a prayer produces, it *will save the sick man, and the Lord will raise him up.* In other words, he seems to speak of faith not as commitment to the will of God, but as conviction that it is the will of God to perform this healing.

The Lord Jesus included this sort of praying among all the other rich teaching on prayer that he gave. We might take Mark 11:22ff. as an example. God can do absolutely anything he wishes and we can trust him absolutely, no matter if the problem is as great as moving a mountain (22). But there is also a specific faith, whereby we are enabled in making our request to 'believe that you receive it'. From such a prayer, the result is certain: 'and you will'. This is obviously an important matter, but it is also one full of complications and beset with great dangers. We must be careful. The Lord Jesus is not to be understood as saying that this is the whole truth about prayer, and that all prayer must be a prayer of faith in this sense. The majority of our prayers are, in fact, prayers of rest – and rightly so. Very often we do not know what to ask either for ourselves or for others, whether through lack of wisdom (to know what is right) or of knowledge (to know what is needed), and we are glad to fall back on the great plea 'Lord, bless . . .'. The word 'bless' is a conscious shorthand for 'Lord, I do not know what to ask, but you know what is needed'. Nor is the Lord Jesus saying that we can pray only when we possess this special certainty of faith regarding what we ask. In Mark 9:21 he himself responded in power to a faith which was by its own confession far from certain. Nor yet is he saying that his response to our prayers will go only as far as our faith stretches, for he does 'far more abundantly than all that we ask' (Eph. 3:20). And he is certainly not saying that we should try to whip up a believing spirit, or pretend that we have it when we do not. But he does seem to be teaching that we should always be alert in our prayers to the fact that he may wish to give us a particular gift of faith in relation to something which we ask him.

If this is even part of the meaning of James 5:15, then it points to the seriousness with which the elders must ponder their response to an invitation to prayer over the sick with anointing in the name of the

Lord. Is the Lord, in mercy, granting them that special unction of faith whereby in praying for healing they can also believe that they have what they ask? It would seem that the element of self-examination and self-awareness on the part of the praying elders could be much more demanding than the self-examination suggested for the sick person. Furthermore, if the elders are as mature in fact as their office would demand, they will know the deceitfulness of their hearts and hold themselves in readiness to be mistaken. Nowhere is a spirit of jaunty confidence more misplaced than in the sick-room. It is no time for unconditional predictions of what the Lord will do. Precious in his sight is every affliction of his people (Ps. 56:8), not just their death (Ps. 116:15), and he keeps his secrets to himself. In ordinary, common or garden matters we find that we are too often misled by our convictions of what the Lord will or will not do, and the tender spirit of the sick must be protected from, rather than exposed to, the brashness of confident prognostications.

We need to turn, therefore, from what a unique phrase may mean to what the whole verse must mean. Prayer is a commitment to the will of God, and all true prayer exercises its truest faith in patiently waiting to see what he has determined to do. The unqualified statement that *the prayer of faith will save the sick* stands alongside many similar affirmations regarding prayer. In fact it is the standard way in which the Bible makes its prayer promises. We think, for example, of Matthew 18:19, 'If two of you agree on earth about anything they ask, it will be done for them by my Father in heaven'; or John 14:13, 'Whatever you ask in my name, I will do it.' Such promises are intended to bring us with confidence into the place of prayer; they speak to us of a God who can do all things, who is so generous that he will withhold nothing from us that is good and whose ears are open to our every word. But the one thing the promises do not encourage or allow is that we should come into the place of prayer in a stubborn insistence that we have got it right, and that our will must be done. Indeed, if the promises really meant that we always got what we asked, as soon as we asked it, and in the measure in which we asked, we would speedily stop praying and our friends would petition us to stop praying for them. What an intolerable burden such praying would impose on our frail wisdom! And what a weight of unhelpful and mischievous answers to prayer we should pull down on our own heads, and on the heads of those who were unfortunate enough to figure on our prayer list! Verse 13 taught us that the essence of prayer is 'not my will, but thine, be done' (*cf.* Lk. 22:42). The Lord Jesus put

199

this petition in the forefront of the model prayer (*cf.* Mt. 6:10) and, when his own prayers reached their Gethsemane maturity, he said virtually nothing else. In *the prayer of faith*, our faith is not that 'the promises' will be fulfilled just like that; it is the faith which rests trustfully in the will of a sovereign, faithful and loving God. Neither the sick person nor any of the elders is there to insist that his or her will be done, but to put the sick one within the total, eternal security of the unchangeable and unchangeably gracious will of God.

Is it to accommodate this precious thought – even, perhaps, to lead us to it – that there is a hint of ambiguity in the words James uses? In verse 15 he uses, in connection with the earthly benefit of healing, words whose fullest meaning is concerned with our eternal salvation: *save . . . raise up*. Similarly, in verse 16 he uses in connection with restoration of spiritual well-being a word whose first bearing is on bodily health: *be healed*. The perfect will of God may be done in the lesser benefit of a return to bodily health, or in the supreme benefit of fullness of life in the immediate presence of Jesus. For this reason we must always say – in all our prayers, not just those concerned with healing – 'Thy will be done'. The effect of this petition is to take away from our prayers the limitations imposed by our knowledge of what our needs are, by our proposals of what will meet them, and by our sense of what is best. Its effect is to place ourselves unreservedly into the hands of that infinite wisdom, love and power which belong to our heavenly Father. To say 'Thy will be done' does not impose a restriction on what we ask; rather, it lifts all earthly restrictions. And we must say that this is, if anything, more important in the case of a sick person than in almost any other case. The disposing of the welfare of the child of God cannot be left with greater confidence anywhere else than in the Father's hands, nor can any solution of the plight be more fitting, beneficial and glorious than that which he has in mind.

The friends at prayer: a spirit of reconciliation (5:16a)

Therefore confess your sins to one another, and pray for one another, that you may be healed.

We come away from verses 14–15 with at least this clear in our minds, that prayer is a very powerful thing. It would seem that James intended that we should, for this is the thought which he carries over into the section now before us for study. If we isolate some keywords we shall see the line he is taking: *. . . the prayer of faith will save the* *sick . . . (15). Therefore . . . pray for one another, that you may be healed* (16). [13] Prayer is not the prerogative of elders, nor is it confined to the sick-room. Rather it is the privilege of all believers, and something in which they should rejoice to share fellowship in order that one or the other, or both, may recover from the weaknesses and diseases of the past, and enter into a new spiritual health. If the sick can call the elders to pray, and God has pledged himself to respond so generously to their prayer, then surely we should be enthusiastic to lay hold of prayer in all situations in life. There (14–15) the matter was sickness; here (16a) it is sin which, in line with Scripture, James views as a sickness of the soul which needs to *be healed*. [14] In this too we can involve ourselves in a fellowship of prayer and, as a result, look for the healing touch of God.

Has James some specific situation in mind? It would seem so. He says *Confess your sins to one another, and pray for one another*. It is surely often the case that a Christian who is burdened by some sin will seek out a close friend and confide the problem, so that in prayer together they may bear one another's burdens, and pray through to the place of deliverance, cleansing and healing. [15] But this is not what James is speaking of here, and the wording he uses will not allow this interpretation. When the verb translated 'confess' is used other than of the confession of sin, it never means 'admit sorrowfully', as it would have to do in order to justify the thought of confiding sin to a friend. It can mean 'to affirm', but only in the sense of 'acclaim' — as of affirming loyalty to God or acclaiming him [16] — but the sense 'affirm to each other that you are sinners' is impossible in the light of the way the word is used in the New Testament. The passage therefore is not speaking of the gathering of groups, or the holding of a meeting in which believers tell one another about their sins, nor can such practices be justified on

[13]Readers of the Authorized Version will need to beware of the fact that it has unjustifiably omitted the 'therefore' from the beginning of v. 16 and thus destroyed the connection between these two sections of James' teaching.

[14]*E.g.* Pss. 103:3; 107:17–20; Is. 1:4–6; 6:10; 53:4–5 (see RSV margin); 1 Pet. 2:24.

[15]This was the view taken in the earlier series of studies in James published in 1970 under the title *The Tests of Faith*. I now see that this interpretation is untenable, even though what was written there still remains true regarding 'confiding' sin to a friend, namely that no-one should hear another's admission of sin without a *sole* intention to make it a matter of prayer, and no-one should confide a problem of sin without a *sole* desire and determination to be healed of it.

[16]The verb is *exomologeō; cf.* (in the sense of confessing sin) Mt. 3:6; Mk. 1:5; Acts 19:18; (in the sense of acclaiming or affirming — maybe, even of praising) Mt. 11:25; Lk. 10:21; Rom. 14:11; 15:9; Phil. 2:11; (in the sense of coming to an agreement with) Lk. 22:6.

the ground of James 5:16. For it does not say (even) 'Confess your sins to God in each other's presence', but *Confess your sins to one another*.

The biblical position regarding confessing sin can be summed up in this way. 'Confession must be made *to* the person *against* whom we have sinned, and *from* whom we need and desire to receive forgiveness. . . . There is "secret confession" to God because there are "secret sins" (Ps. 90:8) committed against God alone. Next, there is "private confession", because some of our sins are committed against man as well as God, a private individual, or two or three such, and must be confessed to the offended party. Thirdly, there is "public confession", because some sins are committed against a group . . . a community or the whole local congregation, and must therefore be confessed publicly.'[17] It is in this area of confession that James is moving. We have offended against a brother or sister and we must go to such a one privately and confess in what way we have done wrong, ask to be forgiven, and join in prayer for healing, 'because the biblical principle is consistently that "confession" is due to the party who has been offended'.[18] The believers whom James brings before us have not met to engage in mutual confession of secret sins – for the 'confession' of such is owed to God alone. Rather it is because the one has sinned against the other and is seeking opportunity, in private fellowship, to put things right, or because each has offended the other and they are ready to confess and be reconciled.

As we have seen throughout his letter, James is deeply concerned about fellowship. It is the soil in which a harvest of righteousness comes to full fruition (3:18). Breaches in fellowship are as grievous as war and murder (4:1ff.). It is more than suitable that he who has warned us so plainly about the dangers and causes of broken fellowship should come, before the end of his letter, to teach us the way of healing what has been broken. He looks for three things. First, he looks for a spirit of penitence. However hard and costly it may be, we simply must be prepared to go to the one we have wronged and confess our fault and put things right. Indeed, if we take the teaching of our Lord Jesus seriously (Mt. 5:23), we must be moved not only by our sense that we have wronged a brother or sister, but by our awareness that he or she thinks we have committed a hurtful sin. Some find it harder than others, and none find it easy to say 'I am sorry'. But it is a biblical command that we should do so, and the cause of fellowship must be dearer to us than the humbling of our pride. Secondly, James looks for

---

[17]J. R. W. Stott, *Confess your Sins* (Hodder, 1964), p. 12.   [18]*Ibid.*, p. 28.

a spirit of reconciliation. If we should be, perchance, on the receiving end of someone else's confession of sin, then we must be prompt and unhesitating in our welcome to the brother or sister who comes seeking to put things right. For if, on the one side, pride battles hard against confessing sin, pride battles equally hard against the simple reaching out of a forgiving hand. Sometimes too it is not just pride which holds back from forgiveness, but also fear: fear of trusting oneself to someone who has, possibly, been grievously treacherous or cruelly hurtful. Yet James covers all situations with his assumption that the overtures of the one who would confess are met by the welcome of the one who has been wronged. Rarely, of course, are things nicely clear-cut, and the platitude is true that there are usually faults on both sides. We should then covet nothing more than to get in first with our confession, and to outdo our brother or sister only in this, that we are warmer and more overflowing in reconciliation. Thirdly, James looks for a spirit of prayer, leading to healing. The two who were but recently far apart come into the close unity and harmony of the place of prayer. Mutual concern is expressed and hallowed in the presence of God; the breach is healed. Where spirits have been bruised, or where either has inflicted on the other a blow which has resulted in spiritual decline, then in answer to prayer God will grant restoration to spiritual health. Corporate prayer expresses this determination not only to come together after separation, but to undo the damage to the individual and the fellowship.

The prophet at prayer: a human agent, a supernatural result (5:16b–18)

The prayer of a righteous man has great power in its effects. [17]*Elijah was a man of like nature with ourselves and he prayed fervently that it might not rain, and for three years and six months it did not rain on the earth.* [18]*Then he prayed again and the heaven gave rain, and the earth brought forth its fruit.*

It means much to James that we should really believe all this: that prayer is the truest response to problems (13), even to the problem of serious illness (14–15), and that it has power to heal the sin-sick soul and the sin-torn fellowship (16a). It is to drive home the truth of the power of prayer that he now first states the fact (16b) and then illustrates it from the story of Elijah (17–18).

The fact is that *the prayer of a righteous man has great power in its effects* (16b). In the first place, this teaches us of the inherent power of prayer:

203

it has *great power*. The word (*ischys*) points to inherent strength, the strength which makes a person or thing sufficient for the task. It means potency, power waiting to be released.[19] We might speak of untapped resources. Unpromising tracts of land hide rich deposits of minerals; grey seas cover a wealth of natural gas. Such is the picture suggested by the word – not the unpromising appearance, but the hidden powers. In human terms, we say that 'the situation produces the person' when, in a given set of circumstances, hitherto unsuspected funds of wisdom, leadership, strength of character and purpose come to light. So it is with prayer. It looks unimpressive and it is easy to despise; but it has great resources waiting to be tapped, a huge potency to release.

Secondly, there is the effectiveness of prayer when it is applied to the solution of problems. There is no doubt about the basic meaning of the verb translated *in its effects*: it speaks of a power 'to get things done', effective power. It is used, for example, of the power of the Lord Jesus which actually subdues all things to him (Phil. 3:21). Commentators differ, however, on how we should translate the form of the word found here. Peter Davids seems to prefer the thought that prayer has great power 'when it is activated (by God)', but James Adamson is correct in pointing out that all nine cases where this form occurs[20] demand that 'prayer is mighty in what it is *able* to do, not in what it is *enabled* to do'. He goes on to say (anticipating v. 17) that 'Elijah's prayer carries a mighty punch'. This makes the point as vividly as we could wish! When we pray about something, the inherent power of prayer is released as an effective power which accomplishes its objectives.

In the third place, there is the spiritual foundation of prayer. It is the prayer of *a righteous man*. The word *righteous* has a forbidding ring. It seems to rule us and our poor prayers out of court. And, of course, if we are meant to understand it in the sense of perfect moral character and integrity, it must do so. But this is not what James means, and it

[19]For example, 1 Pet. 4:11 implies that when God gives a 'gift' he makes available also the strength to use it. The verb, *ischyō*, is found in Mt. 5:13 (of salt which has 'lost its strength'); Mt. 8:28 (no-one was 'strong enough' to pass that way); Mt. 9:12 (of the physically healthy); *etc.*

[20]The verb which expresses the idea of 'effective power' is *energeō*. The form found here is *energoumenē*. If this is translated as a passive, it leads to Peter Davids' understanding: *i.e.* something that is 'made effective'. But wherever else the form occurs it must be understood not as passive but as middle: *i.e.* 'in its own effective operation', 'as it makes its effect felt' (Rom. 7:5; 2 Cor. 1:6; 4:12; Gal. 5:6; Eph. 3:20; Col. 1:29; 1 Thes. 2:13; 2 Thes. 2:7). Plumptre would agree with Davids; Alford with Adamson.

is for this reason that he introduces the illustration of Elijah who, he notes, *was a man of like nature with ourselves* (17).[21] He could rise to the heights of faith and commitment (1 Ki. 18:36–38) and fall into the depths of despair and depression (1 Ki. 19:4). He could be brave and resolute sometimes (1 Ki. 18:17–19) and then fly for his life at a whiff of danger (1 Ki. 19:3). He could be selfless in his concern for others (1 Ki. 17:19–24) and then filled with self-pity (1 Ki. 19:10). In other words, he was 'an ordinary person', but he was right with God – or to put things in the sort of terminology that we find in James' letter, his faith was active in his works, and it was reckoned to him as righteousness (Jas. 2:22–23). This is part of the wonder of the way of prayer. Those who by grace have been given the status of righteousness in God's sight have been brought into the realm where effective prayer operates and have been given the right to exercise a ministry of prayer.

Elijah: a person of prayer

James has now cleared the ground by revealing to us both the power of prayer and our God-given right to use this power. Now, with the help of the Elijah illustration, he moves on to the fourth and greatest truth about prayer: its supernatural results. Despite having 'human frailties like our own' (17, NEB), when Elijah prayed there was such a result as only God could bring about. Man prayed, God acted: *... it did not rain ... he prayed again and the heaven gave rain, and the earth brought forth its fruit* (17–18).

Elijah is presented to us in 1 Kings 17 – 19 as the man of prayer. In chapter 17 (see v. 3, 'hide yourself') we read of the secret years of Elijah's apprenticeship, during which the Lord prepared him for his future ministry by bringing him through three testing experiences of ascending severity. The third and greatest was the death of the widow's son (17–24). Through this Elijah was confirmed regarding the power of prayer. Even in the face of death, he learnt, the mighty, inherent power of prayer is effective both to restore the physically dead (22) and to give life to the spiritually dead (24). Now he could be sure that 'the Lord hearkened to the voice of Elijah' (22) – in prayer a mere man can move God. When, therefore, in chapter 18 (see v. 1, 'show yourself') Elijah moves out into public ministry, he proceeds at once to challenge the prophets of Baal and Baal himself precisely on this issue

---

[21]For the word *homoiopathēs* see its only other New Testament appearance, Acts 14:15. Tasker, '... the same nature ... subject to the same emotions, and liable to the same weaknesses ...'.

of prayer. Each party is to call on the name of its God (24), 'and the God who answers by fire, he is God'. It is not the marvel of fire that is the central point. The fire is incidental to the sort of test Elijah proposed – a sacrifice which needed to be ignited. The point is this – which of the contestants, Baal or the Lord, can answer prayer? To this extent Elijah is supremely the man of prayer. He is ready to allow the whole issue of the reality of God to be decided by this one factor: there is a God who answers prayer.

When we come to chapter 19 we move into a different scene altogether. Elijah, exhausted by the strain of the events of chapter 18, is caught off balance and runs away from Jezebel's threats. Physical tiredness, coupled with failure, produced a severe depression, but Elijah has really learnt the lesson of prayer so that even in his depression he talks to God. Anyone who has experienced depression, or who has sought to minister to those who suffer in this way, will pause here to marvel. Prayer must have become ingrained in the prophet. His prayer, certainly, is that his life might be ended immediately – but it is prayer. He is talking to God, not to himself. He does not contemplate suicide, but asks the Lord to act. His prayer is answered with a magnificence which defeats the imagination, for the man who prayed to die at once never died at all (2 Ki. 2:11)! Once again the truth is borne out that a mere human prays and results follow which only God can produce.

As we review the stories of Elijah like this, we see why James selected him as a paramount example of the man of prayer. But what James actually says focuses more specifically on the part played by Elijah and his prayers in the drought which came on the land in his day. At three points James brings an authoritative New Testament interpretation to bear on our understanding of the Old. Like the Lord Jesus (Lk. 4:25), he specifies that the drought lasted *for three years and six months* (17), while 1 Kings 18:1 says only that it ended 'in the third year'. Again, 1 Kings 17:1 quotes Elijah as saying that there will be no rain 'except by my word', and before the actual onset of the rainstorm which broke the long drought, Elijah is pictured as crouching low on Mount Carmel (1 Ki. 18:42–45). James reveals to us that the 'word' of 1 Kings 17:1 is to be understood as the prophet's word in prayer, and that the crouching position is that of a prayerful suppliant. The drought and the rain both came because Elijah prayed.

James sums it all up by saying that *he prayed fervently*, but RSV is not our best guide here to James' meaning. The Greek says, literally, 'with prayer he prayed' and the meaning is not his fervency, nor even his frequency of prayer, but that 'he just prayed' – that, and nothing more! James Adamson puts it correctly when he says, 'Not that Elijah put up a particularly fervent prayer, but that praying was precisely what he did.' The general truth which James is drawing out of the history of Elijah is expressed in verse 17: human prayer, divine results. To withhold rain is something only God can do. Verse 18 draws it out a little further. Prayer operates even in the apparently fixed laws of the natural order. It can master the forces of the heavens (18a). Prayer (18b) is also the key to earthly blessing and fruitfulness. God the Creator orders the life of the world in the light of the prayers of his people.

We have lived with James long enough not to expect him to stop to draw out all the implications of his teaching. He expects that to be part of our response, and also he appears to think that we shall be reasonably quick on the uptake. We may wonder what he would have said by way of application of his teaching on prayer. It may be useful just to draw out one point from verses 16b–18, one point from the immediate context (13–18) in which they are set, and a final point from the wider context of James' concluding section (5:7–20) of which these verses are part. We see in verses 16b–18 that prayer is a thing of power, simplicity and confidence. Its inherent power is great and, when prayer is exercised, its effective power is released (16b). Elijah 'just prayed'. He simply mentioned it to the Lord. We could study with profit his recorded prayers in 1 Kings 18:36–37 and 19:4. They are models of simplicity and brevity. They make their point; they do not fuss or become complicated. They do not confuse reality and earnestness with getting excited; they have a restful confidence that the Lord is near and that he hears. These are lessons we could well learn.

The immediate context of verses 16b–18 is verses 13–18. In a word, James urges that all life should be lived with immediate reference to God (13), bringing its joys to him in praise, and its sorrows to him in prayer. The contrasting states of physical ill (14–15) and spiritual ill (16a) are undoubtedly meant to embrace every distress which may come our way. In fact there is no situation in which prayer is not the proper Christian response, and in which the example of Elijah who 'just prayed' would cease to be appropriate. James does not actually pause after verse 18 to call us to become people of prayer, but the call is surely implicit and plain.

Patience and prayer

But there is also the wider context which holds together the two ideas of patience (7–12) and prayer (13–18), and this also has its message for us. In calling us to prayer James is not cancelling out his call to patience. In fact, he put patience first, did he not? The two belong together. Prayer will minister to us in the experience which demands patience; patience will sustain us as we seek to engage in prayer. Very often the really striking things the Bible records are intended to give a foundation to our faith, rather than a model for our expectations. When we think of the miraculous acts of the Lord Jesus Christ, we know that they are recorded so that we may trust him, not so that we may know what, in every parallel or similar circumstance, we may immediately expect from him. Rightly, we do not expect him to restore our dead as he restored Lazarus (Jn. 11), but as we read the story of Lazarus we become confident that we can entrust our beloved to him who is Lord even over death itself. In miracle after miracle which he performed we can imagine him saying to us, 'I will do it this once so that you will know that I can; after that you must just trust me.' In the same way the story of Elijah is written for our learning. As we read we see what a simple and powerful thing prayer is: it restores the dead (1 Ki. 17), calls fire from heaven and breaks the drought (1 Ki. 18), it calls the angel of the Lord to the side of the downcast (1 Ki. 19). There is a purpose of God in allowing us to see at one glance the simplicity of ordinary human prayer, and the marvel of the divine response. In no other way could the power of prayer be brought home to us. But if we are to take into account all the biblical teaching about prayer, all the examples of people at prayer within the Scriptures, and indeed the evidence of our own experience in prayer, we know that the same rule applies here as in the case of the Lord's miracles: 'I will do it this once so that you will know I can; after that you must just trust me.' Prayer involves the patience which awaits the divine response. It is part of the simplicity of prayer to act in simple faith – faith that the Lord's moment will come, and that he will do 'far more abundantly than all that we ask or think' (Eph. 3:20).

The fellowship of concern: pastoral watchfulness (5:19–20)

My brethren, if any one among you wanders from the truth and some one brings him back, [20] let him know that whoever brings back a sinner from the error of his way will save his soul from death and will cover a multitude of sins.

The words *My brethren* have appeared over and over in James' letter (1:2, 16, 19; 2:1, 5, 14; 3:1, 10, 12; 4:11), and especially since he began to pen his conclusion (5:7, 9, 10, 12). Their reappearance here assures us that, no matter how abrupt verses 19–20 may at first sight seem, they have a real place in the scheme James is developing. There is another verbal link, too, between verses 19–20 and what has immediately preceded. Verses 13, 14 and 19 all begin with the same words, *any one among you.* [22] We must seek ways in which to understand verses 19–20 which honour these indications that James saw them as part and parcel of the whole section.

First we notice the change which occurs between verse 13 and verses 14ff. Verse 13 is concerned with how we are as individual Christians to look after ourselves. Praise and prayer are the key to a fruitful approach to the varying circumstances of our personal lives. But with verse 14 James turns to various aspects of mutual care within the fellowship:

(a) 14–15. Case 1. Sickness, with a possible question of sin in the background;

(b) 16a. Case 2. The sickness of sin; how to deal with conviction of sin and to heal the broken fellowship;

Parenthesis: Prayer has been urged as the key factor in physical and spiritual personal (13) and mutual (14–16a) care. Prayer is indeed of sufficient power and effectiveness (16b–18).

(c) 19–20. Case 3. Someone in the fellowship is slipping away into sin and death. What is to be done?

Throughout all these three case-histories words are used which are capable of physical or spiritual meaning: 15, *save . . . raise up*; 16a, *healed*; 20, *save . . . death.* This shows how James is thinking of all three as belonging together in his concluding teaching on mutual care. But the third case is different from the other two. We have a care for each other not only when someone in physical (14–15) or spiritual (16a) need makes an approach for help, but also when there is no such call. This is when the evidence of our own eyes tells us that someone within the circle of the fellowship is slipping away into the path of sin and death.

We shall consider what James says here under four headings: the evidence, the issues, the agent and the concern.

[22]Notwithstanding RSV, the Greek is the same in v. 14 as in vv. 13, 19.

a. The evidence

Someone who is within the fellowship of the local church (*any one among you*, 19) is seen to wander *from the truth* (19) and to live in *the error of his way* (20). In Titus 1:1 Paul speaks of 'the knowledge of the truth which accords with godliness'. 'Truth' and 'godliness' belong together. It is impossible (in Scripture) to make 'truth' a mere matter of holding some propositions or credal statements in our heads. Truth is a living thing; when it grips our minds it changes our lives. If we claim to know the truth, then the Bible would require us to prove our claim not only by reciting a creed and understanding it, but by the evidence of a way of life matching the truth. The Lord Jesus meant the same thing when he spoke of the truth making us free (Jn. 8:31–32). We learn from Paul of two men named Hymenaeus and Philetus who 'swerved from the truth' (2 Tim. 2:17–18). Their error was primarily intellectual. Jude is roused to write to his fellow-Christians because he sees the faith threatened by those 'who pervert the grace of God into licentiousness' (Jude 4). Their error was primarily moral. But in each case the true faith is denied, and in each case the error spreads. The 'talk' of Hymenaeus and Philetus eats its way into people like a cancer, corrupting and destroying their lives. Jude sees the moral error of his adversaries working in their minds also so that they 'revile whatever they do not understand' (Jude 10).

We can draw out this interweaving of truth and life by quoting Scriptures, but the proof of it is visible in the society in which we live. Going back no further than the memory of the average middle-aged person will carry us, we have seen the professing churches progressively distancing themselves from a serious recognition of the authority of the Bible. More and more, we have witnessed people in leading ecclesiastical positions denying central Christian truth, departing from Christian morality, and yet continuing in office as official teachers of the church. Correspondingly, society has withdrawn from anything but a vague 'folk'-attachment to Christian sentiment. Sunday school attendance has plummeted from that which we remember in the late 1940s and early 1950s. Its descending graph has been matched by the rising graph of juvenile delinquency, just as the churches' abandonment of biblical truth has been matched by the increasingly open licentiousness and lasciviousness of adolescent and adult life-styles. Truth and life belong together. There is a way of life which matches and which grows out of the truth as it is in Jesus, and which cannot be had in any other way. It is one of the crowning follies of the present time that people think they can have Christian standards without Christian convictions. But it is beaten into second place by the folly of church leaders who think that they can deny, or acquiesce in the denial of, biblical truth and still maintain, in the church and in society at large, Christian moral virtues.

James brings us within the local church and urges us to watch for anyone who is losing grip on *truth*, and in whose *way* of life the *error* of sin is showing itself. Of course, we must not sit back and do nothing when we see these things on the wider canvas of society, or of our denomination, though more often than not we find ourselves at a loss what to do. But within the local fellowship we dare not treat truth and life as negotiable. It is our task to care and to rescue.

b. The issues

Rescue is an appropriate word, for issues of life and death are involved. James says that to bring the wanderer back is to *save his soul from death* and to *cover a multitude of sins*. 'Covering' sin is a basic Old Testament idea. When Noah built the ark he was commanded to cover it with pitch (Gn. 6:14). Anyone who has done such work will recall the gradual disappearance of the original woodwork under its new covering, until at length it is all hidden from sight with none of it left, as the painters say, 'grinning through'. It is this same verb (though not in the same form) which the Old Testament uses to describe how God deals with our sin. He covers it over, hides it right out of his and our sight; nothing is left to 'grin through'. But it is more than sweeping sin under the carpet; it is atonement; it is a putting of sin out of sight by the provision of a sufficient sacrifice. In effect we must move away from the illustration of pitch 'covering' the ark, and think rather of the way we use the idea of 'cover' in financial transactions. Perhaps we are planning something for the future and we set aside a sum of money saying, 'That will cover it', so that when the bill comes in it can be paid in full and the thing forgotten. In this way the verb 'to cover' comes to mean a totally sufficient payment, through the blood of sacrifice, by which God has dealt with our sin. And, of course, if we do not avail ourselves of the death of the lamb, then we must forfeit our own lives, for the wages of sin is death.[23]

[23]The Passover record in Ex. 12 perfectly illustrates this. Those who avail themselves of the blood of the lamb by entering the blood-marked houses are safe from divine judgment; those who do not, face the full weight of judgment without protection. The theology of this position can be studied in Lv. 17:11. See G. J.

Every Christian fellowship, as James implies in these verses, is a place of truth and holiness. The truth is held by every member and the life which matches the truth is lived out. We must be watchful all the time for one another's welfare and continuance in truth and life. We know within ourselves how easy it is to slip away from a full commitment to our Lord. We also know (please God, we know) what a blessing it is to have a brother or sister to run after us, minister to us, direct us in the right way and bring us back to God. Such is a scriptural procedure. The leaders of our churches are to keep watch over our souls (Heb. 13:17); we are to stir one another up to love and good works (Heb. 10:24). Yet this is not what James is actually writing about, for the danger which he sees as threatening is one which can never threaten the backsliding Christian. Those who are Christ's are safe at his coming. Death cannot threaten them (1 Cor. 15:20–23). They are his sheep who possess eternal life and cannot be plucked from his hand (Jn. 10:27–30). They look *back* to the day or period of their conversion or to a life which, from the earliest days of infancy and childhood, has belonged to God and whose earliest memories are of loving the Lord Jesus, and they know that they have been 'qualified . . . to share in the inheritance of the saints in light' (Col. 1:12–14). Instructed by Augustus Toplady, they can say that 'the terrors of law and of God with them can have nothing to do; their Saviour's obedience and blood hide all their transgressions from view.'[24] James' point rather is this, that within every fellowship there are those whose profession is not real and whose attachment to Christ is not yet a saving faith. Their true condition, as still held by sin and death, becomes evident to the caring eyes of those who watch within the fellowship. Departure from the truth, and from the life that accords with the truth, gives a revealing testimony to how things really are and calls forth a spirit of concern in every truly Christian heart.

But the question must be asked whether it is in fact possible for us, with our limited wisdom and blinkered perceptions, to discern the difference between the backsliding of a believer who, for all his present slipping away in truth and life, is none the less secure in Christ and will unfailingly be brought back, and, on the other hand, the pretty

---

Wenham, *The Book of Leviticus* (New International Commentary on the Old Testament, 1979), pp. 28–29, 59–63, 245.

[24]With many apologies to A. M. Toplady for this adaptation of some lines from his magnificent hymn, 'A debtor to mercy alone'.

identical evidence which declares that one within the visible fellowship does not truly belong to Christ at all. The fact is that the only evidence we have of each other is what we profess with our lips and live in our lives. We are not privy to the secrets of another's heart, nor to the secret counsels of God. We dare not sit back from any declension in truth or life that becomes evident within the bounds of our local church.

c. The agent

Twice over in verse 19 James uses the vaguest possible word, a word which cannot be pinned on to this person or that. It is *any one* who may depart from the truth, and again it is 'anyone' who brings the wanderer back. The church had its elders (14–15), but they are not named here – just 'anyone'; anyone, that is, who becomes aware of the situation. In other words, the local church is a fellowship of mutual care in which each watches over the other's welfare in the things of God, and is on the alert to minister and rescue. There is just a hint, too, of the delicacy and discretion that is to be used. We understood the phrase about covering a multitude of sins as bringing the wanderer within the embrace of the finished work of Christ. It may have been a special set of sins, or even one single sin, which revealed the departure from the truth and the error of the way. But when a person comes to know Christ as Saviour it is not just one sin that is forgiven, nor even just all the sins of which the sinner is aware, but the whole multitude of all our sins as God knows and has recorded them. The Lord Jesus has offered the one sacrifice for sins for ever (Heb. 10:12). This is undoubtedly the foremost meaning of the expression, but there is another suggestion as well. The idea of covering sins is found in 1 Peter 4:8 (*cf.* Pr. 10:12) in relation to the love we bear for each other, whereby what we happen to know about each other's sinfulness is quietly kept under wraps. When the loving duty falls to any one of us to pursue, care for and rescue some wanderer, we do so because we have become aware of a lapse from the truth or an error in the life. But that knowledge is for ourselves alone: no publicity, no sounding of trumpets before, during or after the rescue bid but, throughout, simply the love which hides a multitude of sins.

d. The concern

We cannot but be struck by the fact that James speaks of the concerned

213

believer as 'bringing back', 'saving' and 'covering the sins' of the one in error. Surely these are things which only God can do? Only God can forgive sins, save us from them and give us the gift of repentance by which we return from our personal far country (*e.g.* Acts 11:18; 2 Tim. 2:25). How can *we* do these things? The answer is that we cannot, but we must act as if we could. The words express the measure of the concern and effort we are called to expend in our spiritual concern for those in spiritual need. Though we cannot convert them, we must labour to do so. Though we cannot save them from death, we must strive for their spiritual welfare as if their eternal destiny rested with us. Though we cannot cover their sins, we must follow the example of the Son of God who can do so, and hold nothing dear to ourselves and no sacrifice too great if only they are saved. For the local church of which James speaks is a fellowship of concern.[25]

[25]In using this 'as if' language James is in line with New Testament ways. *Cf.* Rom. 11:13–14; 1 Cor. 7:16; 9:22. Above all note the example of the Lord Jesus in Jn. 20:23. This verse has suffered much through being made to refer to how ministers act towards church members and has been forced to provide a colour of truth for the error of 'priestly absolution'. But the verse is in fact a missionary mandate. The church is being sent into the world as the Father sent the Son into the world. The question, therefore, is, In what sense can we forgive, or refuse to forgive, the sins of the unconverted world? And the answer is, By giving or withholding the gospel of God's forgiveness. But we are to preach that Good News with all the concern and urgency that arises from acting as if the task and the responsibility of forgiving sins were wholly ours.